Atlantic Transformations

FERNAND BRAUDEL CENTER
STUDIES IN HISTORICAL SOCIAL SCIENCE

Series Editor: Richard E. Lee

The Fernand Braudel Center Studies in Historical Social Science publishes works that address theoretical and empirical questions produced by scholars in or through the Fernand Braudel Center or who share its approach and concerns. It specifically promotes works that contribute to the development of the world-systems perspective engaging a holistic and relational vision of the world—the modern world-system—implicit in historical social science, which at once takes into consideration structures (long-term regularities) and change (history). With the intellectual boundaries within the sciences/social sciences/humanities structure collapsing in the work scholars actually do, this series offers a venue for a wide range of research that confronts the dilemmas of producing relevant accounts of historical processes in the context of the rapidly changing structures of both the social and academic world. The series includes monographs, colloquia, and collections of essays organized around specific themes.

VOLUMES IN THIS SERIES:

Questioning Nineteenth-Century Assumptions about Knowledge: Determinism
Richard E. Lee, editor

Questioning Nineteenth-Century Assumptions about Knowledge: Reductionism
Richard E. Lee, editor

Questioning Nineteenth-Century Assumptions about Knowledge: Dualism
Richard E. Lee, editor

The *Longue Durée* and World-Systems Analysis
Richard E. Lee, editor

New Frontiers of Slavery
Dale Tomich, editor

Slavery in the Circuit of Sugar: Martinique and the World-Economy, 1848–1860
Dale Tomich

The Politics of the Second Slavery
Dale Tomich, editor

The Trade in the Living
Luiz Felipe de Alencastro

Race and Rurality in the Global Economy
Michaeline A. Crichlow, Patricia Northover, and Juan Guisti-Cordero, editors

Power, Political Economy, and Historical Landscapes of the Modern World: Interdisciplinary Perspectives
Christopher R. DeCorse, editor

Atlantic Transformations: Empire, Politics, and Slavery during the Nineteenth Century
Dale Tomich, editor

Atlantic Transformations

Empire, Politics, and Slavery during the Nineteenth Century

Edited by

Dale W. Tomich

FERNAND BRAUDEL CENTER
STUDIES IN HISTORICAL SOCIAL SCIENCE

Cover artwork: Vista General de los Almacenes de Regla y parte de la Bahia de la Habana. Drawing and lithograph by Eduardo Laplante from Justo Cantero, *Los Ingenios. Colleción de Vistas de los Principales Ingenios de Azúcar de la Isla de Cuba* (Havana: Luis Marquier, 1857).

Published by State University of New York Press, Albany

© 2020 State University of New York

All rights reserved

No part of this book may be used or reproduced in any manner whatsoever without written permission. No part of this book may be stored in a retrieval system or transmitted in any form or by any means including electronic, electrostatic, magnetic tape, mechanical, photocopying, recording, or otherwise without the prior permission in writing of the publisher.

For information, contact State University of New York Press, Albany, NY
www.sunypress.edu

Library of Congress Cataloging-in-Publication Data

Names: Tomich, Dale W., 1946– editor.
Title: Atlantic transformations : empire, politics, and slavery during the nineteenth century / edited by Dale W. Tomich.
Description: Albany, NY : State University of New York Press, [2020] | Series: Fernand Braudel Center studies in historical social science | Includes bibliographical references and index.
Identifiers: LCCN 2019049099 (print) | LCCN 2019049100 (ebook) | ISBN 9781438477855 (hardcover : alk. paper) | ISBN 9781438477848 (pbk. : alk. paper) | ISBN 9781438477862 (ebook)
Subjects: LCSH: Slavery—America—History—19th century. | Slave labor—America—History—19th century. | Slavery—Economic aspects—America—History. | Spain—Colonies—America—Economic conditions—19th century. | Slavery—Political aspects—Atlantic Ocean Region—History. | America—Foreign economic relations.
Classification: LCC HT1048 .A88 2020 (print) | LCC HT1048 (ebook) | DDC 306.3/62097—dc23
LC record available at https://lccn.loc.gov/2019049099
LC ebook record available at https://lccn.loc.gov/2019049100

10 9 8 7 6 5 4 3 2 1

In memory of Christopher Schmidt-Nowara

CONTENTS

List of Illustrations	ix
Preface Dale W. Tomich	xi
1780–1880: A Century of Imperial Transformation Josep M. Fradera	1
Slavery in Mainland Spanish America in the Age of the Second Slavery Marcela Echeverri	19
Transatlantic Patriotisms: Race and Nation in the Impact of the Guerra de África in the Spanish Caribbean in 1860 Albert Garcia-Balañà	45
The End of the Legal Slave Trade in Cuba and the Second Slavery José Antonio Piqueras	79
From Cotton to Camels: Plantation Ambitions in Midcentury Hispaniola Anne Eller	105
The Fight against *Patronato*: Labra, Cepeda, and the Second Abolition Luis Miguel García Mora	141
Atlantization and the First Failed Slavery: Panama from the Sixteenth to the Seventeenth Century Javier Laviña	175
Slavery in the Paraíba Valley and the Formation of the World Coffee Market in the Nineteenth Century Rafael Marquese and Dale Tomich	193
Contributors	225
Index	229

ILLUSTRATIONS

Figures

1. José Manuel Restrepo, Carta de la República de Colombia. 1827. Gravado en Paris por Darmet calle du Battoir, no. 3. Escrito por Hacq. (Por José Manuel Restrepo. Paris, Librería Americana, 1827). Available at www.davidrumsey.com — 21

2. Number of voyages in the slave trade between Africa and Cuba (1790–1826) — 91

3. African slaves disembarked in Cuba (1790–1820) — 92

4. Deaths of African slaves during the transatlantic crossing (1790–1820) (percentage of the number of slaves embarked) — 93

5. Prices of African slaves (in pesos) sold in Havana (1790–1844) — 94

6. Evolution of the price of sugar on the London market (1814–1830) (sh/cwt) — 98

7. Map showing emancipation dates, with major projects of indenture, labor control, or indenture emigration in brackets. Map by Annelieke Vries. For clarifications, see note 12. — 110

8. Coffee bean sheller. (*Source*: Catálogo Ilustrado de Tredwell y Jones. AGN-RD) — 118

9. Coffee Exports, 1823–1888 (thousands of metric tons) — 208

Table

1. Evolution of the Population of Panama City, 1575–1607 — 182

PREFACE

The concept of the "second slavery" developed as an attempt to account for the extraordinary expansion of new frontiers of slave commodity production—cotton in the US South, sugar in Cuba, and coffee in Brazil—and their role in the economic and political transformations of the nineteenth-century world-economy. The zones of the second slavery are of special interest because their development runs counter to the prevailing interpretations of slavery in the Americas, which regard slavery as incompatible with a modern industrial capitalist economy or liberal political ideas and values, or both. Such assumptions about the archaic or anachronistic character of slavery in the modern world have long been mobilized in the context of national narratives constructed around notions of linear time and progress. Within such accounts slavery is destined to disappear with the emergence of liberal capitalist modernity, with the result that the persistence or absence of slavery becomes a marker of national backwardness or national progress.

Over the past several decades, the examination of slavery and abolition within the Atlantic system—from the perspective of the "second slavery"—has broken new ground. This approach does not treat slavery as the inevitable repetition of processes that had already been played out in British abolition, the inevitable incompatibility of slavery with an industrialized free market economy and liberal ideas. Rather, it has been attentive to the ways in which Atlantic slavery was expanding and being remade as part of a new global economic and political order; indeed, the battles for and against slavery were being fought on a new terrain. Both liberal ideology and industrial capitalism and the pro-slavery forces arrayed against them were part of this complex and contradictory modernity.

The second slavery is a research perspective that continues to be deepened and broadened as it formulates new research problems and proposes new interpretations; indeed, it has been the subject of two previous volumes in this series and special issues of the journal *Review*.[1] The chapters presented in this book continue to explore these paths, and to address new questions and examine new terrain in order to come to terms with the economic and political transformations of the Atlantic world during the nineteenth century. The point that needs to be emphasized here is that the zones of the second slavery in the US South, Cuba and Brazil are the leading edges of the political and economic changes of the nineteenth century world-economy. They were at once the product of these changes and contributed to making them.

The chapters in this book broaden the scope of the second slavery perspective by examining the mutual interaction of global and local change in different locations and at different spatial and temporal scales. The chapters are particularly concerned with Spain, its colonial empire, and its slave system—especially in Cuba and Puerto Rico—as parts of the Atlantic world. Josep Fradera compares the structure of European empires and interimperial rivalries over the course of the nineteenth century and calls our attention to the interaction of imperial politics, colonialism, and slavery. Marcela Echeverri and Anne Eller extend our understanding of the second slavery by examining how it shaped politics and economy where it did not play as dominant a role as in the US South, Cuba, and Brazil. José Antonio Piqueras examines the legal end of the slave trade to Cuba and the second slavery and traces the ways in which it was intertwined with international, Spanish, and Cuban politics and the colonial relationship between Cuba and Spain. Albert Garcia-Balanyá examines how, in the context of a "colonial public sphere," understandings of race and nation were formed in the course of efforts to raise Afro-Cuban, Catalan, and Basque volunteer battalions to fight in the first Spanish-Moroccan War (1860). Luis Miguel Garcia Mora examines the impact of Cuban slavery, the slave trade on anti-slavery, pro-slavery politics and identity in Spain, Cuba, Puerto Rico. Both these authors contribute to the idea first proposed by Christopher Schmidt-Nowara of a plural "colonial public sphere" that crisscrosses the Atlantic between Spain and its colonies. Javier Laviña moves back in time to examine the failure of the first slavery in Panama. He calls attention to the importance of slave resistance and the ongoing tensions and negotiation between *palenques* (runaway slave communities) and Spanish society in preventing the consolidation of a slave system in Panama. Dale Tomich and Rafael Marquese analyze the interaction between international and local conditions that led to the domination of the world coffee market by producers in Brazil's Paraíba Valley in the political and economic conjuncture of the first half of the nineteenth century. Taken together, these chapters bring to light the variety of forces operating on diverse spatial and temporal scales that were implicated in the formation of the second slavery.

This volume originated in the conference "Politics, Economy, and the Second Slavery" held at The Fernand Braudel Center, Binghamton University (April 29–30,

2016). The conference was dedicated to the memory of our friend and colleague. Christopher Schmidt-Nowara (1966–2015) Chris was a pioneer of the second slavery perspective whose work made a significant impact on Atlantic history and the history of Spain and Spanish America. The majority of chapters in this book originated as presentations at the conference. I would like to thank Richard Lee, Amy Keough, Kelly Pueschel, and Laura Tomich for their assistance in organizing the conference and making this volume possible.

—Dale Tomich

Notes

1. Dale W. Tomich, ed., *New Frontiers of Slavery* (Albany: State University of New York Press, 2016); Dale W. Tomich, ed., *The Politics of the Second Slavery* (Albany: State University of New York Press, 2016): Dale Tomich and Michael Zeuske, eds., "The Second Slavery: Mass Slavery, World-Economy and Comparative Microhistories," *Review: Fernand Braudel Center* 31, nos. 2/3 (2008); Dale Tomich, Flávio dos Santos Gomes, Olivia Gomes da Cunha, eds., "Rethinking the Plantation: Histories, Anthropologies, and Archeologies," *Review: Fernand Braudel Center* 34, nos. 1/2.

1780–1880

A Century of Imperial Transformation

Josep M. Fradera

During the revolutionary times from the 1780s to the 1830s, successive internal crises and constant conflicts among empires seemed to point to the demise of the great European monarchic empires, which were, to all appearances, in their death throes (Klooster 2009; Armitage and Subrahmanyam 2010). However, a century later, two of those empires—the British and the French—governed much of the world, a much larger part than they had ever dominated or held as spheres of influence before. At some distance, the Spanish and Portuguese crossed that period of revolution and war but kept their possessions in the Caribbean, the Philippines, and Africa. The United States of America and monarchical Brazil followed the imperial path inherited from the British and the Portuguese in the Americas. In contrast, most of their rivals and competitors in Europe—the Russians, Ottomans, and Germans—had gone through the cycle of the late eighteenth-century revolutions, or had been impacted by them during the Napoleonic Wars and later conflicts, although the weight and depth of that impact among them was undoubtedly unequal (a general approach may be found in Bayly 2004). If certain events symbolized the imperial fin-de-siècle, these were the Berlin Conference of 1885, the Fashoda Incident (in South Sudan), and the 1898 Samoan Crisis that touched Africa and Oceania, in which the French and British seemed to want to seal their global expansion at the expense of their more direct rivals. The meeting at Berlin was characterized by the consensus of the big boys' club regarding the distribution of the world among those powers that met certain criteria of capitalist modernization (a requisite that kept Spain and Portugal practically from the negotiating table). Continued confrontations between imperial powers showed the limits of a consensus built by birds of prey, where each player sought to define their spheres of influence or sovereignty on the ground.

Let us begin with the cycle of destruction and reconstruction that the monarchic empires underwent through the previously mentioned revolutionary period. The period itself, begun with the Seven Years' War, led to the construction of a new kind of state, described and analyzed by writers such as John Brewer (1990), Jan Glete (2002), Stanley and Barbara Stein (2003), Carlos Marichal (1999), and Josep M. Delgado (2007). Impelled first by the tremendous costs of this and subsequent wars, the fiscal-military state resulted from a tendency that began with the War of Succession and the War of Jenkins' Ear. The North American crisis and the French Revolution, with their huge external impact and their continuation in the Napoleonic Wars, firmly consolidated its bases. This sort of amphibious state, well equipped for war on land, but especially fitted for maritime warfare, was the indispensable instrument for the construction of contemporary empires, the differentiating factor par excellence of European societies, or those with a European matrix, versus the rest of the world (Davies 2011). In this juncture, colonial wars became a scenario upon which European and global hegemony were contested.

For Great Britain, the Thirteen Colonies' independence war and Britain's consequent withdrawal to an inhospitable northern frontier with a majority population of French-speaking Catholics inaugurated the cycle of destruction and reconstruction on a grand scale. On the other side of the globe, Britain also launched the costly operation of imperial stabilization begun in Bengal as well as the war on the Indian subcontinent first against Hyder Ali Khan, and then his son Tipu Sultan, great reformers of the Kingdom of Mysore, who allied with the French against the British East India Company until the total defeat of the French in 1799. Third, the independence of the United States signified the crisis in the Antilles that inexorably led to the 1807 British abolition of the slave trade and the growing criticism of slavery itself, and, consequently, to the need to modulate planters' assemblies' loyalty to the Crown, which then governed the British Caribbean islands. The French did not face minor problems, either. Expelled from North America and the Indian subcontinent by the British, they also had to deal with the spectacular crisis of their Antillean possessions, especially Saint-Domingue and Guadeloupe, as well as the sale of Louisiana in 1802. Despite all this, they kept a stronghold in the Caribbean—with the exception of republican Haiti—and on the two African coasts through Senegal and Reunion/Bourbon Island. Nor did they abandon the minor enclaves that the British did not take from them in southern Asia. Furthermore, they closed this period with the conquest of Algeria in 1830, a territory that had been formally under Ottoman sovereignty. Thus seen, locating the change in the nature of the state at the center of the imperial transformation and crisis makes sense only if we understand how society and war interacted throughout the process. That is, we must understand how interstate competition became a catalyst for social change.

Empires are undoubtedly constituted through violent conquest, but their government must rely on broader means in order to rule. The crux of the matter is how the transformation of the state—its politics of war, finances, and international relations, its bureaucracy and sovereignty—connects with inherently changing societies. In this context we must reflect on what Peter Marshall calls "the making and unmaking empires" (Marshall 2005). As war indeed led to the broadening of the state's basis in terms of military recruitment and fiscal demands, the state's intrusion in the societies formed by the empires, which Joanna Innes defined as the fiscal-military state's "domestic face" in reference to day-to-day governance, was produced inside as well as outside Europe (Innes 2011). This intrusion visibly disarticulated the old equilibrium upheld by the societies within the Atlantic portion of the European empires when other continents were added: enclaves and slave-trading posts in Africa, in the Indian subcontinent, and all the way to Java, Timor, and the Philippines. The foundations of all the old colonial complexes were necessarily altered. It was this that set off the revolutionary crisis across the conquered globe, as the imperial center's demands met with the resistance of defensive local ruling classes. The first of the great crises was that of the British Empire's Thirteen Colonies. This conflict apparently revolved around the increased fiscal pressure that the imperial government tried to impose. The second exploded in the French Antillean colonies with the French Revolution, but it was preceded by a decade of complaints and demands by the colonies' residents against *l'exclusif*, the key imperial fiscal policy on sugar and overseas products. The repeated eruptions of violence in Spanish America, and between Lisbon and the "Paulistas" or São Paulo colonials, responded to the resistance of these empires' American *criollos* to the imperial states' new tributary exigencies. A hypothesis appears: it was not the weight of the new fiscal demands that caused the conflict, but the change in the nexus that tied the colonies with their metropoles, the articulation of policies that increased the imperial center's capacity to intrude more in colonial societies.

The consequences of these conflicts would lead to the complete decolonization of a very significant portion of the monarchic empires, as well as to an important redefinition of center-periphery relations. In every case, the revolutionary crisis signals a moment of decisive imperial change, namely, the transformation of old regime monarchic empires, formed by aggregation, with their multiple jurisdictions and motley constitutional and governmental solutions, and characterized by internal variegation, into empires that are represented as "national" spaces. In effect, colonial elites wish to receive the same political treatment as their counterparts in metropolitan territories. The profound meaning of North American colonists' "no taxation without representation" and their criticism of the so-called virtual representation; the great truth of the period, that "men are born and remain free and equal in rights" of the French Declaration of the Rights of Man; and the idea that "the Spanish nation is the re-union of all the Spaniards of both hemispheres," as the 1812 Constitution of Cadiz proclaims—these are all reflections of the desire to fuse the monarchic empire into the single space of the new nation. Imperial constitutions were the instrument that articulated these demands for inclusion, constitutions that tried to blend the king's domains into the body of the nation, fusing nation and empire into a single political body. Nevertheless, such projects failed. Overseas political communities developed far from their metropoles, and, proud of their origins and their juridical-political cultures, the new obligations forced upon them by the monarchies' dynastic and international compromises dangerously eroded that distance (Greene 2010).

Those distant political communities had been formed on a substratum of colonial relations established with native populations in their original settlements, or populations that had been displaced as slaves or forced laborers, or both. Consequently, imperial protection was essential to the groups at the top of the social pyramid (Tomlins 2010; Morgan and Rushton 2013). They were, from their very origin, multiethnic societies. Only when there are doubts regarding metropolitan loyalty do socially dominant sectors contemplate separation as a reasonable possibility. The colonists' mistrust can be appreciated in the process that led to the Proclamation line of 1763, through which the British imperial government tried to protect the native nations from the colonists' insatiable hunger for land. It can also be observed in the Antillean colonists' reserve regarding the imperial powers' attitude toward the slave crisis and toward "free blacks" as well as the mutual reserve during the protracted conflict regarding the end of the slave trade. The imperial crisis moved in two interconnected planes: the struggle between colonists and the metropole for a greater share of the available wealth, and the multiple struggles that derived from the very nature of colonial societies. In this sense, if we have learned something in the last few years, it has been that the self-liberation of Saint-Domingue's slaves in the summer of 1791 was the replica of North American colonists' great revolution of a few years earlier. They were both part of the same process. As David Geggus and John K. Thornton have shown, cultural and language barriers could not keep news of the equality of men proclaimed in Philadelphia or Paris from reaching the people at the base of that same social pyramid (Geggus and Gaspar 1997; Thornton 2012).

For this reason, the revolutionary cycle of 1780 to 1830 encompassed at the same time the *criollos*' emancipation, secured by colonists from Boston to Santiago de Chile, as well as the reconstruction of imperial frameworks, because empires always strike back. Great Britain reformed and reconstructed its empire in British North America, for instance, where it declared that it would never impose undue fiscal burdens on its colonists, and accepted political representatives for the majority population in Canada, which was of French origin, and Catholic to boot. Those represented included Tories who had fled the Thirteen Colonies (some of them, with their slaves), as well as people who migrated from the British Isles. Across the globe, the armies of the East India Company were simultaneously defeating through force of arms the great powers that succeeded the Mogul Empire in the north and center of the subcontinent, and the reformist sultans that allied with the French in the south. While these episodes of consolidation were taking place, the most complicated problem faced by the Georgian empire was that of Antillean slavery. The empire's desire for moral regeneration led to the abolition of human trafficking, as Cristopher Brown has shown, but the interests of property tied up in slavery in the islands and in Great Britain itself marked the limit of that regeneration (Brown 2006). The alliance between the religious-humanitarian campaigns and the eighteenth-century sensibility against the purchase and sale of human beings (that of children had already led to the abolition of the slave trade in the Indian Ocean) and the intentions of the military and political establishment was a crucial aspect of the British imperial reform (Allen 2009). In the end, what becomes clear is that between the Quebec Act of 1791 and the parliamentary reform of 1832, which liquidated the parliamentary lobbies of Caribbean planters and nabobs in Westminster, the empire finally released ballast and readied itself for its future expansion.

France followed a different route: after all, it had been defeated in the war for continental and global dominance. For a moment, it seemed that revolutionary élan would carry the empire over the challenge of self-emancipation presented by Saint-Domingue and its shock wave across the rest of its Caribbean possessions, Senegal, and the Mascarene Islands. The participation of free mulattos and former slaves in metropolitan institutions guaranteed national unity until the neo-Jacobin period of 1797–98. However, as first consul, Napoleon nipped that path of revolutionary integration in the bud through two key policies. The first was placing the colonies beyond the reach of the metropolitan constitutional framework of 1799; and the second, the infamous reestablishment of slavery in 1802. Both decisions were part of a project to restore the old order in the Antilles and the Mascarene Islands. However, this meant rolling back the gains of unity and equality of the revolutionary period, notions that had completely transformed France and its overseas world. It is easy to understand then why one of Napoleon's greatest defeats was the debacle of the army that he sent against the infant Republic of Haiti, and why the stabilization of the French Empire after Waterloo was so grueling and oppressive.

There was a second cycle, from the 1830s to 1870, related to the triumph of "specialness," that formula that Napoleon clairvoyantly announced, and which his heirs developed in France and other countries with imperial pretensions. For contemporary jurists, the French in 1799, the Spanish in 1837, and the Portuguese in 1838, the meaning behind government by "special laws" was clear. They referred to this formula as a "double constitution" system. This was a fallacious rhetorical device because there was only one constitution: special laws were an ersatz series of ordinances and decrees characterized by arbitrariness and even military despotism, which starkly revealed the absence of legislative unity between the metropole and the colonies. David Bell explained that the Napoleonic use of specialness was a strategy to "*créer un état qui peut imposer des normes administratives, judiciaires et fiscales—par exemple le Code Napoléon—sans l'obligation de fondre tous les citoyens dans une même nation*" (create a state that can impose administrative, judicial, and fiscal norms—for example the Napoleonic Code—without the necessity of merging all citizens into a single nation) (Antoine et al. 2014, 27). In time, other European powers imitated and followed the quintessentially French idea of *specialité*, so that it acquired a superior coherence. Indeed, while in the metropolis elected parliamentary chambers debated and passed laws, embodying the essence of liberal-representative politics, colonial legislation was generated by the executive at the margin of the legislature through imperial edicts, *senatus-consulte*, *arrêtés*, ordinances, and decrees. If we look at the global postrevolutionary period, we will see a generalized coherence between the contraction of the idea of the citizen, as the political subject par excellence, to a mere qualified elector, in the metropolis, and the literal collapse of the idea of citizenship in colonial spaces.

The deep logic of the distinction between two types of legislation, one linked to deliberation, political and electoral struggles, and the composition of parliamentary chambers, and another, discretional, colonial, and essentially repressive, dictated as it was by political-military rule, as opposed to the rule of law, goes beyond the sphere of decisions and legislative activity. It is in colonial practice, in each and every one of an empire's corners, that the imposition of a logic that separated and distinguished between subjects and situations under a single sovereignty was felt. In the French Antilles, Senegal, and Reunion Island, where slavery was legal until the Second Republic, the universal emancipation of 1848 gave French citizenship back to the slaves (Tomich 1990; Jennings 2000). However, since those territories had been placed outside the reach of the French constitution since 1799 and the departmental changes that it later encompassed, residents of these territories were second-class citizens. The so-called old colonies remained under rules of specialness until 1947. As we will see, for the named new ones, colonial policies can be worse.

We can find similar contrasts of lights and shadows in France's rival empire, particularly, in Jamaica's Morant Bay Rebellion of 1865, in which soldiers and militias repressed and killed hundreds of black rioters and the government executed hundreds more, eventually arresting and killing a mulatto political opponent and local businessman. This bloody incident galvanized and divided British public and intellectual opinion (Heuman 1994). Faced with the impossibility of clearly defining the limits and content of personal freedom in colonial conditions, the great Liberal empire decided to suspend the first empire's old system of local representation, accentuating rather than decreasing specialness. As is well known, the only exception was found in Barbados, where land scarcity and the planters' iron grip rendered this measure unnecessary.

In the Spanish case, the dilemma of keeping Cuban sugar interests on a short leash within an unstable Liberal framework led to the expulsion of the overseas representatives from the Spanish Cortes in 1837 (Fradera 1995, 334–39; for an enlarged version on Spanish colonial policy and the general context in the Spanish Antilles and the Philippines, see Fradera 2005). The legal and political vacuum thus generated was filled by a combination of military despotism and special laws, which were in place until very late in the Caribbean, and practically until the "emancipation" of 1898 under US neocolonial tutelage in the Philippines (McCoy and Scarano 2009).

If the development of specialness can be traced back step by step in colonies governed by Europeans for centuries, it is even clearer in those places where the imperial machinery came into contact with highly organized societies whose religious and legal systems, social life, and political hierarchies were as ancient and complex as those of the Europeans themselves, and were acknowledged as such by the colonizers. The examples of British India and French Algeria are enough to demonstrate this. Algeria was the counterpoint to the "old colonies," where the Napoleonic involution reestablished slavery during the early nineteenth century. If in those old colonies, French imperial policy led to the construction of a second-class citizenship, in Algeria it led to what French jurists called a "juridical monster." Constituted by a dual regime, the North African possession was divided into three departments for *français de souche* citizens, and a territory of Berber and Arab residents administered under a totally different regime. The long and violent military conquest and plunder that brought Algeria under French sovereignty was followed by the establishment of a set of repressive norms (that included collective punishments, deportations, and reprisals) that would have been unthinkable in the metropole's penal system, given their absolute lack of proportion and guarantees. Finally codified in the Code d'indigénat of 1881, they were exported *prêt-a-porter* to Indochina and New Guinea. The state's highest magistrate periodically confirmed this repressive instrument, with practically no parliamentary debate. Meanwhile, Algeria's "dual constitution" excluded "Muslim" subjects from even the narrowly defined citizenship, even more narrow than that which the residents of the Antilles, Senegal, and the Mascarene Islands enjoyed (Blévis 2004; Thenault 2014). In Algeria, the Third Republic created French citizens in three departments at the same time as it generated phantasmagorical French subjects who could not be citizens due to religious reasons, which was in stark contradiction to the regime's euphoric secular character. Even more shocking was that, first Jews, and then Italians and Spaniards, could ask for French citizenship, while Muslim Algerians had no legal means of attaining it.

During the Indian Rebellion of 1857 against the East India Company, the British nearly lost their immense Asian domains. A mix of peasant insurgency, officer and sepoy mutiny within the Company's large private army, and anti-British conspiracies of provincial dignitaries came close to putting an end to a century-old British domination and administration. To prevent something like this from happening again, the empire was nationalized within the empire. Until then, the East India Company had governed its territories with an able combination of proconsular despotism and long-established and efficient regularization of land taxation systems. But after this narrow escape, the Victorian Crown institutionalized the Indian Raj and made some concessions to the regional ruling classes (Baxi 2003). In the apotheosis of the so-called responsible governments of the large white settler colonies, the empire did not give in to the temptation of satisfying the autochthonous upper classes' demands for self-government, which was the key demand of the Indian National Congress, founded by liberal Indian and British subjects in 1885 (for more on the Indian perspective, see Bayly 2012). In *Considerations on Representative Government*, John Stuart Mill, an East India Company employee until the very last day, articulated the enlightened thought of his day when he argued that the principles of self-government were not viable without a process of education and emulation that the Indians were far from achieving (1861, 77–78). Unfortunately, there was no equivalent in India of the citizen, placed at the center of the British political system by the political reforms of 1832 and 1867. Indian and British subjects could not be judged by the same tribunals, something that angered and humiliated the autochthonous ruling classes of the subcontinent and led them to raise constant complaints.

The development of the political and juridical culture of specialness (with or without the explicit use of the term) inexorably led to a progressive distinction between sovereignty's national and imperial contexts. The nation in the metropolis tended to forge moral and cultural unity, locating the citizen and his rights at the center of the majority population's aspirations. Moreover, the condition of citizenship increasingly exceeded the subjects' strict political capacities (adult males, with fixed legal residence and a clean legal background), and encompassed certain duties of the state, such as social assistance, job security, and primary and secondary education, that set of political and social rights that Gérard Noiriel defined as the French Third Republic's "social citizenship" (Noiriel 1999; also by Saada 2007). In the colonies, however, political organization and the position of their residents was fragmented and atomized, according to the rules of specialness, between the social realities of each place and the way in which they were governed. From the opposite side, the metropolis tended to concentrate more than often extraordinary powers to display at their will (Yusuf 2014). Nobody was deceived as to where the threshold of social and political rights lay, that high point that established the hierarchy of situations in the framework of the nation and the empire.

The third cycle of imperial transformation began in the last decades of the nineteenth century and ended with the First World War. It corresponds to the apex of the imperial nation, the moment of the great imperial expansion that we spoke of in the beginning. Very different political entities participated in this great cycle of expansion: great imperial nations, old empires, and countries with colonies. Among them, the imperial nation, that is, the sum of the national communities that emerged in the nineteenth century and its possessions, governed by rules of specialness, was at the center of global transformation. Without pretending to equate the incomparable, the two great empires of that period, France and Great Britain, as well as Spain, Portugal, the Netherlands, Denmark, and the recently arrived Belgium and the German Kaiserreich, more or less fit this model after 1885. We must also include in this family the United States of America, heir of the British Empire in North America, and an ardent practitioner of rules of specialness between north and south; with relation to the Indian nations; and the Hispanic-Mexican world, all of these within its continental territory, but even more accentuated after it erupted outside its continental frontiers in the late 1890s. These imperial nations were not alone: alongside them, as rivals and competitors, were the Viennese Habsburgs, Tsarist Russia, China under the Qing dynasty, Meiji Japan, the Persian Qajar dynasty, and the Ottomans, political entities that fluctuated between old, autocratic forms of government of monarchic empires and the great national transition.

Let us look again at the greatest power of that period. Between 1880 and 1918, the Victorian British Empire had left its contemporaries and competitors behind in terms of imperial expansion. In the metropole, the combination of electoral reforms and social conflict placed the community of citizens at the center of political life. At the same time, thanks to technical advances in printing and communication, with the proliferation of newspapers and popular journals, information regarding the empire and its conflicts impregnated British social life. There are many examples of the connection between empire and nation, which albeit not limited to the third cycle of imperial transformation, saw an exponential increase in their significance during this period. For instance, the combination of popular antislavery sentiment and nonconformist church antislavery campaigns in connection to the Antilles, deftly explored by Catherine Hall; the weight of the British Raj and Africa in the career of countless young middle class men; Ornamentalism's pomp and splendor, as studied by David Cannadine; the importance of the domestic replicas that were Australia, Canada, and South Africa's white settlements; and finally, the weight that interimperial rivalries acquired in metropolitan cultural and social life, from the Napoleonic Wars to the Crimean War (Hall 2002; Cannadine 2002; Darwin 2009).

As the nation was placed at the center of collective life, rules of specialness were expertly applied to the empire, so that the assimilation of new populations and territories was carried out without excessive conflicts, according to a well-practiced score of constitutional and administrative formulas. An axis formed by the metropolis and the white settlements—the Canadian and Australian federation, and later South Africa—were at the center of the imperial nation. These overseas territories governed themselves and financed themselves, and were perhaps happy to defend the empire, as the Boer Wars and later the Great War revealed. Crown colonies came next, with varied formulas of self-government and rule of law, in John McLaren's conceptualization (McLaren 2010). They had come up with successful political formulas for spaces that were not "ethnically" homogenous, spaces of European colonization with policies for non-Europeans that went from pure and simple genocide (as in the Australian case) to paternalism that excluded (regarding the Indian nations in Canada), all legitimated by the geographical morality spoken of by Edmund Burke (Bell 2006, 283). The third concentric circle was occupied by colonial empire par excellence: the new possessions in the Pacific, Southeast Asia, and Africa. Myriad imaginative gradations characterized policies in this last continent, from the Egyptian Protectorates to the colonies administered directly by British officials in the Lower Nile, the Gulf of Guinea, and Rhodesia, ending with the great discovery of "indirect government" practiced in Nigeria. Instead of attempting to find an ideal political or administrative solution, the British had the capacity and experience to devise and implement government formulas that were relevant to the local contexts. In any case, the evidence of a flexible, albeit hierarchical, system should warn us against the widespread idea that the global British imperial integration lacked a methodology or was solved through pure empiricism.

From the 1880s to the fateful year of 1914, new factors were added to the imperial transformation described so far. Undoubtedly, the first was the absolute centrality of the nation—the community of citizens at the center of the imperial power complex. The second was the influence of racial(ist) factors at the very heart of imperial politics and perceptions. These processes are intimately related. At the center of both nation-state consolidation and imperial expansion stood the nation, the most dynamic factor in the equation thanks to its weight as both a political and a cultural community. Starting in the 1870s and 1880s, the nation, which was capable of (re)defining the nature of the state that it inherited as well as the nature of its empire as a project of expansion, was the ideal and the referential framework imposed (and supposed) by the imperial nation on the great capitalist, liberal societies. For example, the values of the Victorian "gentleman" became interwoven with serving a Great Britain that had successfully passed the double text of democratizing political life at home and consolidating its imperial expansion abroad in spite of the fierce competition of its rivals (Parry 2006, 20). The same thing happened in France, where republican ethos, social citizenship, and the *mission civilisatrice* constituted a single project that would prolong itself in various tones and shapes through the two Frances of 1940–45. This project was etched in the republican soldiers' spirit of service, as Marshal Lyautey's declaration in 1891 revealed, when he defended his role at the service of the great national project of his day (Lyautey 2009).

The idea of "white" "racial" superiority would increasingly gain an important place in this history, but it is not easy to discern just how important it was. It took time for the idea that biological inferiority was hereditable to become part of the cultural common sense. Nevertheless, the long validity and use of slavery constitutes a key factor. Indeed, European ethnocentrism, investigated by Douglas Lorimer and Catherine Bolt, resisted its transformation into a race-centered belief system until very late, and with great hesitancy. Nevertheless, there were inklings of white racial superiority in plantation colonies, and reverberations of it across Europe for more than a hundred years. Slavery provided a legitimate framework for exploiting transplanted Africans and their descendants without a need to define their inferiority ethnographically or racially. Things changed when that institution was progressively abolished in the various colonies, in 1833, 1848, 1865, and from 1886–88. Manifestations of an openly biological and phenotypical racism began gaining ground. Since that moment coincided with the increase in the gap between the great metropolitan centers and societies in other continents, the confluence of these perceptions seriously eroded the notion that there was a single humanity, albeit in different stages of development, which had been for a long time the shared framework of classic liberalism and Christian ecumenism (Lyautey 2009, 22). The transformation of the archetypes of racial distinction and their association with scientific thought in the spiraling process of their fabrication and legitimation was slower and more tortuous than one may think (Mandler 2000, 224–45). When Alexis de Tocqueville—author of the striking chapter on the three races in *La Démocratie en Amérique*—writes to his relative Arthur de Gobineau that the latter's rigid vision of "human races" was worthy of a horse trader, he represents a sector of public opinion. Equally representative was Charles Darwin's sympathy for the position adopted by John Stuart Mill (an ethnocentric, but not racist, diffusionist) regarding the 1865 Jamaican conflict, and his refusal to extrapolate his ideas to the human species (that heated debate is summarized in Semmel 1962). Nevertheless, racialist sensibilities increased first in the context of stark colonial relations, where significant populations of former slaves and a lack of rights generated open conflicts, before expanding throughout the respective empires. Examples easily come to mind: the emergence of the one-drop rule in the southern states after the Civil War; the anti-Asian immigrant laws passed in California; Australia and its genocidal treatment of aborigines (Lake and Reynolds 2008). If to all this we add the large-scale colonization of Africa by several countries, we can trace the way racial archetypes consolidated and expanded. However, that does not mean that we can trace with the same accuracy the ways in which they affected the formulation of colonial policy, which, as Jane Burbank and Frederick Cooper warned, is a very complex issue (Burbank and Cooper 2010, 325). In any case, it is very difficult to remove these efforts at racial classification from the historically simultaneous definition of the basic cultural consensus of the modern nation, which was based on the search/construction of a homogeneity that would solidify and discipline the national body, vis-à-vis mass politics and political competition. It was in this connection that the precocious biologism of the Scandinavians and the Germans found its logical replica in the imperial lucubration of the precursor empires that we have been analyzing.

The notions advanced so far suggest a couple of conclusions. The first closes the circle that was opened with the initial question. The monarchic empires of the seventeenth and eighteenth centuries became the perfect framework for the development of the great nations of America and Europe in the contemporary world to the degree that they were able to close the cycle of broken promises that characterized the revolutionary moment of the 1780s to the 1830s and open it again unequally for colonial and metropolitan subjects. The second conclusion is that the imperial nation became the model that those countries that were behind in the imperial race sought to replicate. Although other cases could be cited, the most exemplary is that of Germany after the colonial turn taken by Chancellor Otto von Bismarck in the 1880s. If before, the monarchic-imperial project related to Prussia had centered on inter-European power games, the Kaiserreich now added the desire to expand globally, particularly to Africa and Oceania. A late and compulsive nationalization, and a speedy entry into the colonial race outside Europe, are two sides of the same coin. Recent texts by Sebastian Conrad and Jürgen Osterhammel have shown the real dimension of what the incorporation of Wilhelmine Germany in the colonial race meant for Europe and the world (Osterhammel 2014 Conrad 2010, 2011). The importance of what happened was not limited to the simple incorporation of Germany into the select club of countries that distributed the world among themselves. I dare suggest that it had to do with the incorporation of a model of nation and empire whose constitutional and political interrelations and solutions had taken a century to form.

All empires are built upon colonial foundations. Writing about empires is a clever subterfuge for writing about the world without having to descend into the messy universe of labor in colonial conditions, the forced and voluntary displacement of human beings, and social lives and problems that were even worse than what they were in metropolitan societies. However, it is not a subterfuge when such writing addresses the political and cultural integration of diverse colonial complexes, often quite diverse. It makes even more sense if that reconstruction includes the integration, by nature unequal, between metropolitan society and the colonial worlds under its sovereignty. In these few pages I have tried to show the complex ways through which those two planes of integration were articulated from the crises at the end of the eighteenth century through the early twentieth century. If I am capable of discerning a primum mobile in this long century of imperial destruction and reconstruction, it is in the complexities of imperial government, by which a few "equals" governed millions of "non-equals."

Works Cited

Allen, Richard B. 2009. "Suppressing a Nefarious Traffic: Britain and the Abolition of Slave Trading in India and the Western Indian Ocean." *William and Mary Quarterly* 66, no. 4: 873–94.

Antoine, François, Jean-Pierre Jessene, Annie Jourdan, and Hervé Luewers, eds. 2014. *L'Empire napoléonien: Une experiénce europeénne*. Paris: Armand Colin.

Armitage, David, and Sanjay Subrahmanyam, eds. 2010. *The Age of Revolutions in Global Context, c. 1760–1840*. Houndmills: Palgrave Macmillan.

Bayly, Christopher A. 2004. *The Birth of the Modern World, 1780–1914*. Malden, MA: Blackwell.

Bayly, Christopher A. 2012. *Recovering Liberties: Indian Thought in the Age of Liberalism and Empire*. Cambridge: Cambridge University Press.

Baxi, Upendra. 2003. "The Colonialist Heritage." In *Comparative Legal Studies: Traditions and Transitions*, edited by Pierre Legrand and Roderick Munday. Cambridge: Cambridge University Press.

Bell, Duncan S. 2006. "Empire and International Relations in Victorian Political Thought." *Historical Journal* 49, no. 1: 281–98.

Blévis, Laure. 2004. *Sociologie d'un droit colonial: Citoyenneté et nationalité en Algérie (1865–1947); Une exception republicaine*. Marseille: Université Aix, Marseille.

Brewer, John. 1990. *Sinews of Power: War, Money, and the English State, 1688–1783*. Cambridge: Harvard University Press.

Brown, Christopher L. 2006. *Moral Capital: Foundations of British Abolitionism*. Chapel Hill: University of North Carolina Press.

Burbank, Jane, and Frederick Cooper. 2010. *Empires in World History: Power and the Politics of Difference*. Princeton: Princeton University Press.

Cannadine, David. 2002. *Ornamentalism: How the British Saw Their Empire*. Oxford: Oxford University Press.

Conrad, Sebastian. 2010. *Globalisation and the Nation in Imperial Germany*. Cambridge: Cambridge University Press.

Conrad, Sebastian. 2011. *German Colonialism: A Short History*. Cambridge: Cambridge University Press.

Darwin, John, 2009. *The Empire Project: The Rise and Fall of the British World System, 1830–1870*. Cambridge: Cambridge University Press.

Davies, Brian. 2011. *Empire and Military Revolution in Eastern Europe: Russia's Turkish Wars in the Eighteenth Century*. London: Bloomsbury Academic.

Delgado, Josep M. 2007. *Dinámicas imperiales (1688–1796): España, América y Europa en el cambio institucional del sistema colonial español*. Barcelona: Edicions Bellaterra.

Fradera, Josep M. 1995. "Why the Special Overseas Laws Were Never Enacted." In *Spain, Europe and the Atlantic World: Essays in Honour of John H. Elliott*, edited by Richard L. Kagan and Geoffrey Parker, 334–49. Cambridge: Cambridge University Press.

Fradera, Josep M. 2005. *Colonias para después de un imperio*. Barcelona: Edicions Bellaterra.

Geggus, David P., and David B. Gaspar, eds. 1997. *A Turbulent Time: The French Revolution and the Greater Caribbean*. Bloomington: Indiana University Press.

Glete, Jan. 2002. *War and the State in Early Modern Europe: Spain, the Dutch Republic and Sweden as Fiscal-Military States, 1500–1660*. London: Routledge.

Greene, Jack P., ed. 2010. *Exclusionary Empire: English Liberty Overseas, 1600–1900*. Cambridge: Cambridge University Press.

Hall, Catherine. 2002. *Civilizing Subjects: Metropole and Colony in the English Imagination, 1830–1867*. Chicago: University of Chicago Press.

Heuman, Gad. 1994. *"The Killing Time": The Morant Bay Rebellion in Jamaica*. Knoxville: University of Tennessee Press.

Innes, Johanna. (1997) 2011. "The Domestic Face of the Military-Fiscal State: Government and Society in Eighteenth-Century Britain." In *An Imperial State at War: Britain from 1698–1815*, edited by Lawrence Stone, 96–128. London: Routledge.

Jennings, Lawrence C. 2000. *French Anti-Slavery: The Movement for the Abolition of Slavery in France, 1802–1848*. New York: Cambridge University Press.

Klooster, Wim. 2009. *Revolutions in the Atlantic World: A Comparative History*. New York: New York University Press.

Lake, Marilyn, and Henry Reynolds. 2008. *Drawing the Global Colour Line: White Men's Countries and the Question of Racial Equality*. Melbourne: Melbourne University Press.

Lyautey, Maréchal. 2009. *Le rôle social de l'officer*. Paris: Bartillat.

Mandler, Peter. 2000. " 'Race' and 'Nation' in Mid-Victorian Thought." In *History, Religion, and Culture: British Intellectual History, 1750–1850*, edited by Stefan Collini, Richard Whatmore, and Brian Young, 224–45. Cambridge: Cambridge University Press.

Marichal, Carlos. 1999. *La bancarotta del veirreanto: Nueva España y las finanzas del Imperio español, 1780–1810*. México: Fondo de Cultura Económica.

Marshall, Peter J. 2005. *The Making and Unmaking of Empires: Britain, India, and America, c. 1750–1783*. Oxford: Oxford University Press.

McCoy, Alfred, and Francisco Scarano, eds. 2009. *Colonial Crucible: Empire in the Making of the Modern American State*. Madison: University of Wisconsin Press.

McLaren, John. 2010. "The Uses of the Rule of Law in British Colonies in the Nineteenth Century." In *Law and Politics and British Colonial Thought: Transpositions of Empire*, edited by Shaunnagh Dorsett and Ian Hunter, 71–90. Basingstoke: Palgrave Macmillan.

Mill, John Stuart. 1861. *Considerations on Representative Government*. London: Parker, Son and Bourn.

Morgan, Gwenda, and Peter Rushton. 2013. *Banishment in the Atlantic World: Convicts, Rebels and Slaves*. London: Bloomsbury.

Noiriel, Gérard. 1999. *Les origines républicaines de Vichy*. Paris: Hachette.

Osterhammel, Jürgen. 2014. *The Transformation of the World: A Global History of the Nineteenth Century*. Princeton: Princeton University Press.

Parry, Jonathan. 2006. *The Politics of Patriotism: English Liberalism, National Identity and Europe, 1830–1886*. Cambridge: Cambridge University Press.

Saada, Emmanuel. 2007. *Les enfants de la colonie: Les métis de l'Empire français entre sujetion et citoyenneté*. Paris: Éditions la Découverte.

Semmel, Bernard. 1962. *The Governor Eyre Controversy*. London: MacGibbon and Key.

Stein, Stanley, and Barbara Stein. 2003. *Apogee of Empire: Spain and New Spain in the Age of Charles III, 1759–1789*. Baltimore: Johns Hopkins University Press.

Thenault, Sylvie, 2014. "1881–1918: L' 'apogée' de l'Algérie française et les débuts de l'Algérie algérienne." In *Histoire de l'Algérie à la periode coloniale (1830–1962)*, edited by Abderraman Bouchène, Jean-Pierre Peyroulou, Ouanassa Siari Tengour, and Sylvie Thénault. Paris: La Découverte.

Thornton, John K. 2012. *A Cultural History of the Atlantic World, 1250–1820*. Cambridge: Cambridge University Press.

Tomich, Dale W. 1990. *Slavery in the Circuit of Sugar: Martinique and the World Economy.* Baltimore: Johns Hopkins University Press.

Tomlins, Christopher L. 2010. *Freedom Bound.* New York: Cambridge University Press.

Yusuf, Hakeem O. 2014. *Colonial and Post-Colonial Constitutionalism in the Commonwealth: Peace, Order and Good Government.* New York: Routledge.

Slavery in Mainland Spanish America in the Age of the Second Slavery

Marcela Echeverri

I

The historiography on the second slavery, inspired by Dale Tomich's 2004 conceptual analysis of the links between slavery and capitalism in the nineteenth century, has had an important influence on ushering in a wave of scholarship on the political economy of Atlantic slavery.[1] It has also been a very generative arena for rethinking questions of teleology and temporality in the study of slavery's simultaneous expansion and extinction in different parts of the Atlantic world during the so-called Age of Abolition. In this framework, the second slavery regimes are the Spanish island of Cuba, southeastern Brazil, and the cotton economies of the US South. What joins these regions together conceptually and historically is that they all experienced huge technological and ideological transformations around slavery, whereby the rise of massive plantation economies based on enslaved labor, and their production, were articulated to the emergence of global industrial and financial economies. Ideologically, in the context of the rise and spread of liberalism, abolitionism, and of the principles of civil equality, these societies of the second slavery also had to redefine bondage. That was done by justifying in new terms slavery's economic and social foundations—exploitation and inequality.

This chapter seeks to contribute to these fertile conceptualizations and debates by expanding the geographic frame and including mainland Spanish America, the continental region of the Spanish Empire that between 1810 and 1825 broke off from Spanish rule and created independent republics. This extensive region from

Mexico to Rio de la Plata (contemporary Argentina) until now has not been examined within these discussions. Here I suggest why and how it constitutes a central node for our historical understanding of the links between the politics and varied local and social dimensions of Atlantic antislavery and the emergence of global capitalism in the nineteenth century. My rethinking of the analytical boundaries of this history from the perspective of mainland Spanish America is in line with current global studies of abolition that are unearthing the particularities of slavery and abolition in Asia or eastern Europe, giving a fuller picture of what is effectively a global as well as a multiple process (Suzuki 2015). I will illustrate my argument with an emphasis on the case of the Republic of Colombia created in 1821, which I call "Old Colombia" to differentiate it from the smaller, contemporary one.[2]

After a long independence war against Spain, military commanders, intellectuals, and political leaders established a constitutional congress in Cúcuta where they gave life to the Republic of Colombia, which encompassed two of the northernmost Spanish possessions in South America: Venezuela and the Viceroyalty of New Granada, the latter including the Quito and Panama *audiencias* (see figure 1). Along with declaring independence from Spain, the Colombian law of July 21, 1821, sanctioned under the Cúcuta Constitution, decreed the abolition of the slave trade and a Law of Free Birth across its territory. These abolitionist laws were, no doubt, a progressive move on the part of the Colombian legislators, reflecting a commitment on the part of elites such as Simón Bolívar to the abolition of Atlantic slavery: they aligned with the Haitian Revolution both in the principles of republicanism and antislavery and with the British monarchy's campaign to stop the African slave trade. They were, moreover, a clear consequence of the mobilization of enslaved people in the armies fighting for independence.

As a result of the combination of these factors, the Spanish American mainland antislavery republics constitute one of the three paradigms of abolitionism in the Atlantic world alongside the British intellectual, civic, and diplomatic abolitionism (C. Brown 2006; Davis 1991; Drescher 2002) and the Haitian-centered abolition of slavery born out of slave rebellion that shifted the focus from enlightened publics to the incidence of radical Afro-diasporic politics in the destruction of slavery (Dubois 2004a, 2004b; Popkin 2010). The third paradigm is characterized by gradual abolition in mainland Spanish America, stemming from the military dynamics of the independence wars. Indeed, this is how the historiography on Atlantic abolitionism currently understands and defines the place of Latin America in that process, based on recent scholarship on the wars of independence in Latin

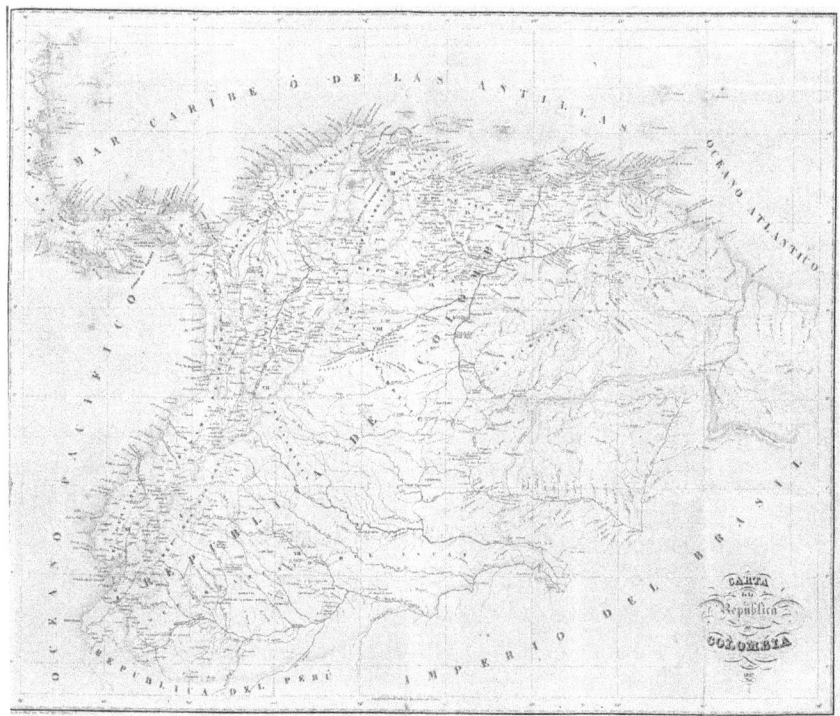

Figure 1. José Manuel Restrepo, Carta de la República de Colombia. 1827. Gravado en Paris por Darmet calle du Battoir, no. 3. Escrito por Hacq. (Por José Manuel Restrepo. Paris, Librería Americana, 1827). Available at www.davidrumsey.com.

America that has brought attention to the links between the military and political processes of the wars and the mobilization of enslaved people (Blanchard 2008; Drescher 2009, 181–204; Echeverri 2016; Ferrer 1999).

Although there is growing awareness about the significance of the gradualist abolition laws of the Spanish Main (Central America and the Northern Coast of South America), the region stands as marginal to the historiography of the second slavery that takes up the rise and fall of slavery in other places of the Spanish Atlantic, namely Cuba and Puerto Rico. Focusing on Old Colombia between 1820 and 1830, and on Ecuador, Venezuela, and New Granada after 1830, I argue that rather than seeing mainland Spanish America as peripheral to the history of Atlantic slavery and antislavery, historians should consider the region as the epicenter of larger historical dynamics that shaped the meanings of freedom and republicanism in the American continent. For example, the deep and long-lasting effects of slaves' military service on nation-state formation in the Spanish American republics foreshadowed the links between slavery's abolition and the independence war in Cuba in the late nineteenth century (Fradera and Schmidt-Nowara 2013, 7; Lasso 2007, 1–15).

I will explain how within the conceptual framework of the second slavery we find fruitful tools for rethinking the traditional interpretations of the aspects of mainland Spanish America's history that have been thought to exclude the region from the second slavery economies' historical plane. I will also explore why taking the step of establishing this dialogue, in turn, has a major impact on our understanding of slavery and slave societies in the Atlantic world. As this volume suggests, the spirit of inquiring about the Atlantic transformations during the age of the second slavery is to reconstruct how the global was produced in the local throughout the nineteenth century, thus all specific regional articulations are of the utmost importance and deserve attention (Tomich 2004).

In spite of its location at the crossroads of pro- and antislavery forces, given its status as a failed republic, Old Colombia as a unit has received little attention. Most of the scholarship reproduces post-1830 geopolitical frontiers and focuses on Venezuela, Panama, Ecuador, or Colombia separately. Additionally, these nation-based histories of abolition overlook the Atlantic ideological context in which both proslavery and antislavery factions participated.

Just as looking at the ambitious Colombian project during the years in which it existed is important, the fact that by the end of the decade the Republic of Colombia underwent serious crises that led to its dissolution in 1830 is another interesting element for analysis as well. Though the resulting republics of Ecuador, New Granada (including Panama), and Venezuela continued to uphold the legal framework that was driving their societies and economies out of slavery, the institution did not legally end in either of these nations until the early 1850s: 1852 in New Granada and in Ecuador, and 1854 in Venezuela. Thus, rather than a linear history of abolition between the 1820s and 1850s, together these countries illustrate the erratic process through which abolition came about in the Spanish Main and in the Americas more broadly.

The principal reason why mainland Spanish America has been at the margins of the history of the age of the second slavery is that the regions it encompasses (with few exceptions like some areas in Venezuela and Peru) did not develop plantations on a massive scale either in the eighteenth or nineteenth centuries.

From that distinction derives the premise that those regions were not as relevant to the forging of global capitalism. Based on the particular trajectory of mainland Spanish American societies over the course of the wars of independence, scholars have also assumed that in that region the institution of slavery was historically of secondary or minor importance and, moreover, in decline in the early nineteenth century, explaining its early abolition.[3] Scholars have drawn these conclusions and produced such representations of slavery and antislavery in mainland Spanish America from two aspects: the low percentage of enslaved populations and the ties between political dynamics stemming from independence and abolitionist processes between 1810 and 1830. Taken together, these two factors have made mainland Spanish American slavery seem unimportant and its abolition inevitable.

I argue that only the first point of contrast (the absence of massive plantations) truly distances mainland Spanish America's trajectory from the singular path of second slavery regimes, which if seen in a wider context are the true exceptions. On closer inspection, however, slavery's historical transformation in mainland Spanish America was not as linear as it has been assumed either temporally or geographically. During the nineteenth century, mainland Spanish America was a region where the forces of both pro- and antislavery intersected due, precisely, to the central place that slavery actually had in those societies that led to the difficulty in dismantling it—an importance that should be accounted for by looking beyond demography or economics.

It is certainly true that at the turn of the nineteenth century in New Granada or Rio de la Plata slavery did not have the numerical weight of places such as Brazil or Cuba. The number of slaves was not higher than 10 percent of the population across the Spanish Main, but slaves were concentrated in certain regions and in urban centers where they continued to have a significant importance both economically and socially (Blanchard 2008, 8; Schmidt-Nowara 2011, 93, 108). Just like in Brazil, the enslaved populations were unevenly distributed and linked to particular regional economies that had been specifically tied to slavery.

At the economic and social levels, Old Colombia had been an ambitious attempt to unite three very disparate regions. At the eve of independence Venezuela, the foremost Caribbean region of Old Colombia, held the third largest population of slaves in Latin America (after Brazil and Cuba) and it had developed an economic project closest to the plantation economies of the Antilles, mainly in the provinces of Caracas and Maracaibo (Lombardi 1971; Pollak Eltz 2004; Rodriguez Arrieta 2002). New Granada had an important economy based on gold extraction that was dependent on enslaved people's labor in the western provinces of Chocó, Antioquia, and Popayán (Colmenares 1999; Jiménez 2004; Romero 1995); in the audiencia of Quito, slavery was mainly important around the Chota valley (cane) and Guayaquil (shipyards) (Chaves 2010, 130–49; Hamerly 1973; Townsend 1993).

The centrality of slavery to the regional economies of Old Colombia, and to the political projects woven around these, suggests that the importance of slavery in Old Colombia was not just a question of numbers. Indeed, while slavery across Old Colombia never reached the proportions it had in the plantation economies of the Caribbean and Brazil, it was nonetheless very entrenched both ideologically and economically following independence. Slavery was a key institution through which state power was articulated. In the decades between 1810 and 1860, the battles over slavery, among regional elites and between them and the Afro-Colombian populations, had consequences for the tensions that developed at the core of Old Colombia as a republican project.

When thinking through numbers, on the other hand, a significant particularity about these societies in terms of demography—and one that weighs heavily on the importance of studying mainland South America's slavery and antislavery, especially in places like New Granada or Venezuela—is that in Old Colombia free people of African origin and descent had proliferated as a result of the manumission laws of the Spanish monarchy. Certainly, this is an important fact when one considers that, on the eve of independence, in Venezuela the population of free people of African descent ascended to 50 percent and in New Granada it was 30 percent. This is in itself an important reason to account for the place of those freed people in the genealogy of freedom across the Americas (Fradera 2013, 260, 263, 266, 276; Garavaglia 2013, 74–100; Klein 2012, 206–22; Klein and Vinson 2007).

People of African descent had carved out spaces of freedom during the colonial period, and these left marks on the labor structures of mainland Spanish American regions. By escaping forced labor, and in inhabiting the spaces of free laborers, they also shaped the transformation of the economic dynamics of production. This was particularly the case in places like Cartagena and Antioquia in New Granada, Esmeraldas in Quito, and in Venezuela as a whole. Their importance was not, in any case, only economic. The establishment of towns of free people since the colonial period had been a crucial instance of state formation and it continued to impact the process of the rise of political institutions such as political parties and citizenship (Laviña and Zeuske 2008; McGraw 2014; Rueda 2010; Sanders 2004; Zahler 2013).

Additionally, all across mainland Spanish America indigenous people were core actors in the evolution of labor markets, from Mexico to Argentina, and Old Colombia was not an exception. In the colonial period, indigenous people had been objects of state legislation that sought to control them and to exploit their labor. In some cases, they were enslaved. In other cases, as free vassals, they were an example to the enslaved and free people about what freedom might mean, within the Spanish monarchy, in economic and legal/political terms (Echeverri 2016; O'Toole 2012). In that sense, incorporating the indigenous people of the Spanish Main into the history of nineteenth-century slavery and antislavery is a crucial step for expanding the study of slavery and abolition in the Atlantic world. Specifically, the demographic composition of Old Colombia is an interesting laboratory for exploring the differences between places as dissimilar as Ecuador and Venezuela, because Ecuador's Andean society had the largest population of indigenous people while Caribbean Venezuela, as already mentioned, had an exceptionally significant and growing population of free blacks (Gómez 2013, 35–48; Hamerly 1973; Lombardi 1971).

II

From the macro perspective, historians exploring the links between the second slavery regions and global capitalist developments in the nineteenth century have been particularly interested in the financial and trade connections between Britain and Cuba, or the US global cotton market. For example, Spain's involvement in the contraband slave trade, as Michael Zeuske has shown, was at the base of Catalonian industrialization. Though not centered on plantation economies, the Spanish American mainland, as much as the Spanish Caribbean, maintained parallel relations with Britain and its Caribbean colonies that were crucial in the uneven expansion of its trade and financial capital. What this suggests is that the marginality of the Spanish Main is far from clear. And we should avoid a narrow focus on the second slavery regions that results in ignoring the bonds between Latin America and Britain that are well known. Historians of the British Empire have long debated whether Britain's advance south in the nineteenth century constitutes an informal iteration of British imperialism (C. Brown 2006; Gallagher and Robinson 1953; Neil and Williamson 2014; Owen and Sutcliffe 1972; Zeuske 2014).

Here it is useful to consider John Tutino's noteworthy effort to situate Latin America in the most recent narratives about the rise of industrial capitalism.

Tutino challenges the exclusion of the region from that history by pointing to the foundational dynamics of circulation across global markets of resources extracted across Spanish America, mainly silver from the mines in Mexico and Peru and gold from New Granada. The channels that enabled the flow of Spanish American resources structured the global economy from the sixteenth up to the nineteenth centuries. In Tutino's words, from the sixteenth century onward, "the profits of silver stimulated new ways of production and consolidated European rule across Spain's Americas." The mining economies at the heart of Spanish imperialism "stimulated [and powerfully shaped] global trade" and were linked to the rise of sugar slave economies in the Atlantic world, although they "often appear separate" (Tutino 2016).

From this broader chronological perspective it is possible to see that the links between the Spanish Main and Britain had deep roots, for instance in the eighteenth century when Jamaica was the nodal point of trade across the Spanish Caribbean. Ernesto Bassi's work illustrates the increased historiographic interest in connecting "British imperial history with Latin America and the American Revolution with the Americas" (Bassi 2016, 117; Costeloe 1981; Goebel 1938). What this analysis offers is a view of how the British Empire became articulated around the interests of Jamaican merchants and planters and what Bassi calls imperialist adventurers who negotiated with a variety of Spanish and Spanish American agents whose interests lay precisely in receiving British support for projects of economic development. Before the Spanish monarchy's crisis in 1808, such relations fostered cotton production in New Granada's Caribbean coast and later in the nineteenth century a more significant production of tobacco for export that signaled its integration into the world economy (Bassi 2016, 134–39; Borucki 2012; Safford 1993, 105).

Thus, in the late eighteenth century mainland Spanish America represented a crucial ground for the British Empire's recomposition in the Atlantic context after the American Revolution. To that extent, Britain's commercial relations with mainland Spanish America were as central to the development of world capitalism as its relations to the plantation societies of the second slavery. Because capitalism is by definition a global phenomenon, the Spanish American mainland cannot be excluded from its historical development. More to the point, the political and economic transformations in the Spanish Main were driven by the same forces that fostered the second slavery.

Additionally, the evident uneven development articulated across the Spanish Main are an important expression of capitalism's variability and complexity. At the same time, capitalism's development hinged on political relations that are crucially important to understand, namely diplomacy and state formation. These are two sides of the same coin: the anti-slave-trade diplomacy of the British Empire was as significant for the eventual abolition of slavery in the Atlantic world as was the diplomacy of the emergent Spanish American republics in the process of their international recognition (Blaufarb 2007; Gutiérrez 2012).

III

A rich historiography has investigated (and continues to investigate) the process leading to abolition in the Spanish Caribbean in the late nineteenth century in the works of scholars such as Ada Ferrer, José Antonio Piqueras, Christopher Schmidt-Nowara, and Rebecca Scott (Cowling 2013; Ferrer 1999, 2016; Finch 2015; Piqueras 2011; Schmidt-Nowara 1999; Scott 1985). Yet for the Spanish American mainland the politics of the abolition of slavery before and after independence is still a question largely unexplored (Bierck 1953; Blanchard 1992; Clementi 1974; Lombardi 1971; Pita Pico 2014; Tobar Donoso 1959, 5–38; Tovar and Tovar 2009; Townsend 1993). In part this is a result of the prevalent supposition that British diplomatic pressures paved the way for abolition in the emergent republics across the region (Bethell 2009; Murray 2002). Indeed, the history of freedom in the Atlantic world is generally (or still is) portrayed as especially tied to Anglo-Atlantic liberalism. And though British involvement in the dismantling of the slave trade and slavery is unquestionable, mainland Spanish America's importance in the process of Atlantic abolition has been seriously underestimated.

A related presupposition that historians need to revise, therefore, is that mainland Spanish America simply was a recipient of antislavery thought from other regions. It is certainly true that the Spanish Main was a site of intense diplomatic activity especially as part of Britain's crusade to abolish the slave trade. But relations between Britain and the Spanish Main were not unidirectional nor were these the only relevant connections that we need to explore to have a complete picture of the strategic place of mainland Spanish America in the politics of slavery and antislavery in the nineteenth century. The position of the Spanish Main in the competing networks of slavery and antislavery activism in the nineteenth century was a byproduct of its deep historical connections—economic, political, and diplomatic—with the major players understood to be driving the transformative dynamics in the nineteenth-century Atlantic. Thus, aside from revising the Anglo-centric paradigm in the field of Atlantic antislavery through recasting mainland Spanish America's relations with Britain and the United States from a wider chronological perspective, it is necessary to explore the relationship that the emerging Spanish American republics simultaneously developed with Spain and among themselves, highlighting local dynamics across the Spanish American mainland's societies.

Until recently, the consensus in the historiography of Atlantic abolitionism was that Spanish abolitionism (including in Spanish America) did not exist. This conclusion resulted from measuring the Hispanic experience with the standards of the North Atlantic abolitionist movements in France, the United States, and particularly Britain. Studies of Spanish and Spanish American slavery and antislavery have begun to undo this approach, decentering Atlantic history from the North Atlantic and uncovering transimperial dynamics and connections, especially by including the Iberian Americas and Africa (Berquist 2010; Blackburn 2011; Everill 2013; Ferreira 2014a, 2014b). For instance, as Ada Ferrer has conspicuously argued, from the perspective of Cuban history it is reductionist to understand the nineteenth century as the British-centered "age of abolition." As Ferrer's insight suggests, discussions regarding the relevance of the second slavery regions like Cuba and Brazil have led to an increasingly sophisticated understanding of multiple chronologies of nineteenth-century slavery and anti-slavery (Ferrer 2013, 134–57; Zeuske 2014).

A revitalized historiography on the Spanish Main in Latin America can emerge from a dialogue with this debate and simultaneously contribute to making it richer. The historiography on the second slavery is an interesting tool for rethinking Anglo-centric narratives, because it illustrates the premise that nationally or imperially bounded histories are not appropriate or generative to the study of slavery and abolition.[4] The case of Old Colombia precisely offers an opportunity to think outside contemporary national frames, not just because it implies looking at Venezuela, Colombia, Panama, and Ecuador together but also because the diplomacy of the Colombian statesmen was vitally linked to republics all across the hemisphere, including Mexico, Central America, Rio de la Plata, Chile, Peru, Haiti, and the United States. Therefore, it is absolutely necessary and enriching to account for such influences, relationships, and—in some cases—antagonisms, to understand the economic and ideological contours of slavery's fundamental place in the history of the emergent Latin American republics in the nineteenth century.

It is possible to explore two sets of connections: with the strands of British, US, Mexican, and Haitian abolitionism, on the one hand, and with proslavery forces in Brazil, Cuba-Spain, Peru, and the United States South, on the other. This means acknowledging that the Old Colombian abolitionist project did not emerge or evolve in a vacuum. Like the second slavery regions that embarked on redefining slavery economically, and reimagined the arguments in favor of slavery ideologically and morally, proslavery elites in Colombia were doing the same thing, and they were doing so by establishing links to that broader contemporary reality of the simultaneous growth of Atlantic slavery and antislavery.

The local political processes leading to the antislavery legislation across the Spanish Main were essentially transnational and they go back to the beginning of the wars of independence in 1810 in Chile and Buenos Aires, both in South America. These were at the forefront of developing a model of gradualist legislation for state abolitionism.[5] In New Granada, in 1813 José Felix Restrepo drafted the first proposal of a partial reform to gradually abolish slavery in the province of Antioquia. In 1814 Juan del Corral, president of an autonomist junta in Antioquia at the time, turned the proposal into a law. Del Corral justified this radical project by referring to the Chilean law of 1811 that abolished the slave trade and instituted a free womb law (that is, children born of enslaved women would not be enslaved). In these and other early experiments with abolition across the Spanish Main we see why the flow of ideas and institutional examples among South American regions are relevant, and not just influences from the North Atlantic. Indeed, other fundamental local social forces were the enslaved and free people of African descent who shaped the abolitionist processes. They weakened the slave economies by expanding free labor (both its social and economic components) and exercising political pressure over nation formation as participants in the independence war, creating similar pressures across mainland Spanish America (Y. Barragán 2016; Blanchard 2008; Di Meglio 2007; Echeverri 2016; Feliú Cruz 1973, 10, 38; Gutiérrez 2015; Laviña and Zeuske 2008; Mallo and Telesca 2010; Thibaud 2013, 235–37).

It is equally true that the understanding of a unidirectional relationship between British initiatives and Colombian receptiveness is incorrect. As Yesenia Barragán has shown, on closer inspection, Colombia's importance in the process of Atlantic abolition has been misrepresented: in the crucial decade between 1820 and 1830, British abolitionists were aware of and very interested in Colombia's abolitionist policies. They considered Colombia exemplary, with one member of parliament ranking Colombia's "government high in the scales of civilized states" due to its abolitionist policies, and another one advocating for "a measure something like that which had been agreed to in Colombia." For example, in his petition for abolition in the British West Indies before the House of Lords in March 1823, Sir Robert Thomas Wilson of Southwark noted that "our conduct in regard to slaves [contrasts] with that of the new republic of Colombia" (Y. Barragán 2016, 3–4; Hansard 1823, 768; Hansard 1824, 980).

Other significant dimensions of Colombia's international presence in the history of antislavery revolve around its particular place in the history of republicanism. Since its first conception by Francisco de Miranda between 1788 and 1804, Colombia had been a republican project framed in the grandiose scheme of hemispheric emancipation from European rule, pioneered by the United States (del Castillo, forthcoming; Racine 2003, 49). In the struggle that Simón Bolívar embarked upon decades later, New Granada's and Venezuela's independence became inextricably linked to Haitian republicanism, and thus to antislavery as well. As is well known, after finding himself unable to secure support in Jamaica, Bolívar traveled to Haiti where Alexandre Pétion openly became an ally of the South American independence cause (Bassi 2016; Fischer 2013). The independence of Old Colombia and of mainland Spanish America more broadly was thus a crucial arena for the definition of republicanism in the hemisphere and, as such, it is necessary to see it within the frame of the rise and development of republicanism in the Atlantic world (Sanders 2014).

The contrasts between Old Colombia and the United States were not predictable nor were connections among them simply unidirectional. For example, with regards to Old Colombia's commitment to abolitionism, Caitlin Fitz has shown that the Bolivarian project had a significant impact in the United States press and shaped evolving ideas about race and republicanism among publics in both the North and the South. While the United States was a republic that had left the question of slavery unresolved, Old Colombia and the other Spanish American republics in the Spanish American mainland gave shape to an alternative vision of republicanism that embraced the principle of racial equality. Perhaps counterintuitively from our perspective, during the Spanish American independence wars and the early years of nation-state formation, newspapers in the US South represented the South American antislavery republics as allies in the republican cause and their explicitly radical origin in racial alliances as inspiring (Fitz 2016; Lasso 2007).

Aside from Old Colombia's republican antislavery politics being central to its hemispheric diplomatic fronts, the way in which it maneuvered in the field of antislavery had significant consequences for the transformation of Spain's empire vis-à-vis slavery. Though historians today separate mainland Spanish America from the Spanish Empire when it comes to analyzing the abolition of slavery, it is rather necessary to think about the two together as part of a linked process. The historiographic gap has prevailed because antislavery in the Spanish American mainland republics is understood to be a corollary of the anticolonial wars, as an essential factor in their break from Spain.[6] Yet, in fact, both slavery and abolition in mainland Spanish America need to be framed in the Spanish imperial context that defined them historically. That is, aside from the foundational link of Spain and Spanish America regarding slavery, mainland Spanish America's turn toward abolition in the early nineteenth century grew in relation to Spain's own history of antislavery (especially in Cádiz) and developments in mainland Spanish America itself defined Spain's relation to slavery once it lost most of its American possessions.

The early abolitionist positions in the first Venezuelan revolutionary project and, later, in Old Colombia did express the way in which substantially abolitionism stood as a symbol of the Spanish American anticolonial struggle against Spain. But that development is even more significant if we take into account that in the late eighteenth century elites on the Spanish American mainland had strongly supported the project of free trade in slaves that was meant to enable Spain's investment in the growth of its Caribbean plantation economies, for example, in Venezuela and in the hinterland of Cartagena. It is important, therefore, to ponder the changes in the elites' positioning: that is, their embrace of a policy of expansion of the slave economies within the Spanish Empire in the 1780s in contrast to the first Venezuelan Constitution of 1811, which proscribed legal differences among races and banned the slave trade. Cartagena, as Marixa Lasso has shown, upheld principles of racial harmony and established institutions that gave representation to *pardos* (free people of African descent), precisely as a means to counter the Cádiz imperial project's exclusion of people of African descent from citizenship (Lasso 2007). This abolitionist project had continuity during the 1820s, when Old Colombia aligned with Britain's anti-slave-trade crusade (King 1944; Pérez Morales 2012; Straka 2016, 3; Zeuske 2013).

Thinking transversally about the aspects that I have discussed up to now with regard to the Spanish Main—the links between slavery and politics (nation-state formation and diplomacy), slavery's articulation to different forms of free and unfree labor (the economic and political institutions that managed indigenous populations and emergent communities of free blacks)—it is possible and necessary to establish parallels with the history of Spanish slavery and abolitionism.[7]

For instance, understanding Spanish slavery and abolitionism through the lens of regions where indigenous people coexisted with enslaved Africans is a project that has the potential of tracing Iberian historical precedents to the nineteenth-century Anglo-abolitionist debates and policies. This question has been discussed by historians in recent years; Christopher Schmidt-Nowara's trajectory is illustrative in that regard. Schmidt-Nowara raised our awareness that Spanish abolitionism had a deeper history that had not been appreciated in the historiography of Atlantic abolition, leading us to ask unconventional questions about prevalent definitions of Spanish antislavery. In the volume that Schmidt-Nowara coedited with Joseph Fradera, *Slavery and Antislavery in Spain's Atlantic Empire*, these authors laid out a critical argument: that antislavery in the Iberian empires went back to the sixteenth century and that taking into account its actors (including Indians), debates (among Jesuits, for example), and institutional impact (legislation against Indian slavery) intrinsically transforms the history of antislavery and abolitionism in the Atlantic world.[8]

Deeper scrutiny on the subject of forced labor, and the ambiguous legal status of Indians in the Americas, also speaks to the relationship between liberalism and Indian labor in Spain's Atlantic empire, and in the Spanish American republics, in the late eighteenth and early nineteenth centuries. This is clear from the South American perspective. Rossana Barragán has recently taken up the issue of political disputes around forced labor in Upper Peru (now Bolivia), where discussions about the *mita* had shaped perspectives over Bourbon reformism's imperial reach and how these, in turn, were crucial precedents to the contentious debates about Indian citizenship in the Cortes of Cádiz between 1810 and 1814 (Barragán 2013, 151–78).

Also in this early nineteenth-century context, the transformations in visions about Indian rights and Indian labor that characterized the independence processes across mainland Spanish America (1810s–1850s) were entangled. From Mexico to Argentina, when republics were founded, these were antislavery republics that produced laws to dismantle slavery as part of their constitutional and economic project of nation building. Everywhere they emerged after the independence wars that had laid the foundations of interracial alliances between Creoles (Americans of Spanish descent), Indians, and people of African descent, both free and enslaved.

Those interethnic alliances had crucial consequences for the fate of slavery and for the development of citizenship across the region. Guided by liberal principles, evolving views about the need to dismantle the category of "Indian," between the 1810s and 1850s, had contradictory consequences yet they were always consistently tied to the abolition of African slavery and to the search for equality (Echeverri, forthcoming; Helg 2004; Larson 2004; Lasso 2007; Sanders 2004; Thompson 2002).

Parallel developments in Spain and its relationship to the Caribbean colonies should be framed within the broader context that includes the Spanish American republics. In other words, that Cuban slavery became the core link to Spain at the same time that the Spanish Empire was imploding is not a coincidence. Interrogating that relationship we can uncover how Spanish American mainland abolitionist politics had a crucial impact on the Spanish Empire's own redefinition in the nineteenth century and analyze why, ultimately, Cuban loyalty produced beneficial results when it touched upon the structural connection between slavery and imperial belonging. As Anne Eller has explored, Spain's imperial commitment to slavery was clear in its 1861 recolonization of Santo Domingo (Eller 2016; Surwillo 2014).

On the other hand, the way in which Old Colombia and Mexico were also involved in an ultimately fruitless campaign to liberate Spain's Caribbean possessions poses a different problem. Colombia and Mexico articulated with local Cuban nationalist movements that were, in the 1820s, seeking to become part of the anticolonial wave that those republics represented. We know about those incipient and fragile alliances both through the explicit declarations of Bolívar about the project of liberating Cuba as he navigated diplomatic goals and priorities vis-à-vis Britain and the United States, and because of the conspiracies that were discovered on the island that proclaimed Bolívar as a symbol and a leader of their own ambitions to become independent. It is less clear what role Mexican and Old Colombian abolitionism played in that project, largely based on the current historical understanding of Cuban antislavery in this period as practically muted. Though Old Colombia and Mexico had laid the constitutional ground for dismantling slavery, that was a project that could have been perceived by contemporaries as unstable, founded as it was in weak regional alliances within each of those republics (Fradera 2005; Garrigó 1929; González 1985; Morales y Morales 1931; Piqueras 2007; Pividal 2009; Rojas 2001; Sartorius 2016).

In 1826, when Bolívar convoked the first Pan-American Congress that met in Panama he expected that one of the main points of discussion would be the participating republics' commitment, with Britain, to active policing against the illegal slave trade in the Atlantic (O'Leary 1920; Gutiérrez 2012). Yet this commitment to the international fight against slave trading was paralleled by ongoing contradictions within Old Colombia with regard to the abolition of slavery. The 1821 Law of Free Birth whereby *manumisos* would have to work for their mothers' owners until the age of eighteen was modified in response to slave owners' active involvement in the congress, where they opposed it. In 1830, the reactionary congresses in New Granada and Venezuela extended the period to twenty-one years. This is why the 1821 laws' gradualism has rightly been identified by scholars as a way of instituting and defending unfree labor in a different guise. The law and its malleability in the decades between 1820 and 1850 ultimately accommodated the commitment of Old Colombia's elites to the institution of slavery (Blanchard 1992; Lombardi 1971).

Indeed, after the independent Spanish American republican states legislated slavery's gradual abolition, they did not follow a linear process of slavery's decline. An illustration of the persistence of slavery in mainland Spanish America is the case of the republics of Peru and Argentina, where slavery expanded after the 1820s. Argentina, as Juan Carlos Garavaglia has shown, benefited from its proximity to Brazil and imported slaves after 1820. Peru also opened its trade to other American republics, and engaged in that commerce mostly with New Granada (formerly Old Colombia), when this last republic also authorized slave trading in the 1840s. What is clear in these examples is that in the Spanish Main slavery was not exactly moribund in the mid-nineteenth century. Furthermore, its extinction was far from assured given the deep, intricate, and evolving relation of slavery and politics in the region (Blanchard 1992; King 1944; Kitchens 1979; Garavaglia 1999, 2013).

IV

In the last decade, the works of Edward Baptist, Ada Ferrer, Rafael Marquese, Christopher Schmidt-Nowara, Dale Tomich, and Michael Zeuske, among others, have demonstrated a fundamental principle that simultaneously defines and emerges from the concept of the second slavery: that slavery, as an institution, was characterized by its flexibility and adaptability through time as well as in space. Thanks to the debates sparked around these scholars' work, today we know much about the forms that such flexibility and adaptability took in the contexts of Cuba, Brazil, and the United States, where slavery's massive expansion implied the institution's adjustment to the context associated with the rise of liberal politics (Baptist 2014; Ferrer 2014; Marquese, Parron, and Berbel 2016; Schmidt-Nowara 2011; Tomich 2004; Zeuske 2014).

However enriching, these insights that grow out of the historiography of the second slavery—its portrayal of slavery as changing and adapting to the challenges of economic and political liberalism—coexist with parallel assumptions that grow out of the plantation-centric paradigm. Until today the paradigm that privileges nineteenth-century plantation economies as objects of study, in a narrative that depicts them as leading global economic development, implies that those slave societies that did not develop massive plantations in the eighteenth and nineteenth centuries were historically at the margins of the transformative processes of the age. Indeed, though in the growing scholarship about the second slavery the studies on Iberian abolitionism are at the forefront, for the Spanish Empire the emphasis is on the late abolition of slavery in the Spanish Caribbean colonies of Cuba and Puerto Rico.

My argument in this chapter has been that the second slavery analytical framework can expand its geographic and chronological scope and connect to the history of the rise of abolitionist republics in the Spanish American mainland. At the same time, I have suggested, cases such as that of the Spanish Main are crucially relevant to illuminate the way in which we understand slavery's persistence and decline in the Atlantic world during the nineteenth century. A basic premise that needs to be the starting point of this project is that the same forces that fostered the second slavery were behind political and economic transformations in the Spanish Main.

In other words, rather than arguing that the particularities of mainland Spanish American societies set them apart on the margins of the historiography of slavery and antislavery in the nineteenth century, these differences can be seen as holding the potential for fully understanding the protean nature of slavery and its consequences for abolition. This aligns perfectly with the second slavery scholarship's challenge to the notion of a single temporality in which the most significant characteristic of the nineteenth century was the transition from slavery to capitalism. In Dale Tomich's words it is possible to reveal, instead, how "although forms of unwaged labor—slavery, serfdom, peonage, sharecropping, and independent commodity production—may have remained unchanged, their role, composition, and significance in the development of the world economy were redefined" in many contexts (Tomich 2004, 52). Thus, studying the articulation of indigenous communal economies, the expansion of unfree labor among Indians and Asian migrants, and the rise of a free-black peasantry in the Spanish American mainland during the nineteenth century is a means to incorporating the variety of labor forms in the Americas to the history of capitalism (Van der Linden and Rodríguez García 2016).

Summing up, placed in the hemispheric and Atlantic dimensions during the nineteenth century, Old Colombia provides a perspective from which to engage the historiography of the second slavery, yielding at least three contributions: to combine seemingly disconnected chronologies of the economic and political histories of slavery and antislavery in the Atlantic world; to revisit and reconsider the generalized equivalence between republicanism and abolitionism in the Americas; and to identify the links between the abolition of slavery and indigenous labor, expanding the debate on slavery, freedom, and abolition through the perspective of South American history.

Notes

1. This chapter grows out of my current research project, "The Politics of Atlantic Abolition in Old Colombia, 1810–1860." For enriching conversations about the themes developed here, I thank the participants in the Gilder Lehrman Center's 2015 annual conference "Anti-Slavery Republics"; the Latin American History Workshops where I presented my work in 2016 at the University of London, Oxford University, and the University of Bristol; the "After Slavery?" conference at the University of Leeds; the Agrarian Studies colloquium at Yale; the Circum-Atlantic Studies Seminar at Vanderbilt University; Ed Rugemer and our students in the "Atlantic Abolitions" graduate seminar in fall 2016; as well as Manuel Barcia, Yesenia Barragán, Alice Baumgartner, David Blight, Alex Borucki, Matthew Brown, Celso Castilho, Roquinaldo Ferreira, Glenda Gilmore, Alejandro Gómez, Toby Green, Daniel Gutiérrez, Jane Landers, Claudia Leal, Jason McGraw, Edgardo Pérez Morales, Jesús Sanjurjo, Rebecca Scott, Barbara Weinstein, and especially Chris Schmidt-Nowara who was my ally and mentor since I began to develop this project, and continues to be an inspiration.

2. In classic historiography, this first Republic of Colombia is called Gran Colombia.

3. Alice Baumgartner demonstrates that the classic argument about decadence obscures contingent as well as structural dynamics in the case of Mexico's abolition (Baumgartner 2015).

4. In their important work on "International Proslavery," Rafael Marquese and Tâmis Parron uncover crucial connections between pro- and antislavery politics in the United States, Cuba, and Brazil. Though they argue that we "need to break with the internal-external

categories in the analysis of the national state-building processes, since all of them were formed in the unified arena of the modern-world system," they do not mention mainland Spanish America or account for its presence in such a system during the 1840s and '50s (Marquese and Parron 2016, 50).

5. In the 1780s, the state of Massachusetts abolished slavery based on court cases that claimed abolition was consistent with the state constitution's declaration of equality of all men. Other North American states such as Pennsylvania passed the first gradualist laws in the Americas. The role of African-descended people in claiming rights to equality in Massachusetts has been studied by Chernoh Sesay Jr. (Nash and Soderlund 1991; Sesay 2014). Early Spanish American antislavery legislation still needs to be studied in relation to those North American precedents (Crespi 2010; Feliú Cruz 1973).

6. This disconnection is visible in Schmidt-Nowara's (2016) chapter "Spain and the Politics of the Second Slavery," in which he writes about Spanish slavery and antislavery in the nineteenth century without a deep analysis of the parallel situation of the Spanish American mainland during and after the independence wars.

7. David Wheat provides a perspective that explores the deeper history of African society in Spanish America and free black communities in the Spanish Caribbean, including Cartagena, which does not assume a plantation-centric teleology to measure slavery's impact in the Americas, and sets a different standard for recognizing the structural weight of African slavery in the Spanish American mainland (Wheat 2016).

8. Andrés Reséndez has documented Philip IV's 1677 antislavery campaign, inspired especially by the enslavement of Indians in Chile and their war against it, and, in the 1680s, Mexico's indigenous people's resistance to enslavement. Speaking about "the other emancipation," Reséndez has critically exposed the parallel realities of Indian and African slavery as well as how the processes of abolition of African slavery were entwined with the spread of Indian slavery across the Americas (Reséndez 2016).

Works Cited

Baptist, Edward. 2014. *The Half Has Never Been Told: Slavery and the Making of American Capitalism.* New York: Basic.

Barragán, Rossana. 2013. "'Indios esclavos': En torno a la mita minera y la igualdad, 1790–1812." In *L'atlantique revolutionnaire: Une perspective Ibéro-Américain*, edited by Clément Thibaud, Gabriel Entin, Alejandro Gómez, and Federica Morelli, 151–78. Paris: Éditions Les Perséides.

Barragán, Yesenia. 2016. "'To the Mine I Will Not Go': Freedom and Emancipation on the Colombian Pacific, 1821–1852." PhD diss., Columbia University.

Bassi, Ernesto. 2016. *An Aqueous Territory: Sailor Geographies and New Granada's Transimperial Greater Caribbean World.* Durham: Duke University Press.

Baumgartner, Alice. 2015. "Rethinking Abolition in Mexico." Paper presented to the Race and Slavery Working Group, Yale University.

Berquist, Emily. 2010. "Early Antislavery Sentiment in the Spanish Atlantic World, 1765–1817." *Slavery & Abolition* 31 (2): 181–205.

Bethell, Leslie. (1970) 2009. *The Abolition of the Brazilian Slave Trade: Britain, Brazil, and the Slave Trade Question.* New York: Cambridge University Press.

Bierck, Harold A., Jr. 1953. "The Struggle for Abolition in Gran Colombia." *Hispanic Historical American Review* 33 (3): 365–86.

Blackburn, Robin. 2011. *The American Crucible: Slavery, Emancipation, and Human Rights.* New York: Verso.

Blanchard, Peter. 1992. *Slavery and Abolition in Early Republican Peru.* Wilmington, DE: S. R. Books.

Blanchard, Peter. 2008. *Under the Flags of Freedom: Slave Soldiers and the Wars of Independence in Spanish South America.* Pittsburgh: Pittsburgh University Press.

Blaufarb, Rafe. 2007. "The Western Question: The Geopolitics of Latin American Independence." *American Historical Review* 112 (3): 742–63.

Borucki, Alex. 2012. "Trans-Imperial History in the Making of the Slave-Trade to Venezuela, 1526–1811." *Itinerario* 36 (2): 29–54.

Brown, Christopher. 2006. *Moral Capital: Foundations of British Abolitionism.* Chapel Hill: Omohundro Institute of Early American History and Culture / University of North Carolina Press.

Brown, Matthew. 2006. *Adventuring through Spanish Colonies: Simón Bolívar, Foreign Mercenaries, and the Birth of New Nations.* Liverpool: Liverpool University Press.

Chaves, Maria Eugenia. 2010. "Esclavizados, cimarrones y bandidos: Historias de resistencia en el valle del Chota-Mira, en el contexto de la revolución de los marqueses quiteños, 1770–1820." In *Indios, negros y mestizos en la independencia,* edited by Heraclio Bonilla, 130–49. Bogotá: Universidad Nacional de Colombia, Editorial Planeta, Instituto Francés de Estudios Andinos.

Clementi, Hebe. 1974. *La abolición de la esclavitud en América Latina.* Buenos Aires: Editorial La Pleyade.

Colmenares, German. (1979) 1999. *Historia económica y social de Colombia, vol. II, Popayán: Una sociedad esclavista, 1680–1800.* Bogotá: Tercer Mundo Editores.

Costeloe, Michael. 1981. "Spain and the Latin American Wars of Independence: The Free Trade Controversy, 1810–1820." *Hispanic American Historical Review* 61 (2): 209–34.

Cowling, Camillia. 2013. *Conceiving Freedom: Women of Color, Gender, and the Abolition of Slavery in Havana and Rio de Janeiro.* Chapel Hill: University of North Carolina Press.

Crespi, Liliana. 2010. "Ni esclavo ni libre: El status del liberto en el Río de la Plata desde el período indiano al republicano." In *"Negros de la Patria": Los afrodescendientes en las luchas por la independencia en el antiguo Virreinato del Río de la Plata*, edited by Silvia Mallo and Ignacio Telesca, 15–37. Buenos Aires: Editorial SB.

Davis, David Brion. (1975) 1991. *The Problem of Slavery in the Age of Revolution, 1770–1823*. Oxford: Oxford University Press.

del Castillo, Lina. Forthcoming. "Colombian Cartography in the Production (and Silencing) of Independence History, 1807–1827." In *Mapping the Transition from Colony to Nation (17th Kenneth Nebenzahl, Jr. Lectures in the History of Cartography, The Newberry Library)*, edited by Jim Ackerman. Chicago: University of Chicago Press.

Di Meglio, Gabriel. 2007. *¡Viva el bajo pueblo! La plebe urbana de Buenos Aires y la política entre la Revolución de Mayo y el Rosismo*. Buenos Aires: Prometeo Libros.

Drescher, Seymour. 2002. *The Mighty Experiment: Free Labor versus Slavery in British Emancipation*. New York: Oxford University Press.

Drescher, Seymour. 2009. *Abolition: A History of Slavery and Antislavery*. New York: Cambridge University Press.

Dubois, Laurent. 2004a. *Avengers of the New World: The Story of the Haitian Revolution*. Cambridge: Belknap Press of Harvard University Press.

Dubois, Laurent. 2004b. *A Colony of Citizens: Revolution and Slave Emancipation in the French Caribbean, 1787–1804*. Chapel Hill: Omohundro Institute of Early American History and Culture / University of North Carolina Press.

Echeverri, Marcela. 2016. *Indian and Slave Royalists in the Age of Revolution: Reform, Revolution, and Royalism in the Northern Andes, 1780–1825*. Cambridge: Cambridge University Press.

Echeverri, Marcela. Forthcoming. " 'Sovereignty Has Lost Its Rights': Liberal Experiments and Indigenous Citizenship in New Granada, 1810–1819." In *Justice in British, Iberian, and Indigenous America, 1600–1825: The Challenge of Legal Intelligibility*, edited by Brian P. Owensby and Richard J. Ross. New York: New York University Press.

Eller, Anne. 2016. *We Dream Together: Dominican Independence, Haiti, and the Fight for Caribbean Freedom*. Durham: Duke University Press, 2016.

Everill, Bronwen. 2013. *Abolition and Empire in Sierra Leone and Liberia*. New York: Palgrave Macmillan.

Feliú Cruz, Guillermo. 1973. *La abolición de la esclavitud en Chile*. Santiago de Chile: Editorial Universitaria.

Ferreira, Roquinaldo. 2014a. "From Brazil to West Africa: Dutch-Portuguese Rivalry, Gold-Smuggling, and African Politics in the Bight of Benin (ca. 1700-ca. 1730)." In *The Legacy of Dutch Brazil*, edited by Michiel van Groesen, 59–77. New York: Cambridge University Press.

Ferreira, Roquinaldo. 2014b. "Measuring Short- and Long-Term Impacts of Abolitionism in the South Atlantic, 1807–1860s." In *Networks and Trans-Cultural Exchange: Slave Trading in the South Atlantic, 1590–1867*, edited by David Richardson and Filipa Ribeiro da Silva, 221–37. Leiden: Brill Academic Publishers.

Ferrer, Ada. 1999. *Insurgent Cuba: Race, Nation, and Revolution, 1868–1898*. Chapel Hill: University of North Carolina Press.

Ferrer, Ada. 2013. "Cuban Slavery and Atlantic Antislavery." In *Slavery and Antislavery in Spain's Atlantic Empire*, edited by Josep Fradera and Christopher Schmidt-Nowara, 134–57. New York: Berghahn.

Ferrer, Ada. 2014. *Freedom's Mirror: Haiti and Cuba in the Age of Revolutions*. New York: Cambridge University Press.

Ferrer, Ada. 2016. "History and the Idea of Hispanic Caribbean Studies." *Small Axe* 51: 49–64.

Finch, Aisha. 2015. *Rethinking Slave Rebellion in Cuba: La Escalera and the Insurgencies of 1841–1844*. Chapel Hill: University of North Carolina Press.

Fischer, Sibylle. 2013. "Bolívar in Haiti: Republicanism in the Revolutionary Atlantic." In *Haiti and the Americas*, edited by Carla Calarge, Raphael Dalleo, Luis Duno-Gottberg, and Clevis Headley, 25–53. Jackson: University Press of Mississippi.

Fitz, Caitlin. 2016. *Our Sister Republics: The United States in an Age of American Revolutions*. New York: W. W. Norton.

Fradera, Josep. 2005. *Colonias para después de un imperio*. Barcelona: Edicions Bellatera.

Fradera, Josep. 2013. "Moments in a Postponed Abolition." In *Slavery and Antislavery in Spain's Atlantic Empire*, edited by Josep Fradera and Christopher Schmidt-Nowara, 256–90. New York: Berghahn.

Fradera, Josep, and Christopher Schmidt-Nowara. 2013. "Introduction: Colonial Pioneer and Plantation Latecomer." In *Slavery and Antislavery in Spain's Atlantic Empire*, edited by Josep Fradera and Christopher Schmidt-Nowara, 1–12. New York: Berghahn.

Gallagher, John, and Ronald Robinson. 1953. "The Imperialism of Free Trade." *Economic History Review* 6 (1): 1–15.

Garavaglia, Juan Carlos. 1999. *Pastores y labradores de Buenos Aires: Una historia agraria de la campaña bonaerense, 1700–1830*. Buenos Aires: De la Flor–IEHS–Universidad Pablo de Olavide.

Garavaglia, Juan Carlos. 2013. "The Economic Role of Slavery in a Non-Slave Society: The River Plate, 1750–1860." In *Slavery and Antislavery in Spain's Atlantic Empire*, edited by Josep Fradera and Christopher Schmidt-Nowara, 74–100. New York: Berghahn.

Garrigó, Roque. 1929. *Historia documentada de la conspiración de los Soles y Rayos de Bolívar*. 2 vols. La Habana: Academia de la Historia de Cuba.

Goebel, Dorothy Burne. 1938. "British Trade to the Spanish Colonies, 1796–1823." *American Historical Review* 43 (2): 288–320.

Gómez, Alejandro. 2013. "La caribeanidad revolucionaria de la 'costa de Caracas': Una visión prospectiva (1793–1815)." In *Las independencias hispanoamericanas*, edited by Véronique Hébrard y Geneviève Verdo, 35–48. Madrid: Colección de la Casa de Velázquez.

González, Margarita. 1985. *Bolívar y la independencia de Cuba*. Bogotá: El Áncora Editores.

Gutiérrez, Daniel. 2012. *El reconocimiento de Colombia: Diplomacia y propaganda en la coyuntura de las restauraciones (1819–1831)*. Bogotá: Universidad del Externado.

Gutiérrez, Daniel. 2015. "La politique abolitionniste dans l'État d'Antioquia, Colombie (1812–1816)." *Le Mouvement social* 3 (252): 55–70.

Hamerly, Michael. 1973. *Historia social y económica de la Antigua provincial de Guayaquil, 1763–1842*. Guayaquil: Archivo Histórico del Guayas.

Hansard, T. C., ed. 1823. *The Parliamentary Debates*. Vol III, February 4–April 13, 1823. London: Printed by T.C. Hansard, Peterborough-Court, Fleet-Street.

Hansard, T. C., ed. 1824. *The Parliamentary Debates*. Vol X, February 3–March 29, 1824. London: Printed by T.C. Hansard of the Pater-master-Row Press.

Helg, Aline. 2004. *Liberty and Equality in Caribbean Colombia, 1770–1835*. Chapel Hill: University of North Carolina Press.

Jiménez, Orián. 2004. *El Chocó: Un paraíso del demonio. Nóvita, Citará y El Baudó, siglo XVIII*. Medellín: Editorial Universidad de Antioquia.

King, James Ferguson. 1944. "The Latin-American Republics and the Suppression of the Slave Trade." *Hispanic American Historical Review* 24 (3): 387–411.

Kitchens, John. 1979. "The New Granadan-Peruvian Slave Trade." *Journal of Negro History* 64 (3): 205–15.

Klein, Herbert. 2012. "The African American Experience in Comparative Perspective: The Current Question of the Debate." In *Africans to Spanish America: Expanding the Diaspora*, edited by Sherwin Bryant, Rachel O'Toole, and Ben Vinson III, 206–22. Chicago: Illinois University Press.

Klein, Herbert, and Ben Vinson III. 2007. *African Slavery in Latin America and the Caribbean*. Oxford: Oxford University Press.

Larson, Brooke. 2004. *Trials of Nation Making: Liberalism, Race, and Ethnicity in the Andes, 1810–1910*. New York: Cambridge University Press.

Lasso, Marixa. 2007. *Myths of Harmony: Race and Republicanism during the Age of Revolution, Colombia 1795–1831*. Pittsburgh: University of Pittsburgh Press.

Laviña, Javier, and Michael Zeuske. 2008. "First Slaveries in Venezuela and Nueva Granada." *Review (Fernand Braudel Center)* 31 (3): 297–342.

Lombardi, John. 1971. *The Decline and Abolition of Negro Slavery in Venezuela, 1820–1854*. Westport, CT: Greenwood Publishing.

Mallo, Silvia, and Ignacio Telesca, eds. 2010. *"Negros de la Patria": Los afrodescendientes en las luchas por la independencia en el antiguo Virreinato del Río de la Plata*. Buenos Aires: Editorial SB.

Marquese, Rafael, and Tâmis Parron. 2016. "International Proslavery: The Politics of the Second Slavery." In *The Politics of the Second Slavery*, edited by Dale Tomich, 57–81. Albany: State University of New York Press.

Marquese, Rafael, Tâmis Parron, and Márcia Berbel. 2016. *Slavery and Politics: Brazil and Cuba, 1790–1850*. Albuquerque: University of New Mexico Press.

McGraw, Jason. 2014. *The Work of Recognition: Caribbean Colombia and the Postemancipation Struggle for Citizenship*. Chapel Hill: University of North Carolina Press.

Morales y Morales, Vidal. 1931. *Iniciadores y mártires de la revolución cubana*. La Habana: Cultural.

Murray, David R. (1980) 2002. *Odious Commerce: Britain, Spain, and the Abolition of the Cuban Slave Trade*. New York: Cambridge University Press.

Nash, Gary, and Jean Soderlund. 1991. *Freedom by Degrees: Emancipation in Pennsylvania and Its Aftermaths*. New York: Oxford University Press.

Neil, Larry, and Jeffrey Williamson, eds. 2014. *The Cambridge History of Capitalism: The Spread of Capitalism: From 1848 to the Present*. Vol. 2. New York: Cambridge University Press.

O'Leary, Daniel Florencio. 1920. *El congreso internacional de Panamá en 1826: Desgobierno y anarquía en la Gran Colombia*. Madrid: Editorial América.

O'Toole, Rachel. 2012. *Bound Lives: Africans, Indians, and the Making of Race in Colonial Peru*. Pittsburgh: University of Pittsburgh Press.

Owen, Roger, and Bob Sutcliffe, eds. 1972. *Studies in the Theory of Imperialism*. London: Longman.

Pérez Morales, Edgardo. 2012. *El gran diablo hecho barco: Corsarios, esclavos y revolución en Cartagena y el Gran Caribe, 1791–1817*. Bucaramanga: Ediciones Universidad Industrial de Santander.

Piqueras, José Antonio. 2007. "El ideario de una revolución frustrada: José Francisco Lemus y la libertad de Cubanacán." *Ibero-Americana Pragensia*, Supplementum 19: 211–21.

Piqueras, José Antonio. 2011. *La esclavitud en las españas: Un lazo transatlántico*. Madrid: Libros de la Catarata.

Pita Pico, Roger. 2014. *La manumisión de esclavos en el proceso de indendencia de Colombia: Realidades, promesas y desiluciones*. Bogotá: Editorial Kimpres.

Pividal, Francisco. 2009. *Bolívar: Pensamiento precursor del antimperialismo*. La Habana: Editorial de Ciencias Sociales.

Pollak Eltz, Angelina. 2004. "Los ultimos años de la esclavitud en Venezuela y su abolición en 1854." *Tierra Firme. Revista de Historia y Ciencias Sociales* 22 (85): 7–15.

Popkin, Jeremy. 2010. *You Are All Free: The Haitian Revolution and the Abolition of Slavery*. New York: Cambridge University Press.

Racine, Karen. 2003. *Francisco de Miranda: A Transatlantic Life in the Age of Revolution*. Wilmington, DE: S. R. Books.

Reséndez, Andrés. 2016. *The Other Slavery: The Uncovered Story of Indian Enslavement in America*. Boston: Houghton Mifflin Harcourt.

Rodriguez Arrieta, Marisol. 2002. "Aportes de la historiografía regional al estudio del proceso de la esclavitud, manumisión y abolición en Venezuela: Caso Provincia de Maracaibo." *Agora* 4 (7).

Rojas, Rafael. 2001. *Cuba mexicana: Historia de una anexión imposible*. Mexico City: Secretaría de Relaciones Exteriores.

Romero, Mario Diego. 1995. *Poblamiento y sociedad en el Pacífico colombiano, siglos XVI al XVIII*. Cali: Universidad del Valle, Editorial Facultad de Humanidades.

Rueda, Rocío. 2010. "De esclavizados a comuneros en la cuenca aurífera del Río Santiago–Río Cayapas (Esmeraldas): Etnicidad negra en construcción en Ecuador, siglos XVIII–XIX." PhD diss., Universidad Andina Simón Bolívar (Ecuador)–Universidad Pablo de Olavide (Seville).

Safford, Frank. 1993. *The Making of Modern Colombia: A Nation in Spite of Itself*. Berkeley: University of California Press.

Sanders, James. 2004. *Contentious Republicans: Popular Politics, Race, and Class in Nineteenth-Century Colombia*. Durham: Duke University Press.

Sanders, James. 2014. *The Vanguard of the Atlantic World: Creating Modernity, Nation, and Democracy in Nineteenth-Century Latin America*. Durham: Duke University Press.

Sartorius, David. 2016. "Cuban Counterpoint: Colonialism and Continuity in the Atlantic World." In *New Countries: Capitalism, Revolutions, and Nations in the Americas, 1750–1870*, ed. John Tutino, 175–200. Durham: Duke University Press.

Schmidt-Nowara, Christopher. 1999. *Empire and Antislavery: Spain, Cuba, and Puerto Rico, 1833–1874*. Pittsburgh: Pittsburgh University Press.

Schmidt-Nowara, Christopher. 2011. *Slavery, Freedom, and Abolition in Latin America and the Atlantic World*. Albuquerque: University of New Mexico Press.

Schmidt-Nowara, Christopher. 2016. "Spain and the Politics of the Second Slavery, 1808–1868." In *The Politics of the Second Slavery*, edited by Dale Tomich, 57–81. Albany: State University of New York Press.

Scott, Rebecca. 1985. *Slave Emancipation in Cuba: The Transition to Free Labor, 1860–1899*. Princeton: Princeton University Press.

Sesay, Chernoh, Jr. 2014. "The Revolutionary Black Roots of Slavery's Abolition in Massachusetts." *New England Quarterly* 87 (1): 99–131.

Straka, Tomás. 2016. "Father Llamozas' Revolution." Paper presented at the "Popular Royalism in the Revolutionary Atlantic World" conference, Yale University.

Surwillo, Lisa. 2014. *Monsters by Trade: Slave Traffickers in Modern Spanish Culture*. Stanford: Stanford University Press.

Suzuki, Hideaki. 2015. *Abolitions as a Global Experience*. Singapore: National University of Singapore Press.

Thibaud, Clément. 2013. "Una constitución perdida: La carta de Nóvita en la Nueva Granada." In *Dos siglos llaman a la puerta (1812–2012)*, edited by Marieta Cantos Casenave and Lola Lozano Salado, 235–37. Cádiz: Universidad de Cádiz.

Thompson, Guy, ed. 2002. *The European Revolutions of 1848 and the Americas*. London: Institute of Latin American Studies.

Tobar Donoso, Julio. 1959. "La abolición de la esclavitud en el Ecuador." *Boletín de la Academia Nacional de Historia* 34 (93): 5–38.

Tomich, Dale W. 2004. *Through the Prism of Slavery: Labor, Capital, and World Economy*. Lanham, MD: Rowan and Littlefield.

Tovar, Jorge Andrés, and Hermes Tovar. 2009. *El oscuro camino de la libertad: Los esclavos en Colombia, 1821–1851*. Bogotá: Editorial Universidad de Los Andes.

Townsend, Camilla. 1993. "En busca de la libertad: Los esfuerzos de los esclavos gualaquileños por garantizar su independencia después de la independencia." *Revista Procesos* 4: 73–85.

Tutino, John. 2016. "The Americas in the Rise of Industrial Capitalism." In *New Countries: Capitalism, Revolutions, and Nations in the Americas, 1750–1870*, edited by John Tutino, 25–70. Durham: Duke University Press.

Van der Linden, Marcel, and Magaly Rodríguez García. 2016. *On Coerced Labor: Work and Compulsion after Chattel Slavery*. Leiden: Brill.

Wheat, David. 2016. *Atlantic Africa and the Spanish Caribbean, 1570–1640*. Chapel Hill: Omohundro Institute of Early American History and Culture / University of North Carolina Press.

Zahler, Reuben. 2013. *Ambitious Rebels: Remaking Honor, Law, and Liberalism in Venezuela, 1780–1850*. Tucson: University of Arizona Press.

Zeuske, Michael. 2013. *Simón Bolívar: History and Myth*. Princeton, NJ: Markus Wiener.

Zeuske, Michael. 2014. *Amistad: A Hidden Network of Slavers and Merchants*. Princeton, NJ: Markus Wiener.

Transatlantic Patriotisms

Race and Nation in the Impact of the Guerra de África in the Spanish Caribbean in 1860

Albert Garcia-Balañà

In February 1860, during the climactic days of the most intense fighting in the first Spanish-Moroccan War, which in Spain had already been christened the Guerra de África or African War (October 1859–April 1860), a certain Martín de Arredondo of Havana presented the captain-general of Cuba, the highest Spanish authority on the island, with a proposal to "form a battalion of volunteers of *pardos y morenos libres* [free mulattos and free blacks] to take part in the African War."[1] We know of this plan to recruit supposed Afro-Cuban volunteers to serve in a Spanish war in Africa—a scheme that went no further than the paper it was written on—thanks to the researches of Michele Reid-Vazquez and David Sartorius (Reid-Vazquez 2011, 140–42; Sartorius 2013, 90–91). We can see from both studies that the captain-general's office dismissed the project with a barrage of objections in rebuttal of Arredondo's argument that, thanks to both their tradition of service in colonial militias and their racial heritage, Cuban pardos and morenos would behave as "good soldiers, valiant against the [Moroccan] enemy," particularly on a battlefield so similar to the "rigors of the tropical climate." Arredondo's references to the "loyal *pardos y morenos* of Havana" did nothing to soften the negative report from the secretary of the recently arrived captain general, Francisco Serrano. His report pointed out the logistical difficulties involved and the potential cost of transporting the men to Morocco, but particularly emphasized two obstacles that were specific to the racial and sociopolitical dynamics of colonial Cuba around 1860.

The first was the expectation that recruitment would not be at all easy given the problems the colonial authorities had already found in filling the ranks of the Batallones de Pardos y Morenos (Battalions of Mulattos and Blacks), which had been reestablished in 1854—having previously been disbanded in 1844—under the name Milicias Disciplinadas de Color (Disciplined Colored Militia). The second obstacle was the potentially disruptive effects of a recruitment of *libres de color*, free people of color, of this kind in the world of midcentury Havana, on its labor market and its racial and social divisions.² If for Arredondo the African heritage of pardos and morenos was what made them especially suitable for fighting in Morocco, for the captaincy-general's report this was, on the contrary, precisely what made it advisable to approach the issue with the greatest prudence and minimal enthusiasm.

The "African War": A View from across the Atlantic

This chapter will put forward a dual reading of this rapid but nevertheless multifaceted rejection by the highest authorities in colonial Cuba of a project to arm Afro-Cuban "volunteers" in order for them to join the Army of Africa of 1860. These readings are based on an awareness of contexts and actors in Cuba, but also, and no less importantly, of the very fluid interaction between the latter and metropolitan and neoimperial contexts and actors, in a Spanish overseas empire with a geography in which Cuba at that time was seen as the undisputed hub, but which was not limited just to the island. It's a dual reading, therefore, that is directly influenced by the pioneering work of Christopher Schmidt-Nowara on the potency and plurality of a "colonial public sphere" in the Spain of the mid-nineteenth century (Schmidt-Nowara 1999, 100–125).

A transatlantic viewpoint can provide us, for example, with a much clearer assessment of just how singular was the rejection of the offer by Captain-General Serrano, given the environment of unbridled bellicose patriotism and support for Africanista intervention in Morocco that existed in Spain in the winter and spring of 1860. Given, too, that Francisco Serrano had been a close ally of the prime minister, General Leopoldo O'Donnell, in his assumption of a leading role in Spanish overseas policy from the summer of 1858 onward, one that would be sustained for some seven years, and that O'Donnell had made the formation and dispatch to the war of provincial militias recruited from among civil society separately from the conventional army, the "Catalan Volunteers" and Tercios Vascongadas or "Basque Regiments," a major factor in encouraging the political legitimization and popular acceptance of the Moroccan war of 1859–60. The transatlantic, and particularly Caribbean, connections of the geopolitics of the Guerra de África would be neither marginal nor insignificant. However, one could also see, as I shall show, the emergence of identifications from across the Atlantic and the Caribbean with the wave of patriotism that inundated metropolitan Spain during the months of the Moroccan campaign. This can be documented among the communities of *peninsulares* or peninsula Spaniards established in Cuba by 1860, but also, in a manner that might be less expected, among sections of the Cuban-born creoles who at that time wished to renegotiate and restructure their links with Madrid. In the cases of both peninsulares and creoles, these expressions of patriotism were loaded with racial imagery and a reinvigorated racial language. When Francisco Serrano dismissed the idea of a battalion of mulatto and free black Cubans fighting shoulder to shoulder with the white volunteers and the Army of Africa, such images and forms of racial language were already taking shape and gaining weight in the "colonial public sphere."

The geopolitics of O'Donnell's ventures in Africa were not disconnected from the circumstances of colonial Cuba. Today we know that the Moroccan campaign was conceived of at the same time as recolonization and the establishment of effective control was initiated in the territories that had formally been considered Spanish in the Gulf of Guinea, the beginning of which can be dated to the so-called Chacón Expedition of 1858, which was rapidly capitalized upon by the first O'Donnell government (García Cantús 2004, 345–406). In 1860 the modest shows of strength made by Spain in Morocco and the islands of the Gulf of Guinea, for all—and despite—their fragility, questioned British hegemony in the Atlantic and, similarly, sought to follow in the wake of and gain the complicity of Bonapartist France and its own reinvigorated imperialism (Garcia-Balañà 2008). And all this was undertaken with one eye on Cuba. Policies conceived with Cuba in mind included the promotion of the supposed system of "contracted emigration" or indentured labor, which had been tested in the French settlements on the Senegalese coast after France's formal abolition of slavery in 1848 and in the course of the 1850s, and which was used by Madrid to justify the sudden Spanish interest in the Gulf of Guinea island of Bioko or Fernando Pó, against the background of a massive demand for fresh labor from the Cuban plantations and the survival of a large-scale illegal slave trade, often under the disguise of formulas of this kind (Garcia-Balañà 2008, 171–76). In addition, around one hundred thousand Chinese "coolies" were also shipped to Cuba on similar terms in the 1850s and 1860s. Equally, Spain's potential new enclaves in Africa were also connected to Cuba through their status as possible destinations for *emancipados*, slaves, and other groups that were to be eradicated from the Cuban colonial order (García Cantús 2004, 433–65, 651–52; Roldán de Montaud 2011, 185–86). At the same time, the increased closeness between Madrid and Paris that smoothed the way for the Spanish campaign in Morocco was inseparable from the albeit-unequal Franco-Spanish collaboration that had begun in the last months of 1858 and early 1859 in such locations as Indochina or the ports of Canton and Macau, and would continue in Mexico in 1861. It was a collaboration in which one can also discover Caribbean considerations: the French merchant fleet, for example, would be the great protagonist and beneficiary of the shipping of thousands of Chinese indentured laborers or coolies to Cuba from 1858–59 onwards, in contrast to the very self-interested abstention and obstructionism of the British (Garcia-Balañà 2008, 176–84).

For all these reasons we should not belittle the multiple implications, both local and imperial, of the wave of celebrations that ran through Spain's overseas colonies following the taking of the Moroccan city of Tetuan on February 4–5, 1860. This wave—as we shall see—swept across Cuba from Havana to Santiago, crossed over to Puerto Rico and finally spent itself in the China Sea. The government of the Philippines organized celebrations in Manila, at the same time as it issued a proclamation full of revealing transoceanic similes addressed to the troops stationed in the islands, who at the time were heavily occupied in completing the process of establishing effective control over the Visayan Islands and, above all, in suppressing the so-called Moro or "Moorish" rebels—since they were Muslims, and so in 1860 equivalents of the Moroccans—in the southern islands of Mindanao and Jolo.[3]

The wave of patriotism that the African War unleashed in Spain has given rise to no shortage of reflections. Two blocks of evidence, which I have been able to document in the case of Catalonia, are of interest here. First is one that shows the existence in abundance of a mass patriotism that was socially heterogeneous and promoted by figures who had themselves emerged from the *pueblo* (the ordinary people) and were often associated with the Progressive (Progresista) and Democratic (Demócrata) political opposition. The five hundred or so Catalan Volunteers who enlisted in Barcelona to fight in Morocco and their popularity in the lower-class Catalonia of 1860—and not only there—are the best example of this. An initiative that had originated with the ambitious General Juan Prim and the traditionally Progressive Catalan circle around him, the Catalan Volunteers capitalized upon "anti-African" patriotism in Catalonia, and not just because of their identification with the "province." Their popularity was also due to the way they were deliberately associated with the Milicia Nacional—from which they inherited both personnel and a variety of symbols—a popular militia that had been much beloved of political radicals in metropolitan Spain and was much missed by 1859, after it had been disarmed and dismantled by the Moderate (Moderato) party counterrevolution between 1856 and 1858 (Garcia-Balañà 2002, 27–50). This image of the battalion as a civilian and popular militia explains why one of the foremost figures in lauding the virtues of the Catalan Volunteers was a man such as Josep Anselm Clavé, a leader of the Democratic Party, promoter of the working men's choirs founded in midcentury Catalonia—known as the Cors de Clavé or Clavé Choirs—and a pioneer in translating the "Marseillaise" into Catalan. This leads us to the second set of evidence we need to consider.

In one of his most acclaimed songs in celebration of the Volunteers, "Los Nets dels Almugàvers" (The Grandsons of the Almogavers), Clavé associated them with the celebrated bands of Catalan warriors of the same name who fought against the Muslims in the Middle Ages, while condemning the Moroccans to the status of a "race of slaves." This inferiority in terms of both political development and general civilization—the Morocco of Clavé, and other Democrats like him, was portrayed as the quintessence of orientalist despotism—conferred a dual legitimacy on the mission of the Volunteers in Africa. First, by reestablishing wounded national honor, but also, and no less importantly, by asserting the political adulthood of the "people," which would be confirmed by their contribution to victory over an empire and people still bound to servitude. It would be confirmed, in effect, by a victory over those who embodied the Democrats' own dystopia (Garcia-Balañà 2002, 57–63). This was a civilizational rather than a biological racism, but nevertheless one that was still able to use phenotypic physical characteristics to clarify the boundaries between active citizens and servile subjects, and to do so in a manner that favored and appeared inclusive for the sections of the common people in Spain who had been expelled from political life in the summer of 1856. Consequently, during the Barcelona Carnival of 1860 the customary degrading lampoons took the form of "various groups of dwarves dressed as diminutive Moroccans" captained by "some sort of black guard" who paraded amid the jeers of the crowd in the shadow of the traditional Carnival giants, dressed as the Volunteers. Nor was there any lack, in the cheap popular chapbooks or *libros de cordel* produced around that time, of stories in which much emphasis was placed on the "almost black" nature of the leading "Moorish" characters, the icing on the cake of a range of other negative attributes.[4]

It is also probable that these political and racial images were additionally nourished by the very many connections that existed between the Caribbean and Catalan society by 1860. It is certainly clear, moreover, that these same images reached (or returned to) the Cuba of the era, where they were picked up afresh for similar but distinct purposes, and where without doubt they did nothing to endorse the idea of a large body of nonwhite volunteers being raised to fight in Morocco. The transatlantic life stories that will be examined in this chapter, of Francisco Fort y Segura and Antonio Serret y Capello, both officers of the Catalan Volunteers in Morocco who a short time later were acclaimed in Havana and Matanzas in Cuba, both demonstrate this fact.

It is useful here to remind ourselves of certain points to introduce us to the worlds in Cuba and the Caribbean within which Francisco Fort and Antonio Serret were celebrated in 1860. First of all there was the rapid demographic increase in the numbers of Spanish peninsulares in Cuba, which took off precisely from 1859–60 onward, in part due to the liberalization of laws relating to emigration from Spain to its colonies in 1858–62 and in part, soon afterward, to the numerous military expeditions—as one form of "migration"—that were dispatched to the region due to the Spanish war in Santo Domingo from 1862 to 1865 and the first Cuban war of independence, the Ten Years' War, from 1868 to 1878 (Moreno Fraginals and Moreno Masó 1993, 69–109). The more than ten thousand Catalans that César Yáñez has estimated were living in Cuba in 1860 constituted a significant element in this takeoff, in view of their well-entrenched position on the island, their quantitative and qualitative weight among the total of over sixty thousand peninsulares (in addition to another fifty thousand from the Canary Islands) and the always potentially vigorous nature of their channels of migration, as would be demonstrated once again during the subsequent decade (Yáñez Gallardo 1996, 83–89; Garcia-Balañà 2012).

The second point to be noted is that the winter of 1859–60 would also be a key moment in the weakening and reversal of the policy of threatened "Africanization" in Cuba that had been brandished in the 1850s by the Captains-General José G. De la Concha (in office 1850–52 and 1854–59) and Juan de la Pezuela (1853–54), a policy conceived as a reply to the challenge of the "annexationist" movement that proposed a union of Cuba with the United States, and its supporters and manifestations among Cuban creoles. This threat of "Africanization" was deployed by an essentially military colonial administration, whose doctrine of a "balance of the races" (*equilibro de razas*) accorded a central position to the existence of libres de color, "free people of color"—in itself a powerful factor in deterring any thoughts of a break with Madrid among creole planters—and one of the principal symbols of which had been, in 1854–55 and still in 1859, the reestablishment of the Batallones de Pardos y Morenos. As Josep M. Fradera has indicated, with the arrival of Francisco Serrano as captain-general of Cuba in 1859–62 "an era of change opened up in the overseas colonies, the direct result of the exhaustion of the model followed by De la Concha during the previous administration, together with the pressure of international circumstances" (Fradera 2005, 614). The racial blackmail exercised by the home country against the island's elites could not be a political solution that would create lasting stability, nor could the framework of African slavery continue to be a politically viable system in the context of the Atlantic world as it entered the 1860s. The rapid eclipse of the battalions of Milicias Disciplinadas de Color after 1859—due also to the reluctance seen among Afro-Cubans to be conscripted into them—would be both evidence of and one of the major instances of these changes in Cuba. The fact that the captain-general who finally abolished the Milicias de Color in 1865 was the perpetuator of Serrano's policies and fellow "reformist" Domingo Dulce (in office 1862–66), the same man who as captain-general of Catalonia in 1859 had given his support to the recruitment of the Catalan Volunteers bound for Africa, is one more of the revealing ironies in this transatlantic story. We also know, however, that this disbandment of the black militia had also been demanded by the creole elites as part of negotiations with Madrid at the beginning of the 1860s, not least because the creoles' demands for political rights sought to gain them room for maneuver in order to gain influence, above all, over the final resolution of the question of slavery and the no less explosive issue of the political rights to be accorded to libres de color, seeking their postponement sine die (Fradera 2005, 652 and 645–64; Reid-Vazquez 2011, 135–44; Sartorius 2013, 87–92).

It was against this dual-faceted background, already visible in 1860, that Serrano rejected the scheme to send Afro-Cuban volunteers to the war in Morocco.

Peninsular Patriotisms: Francisco Fort, from Tetuan to Santo Domingo via Havana

On December 12, 1860 Francisco Milá and Emilio Roig, president and secretary respectively of the Sociedad de Beneficencia de Naturales de Cataluña (Society for the Welfare of Natives of Catalonia), established in Havana in the 1840s, notified the provincial Diputación, or administration, of Barcelona by letter of the results of the "subscription" that the society had organized and collected in Cuba "in order to give aid to the widows, orphans and families of the Catalan Volunteers who had fallen, and those who had been left wounded or disabled defending the Spanish flag on African shores." The "donation from the Island of Cuba" for the Catalan Volunteers from the Moroccan war amounted to the very substantial sum of 11,232 pesos, or 224,640 reales, of which the Barcelona Diputación received 10,067 pesos or 201,340 reales, which it assigned and distributed among the families of the men who had died and among those who had been wounded in Morocco.[5] As a measure of comparison, the total of all the donations collected in Barcelona Province itself by the "Provincial Council of Barcelona for the Support of the Injured from the War in Morocco"—and this not just for the nearly five hundred Catalan Volunteers—amounted by October 1860 to 16,322 pesos, or 326,430 reales.[6] In other words, the amount donated by the approximately ten thousand Catalans in Cuba was equivalent to nearly 70 percent of the donations made by the entire province of Barcelona, with a population of over 720,000; for every three pesos donated by individuals in the province the Catalans in Cuba had given more than two pesos, and that exclusively for the Catalan Volunteers. The more than 200,000 reales received from Cuba provided for an average award of 972 reales among the 202 Volunteers who benefitted from them: 139 wounded men, including 12 who had been left *inutilizados* or "useless," and the families of 51 of the dead.[7]

Francisco Milá requested from the Barcelona Diputación that "once the distribution [of the donations] has been concluded," they should send to Havana "a list of the persons assisted with the respective amounts awarded to them, purely so that the donations may be given the proper publicity here." Still more revealing of the nature of the public zeal for "Cuban" aid is the fact that during these same weeks in the late fall of 1860 the Catalan Welfare Society in Havana also feted lavishly the "valiant Colonel Don Francisco María Fort," a former aide to General Prim and commander of the Catalan Volunteers, who received 510 pesos from the "donation from the Island of Cuba" in his own hands. Francisco Fort y Segura had trained the Volunteers, and had kept the Barcelona Diputación regularly informed of his actions in the Moroccan war. In his letters he had provided lists of the dead and wounded, and extensive accounts of the battles of Tetuan and Wad-Ras (against what he liked to call *la morisma* or the "Moorish rabble").[8] Very significantly,

Fort was not just in Havana at the end of 1860 to receive the public admiration of the Catalans in Cuba. He was also in Havana "en route to Santo Domingo."[9]

Francisco Fort y Segura was in Havana in the fall of 1860 because he was on his way to play—and was already playing—a significant role in the preparations for the Spanish annexation and recolonization of Santo Domingo, which was eventually formalized in May 1861. The annexation of Santo Domingo constituted the second great neocolonial enterprise of the O'Donnell government, its genesis inseparable from the patriotic and imperialistic atmosphere fabricated for and by the Guerra de África. It was also inseparable from the political languages of superiority and racial disparagement that had been fed by the Moroccan war, for it was not accidental that Spain entered Dominican territory—at the "request" of the Dominican president, Pedro Santana—on the pretext of averting the threat of a Haitian invasion that might have enjoyed considerable support among the *gentes de color* or people of color of the eastern half of Hispaniola. It is revealing that Francisco Fort linked Tetuan and Wad-Ras with his mission in Santo Domingo. Equally revealing is the fact that he carried with him to the Caribbean the very vivid and popular image of the Catalan Volunteers who had recently overcome a "race of slaves" in Africa.

In May 1860 Fort had been received as a popular hero at the head of the Volunteers as they returned from Morocco, in Barcelona and in his home town of Tortosa.[10] Scarcely three months later the Madrid press reported that "authorized by Her Majesty's government, Colonel Don Francisco Fort, lately commander of the [Catalan] Volunteers, and several officers, with some 400 individuals, nearly all of them Catalans, are set to form part of the army of Santo Domingo." The report also added, as a guarantee of their worth and to add to their legitimacy, that "more than half of the expeditionaries had already had the opportunity to distinguish themselves in the African campaign."[11] By November 1860 Fort and some of his men were already in Havana, where they received the acclaim and part of the donations from the Catalans of Cuba, before going on to Puerto Rico, where they were similarly "honoured by the Catalans resident there."[12] And by at least February 1861—three months before the annexation—Fort was already in Santo Domingo, taking up positions to oppose the rivals of Santana and the annexationist elites, and combat all those reluctant to accept a return to Spanish sovereignty (a monarchy that still possessed colonies based on slavery on either side of Hispaniola). According to the direct testimony of Ramón González Tablas, an army captain who served in the Dominican campaign, "Colonel Fort, who had acquired a high reputation for courage in the war in Africa, issued a call in Santo Domingo [in March 1861] to all the subjects of her Catholic Majesty to organize a corps of militia" (González Tablas 1870, 40 and 37–41). According to Dominican historians, Fort and his "two companies of Spanish Volunteers" went on to play a key role in the control of the proannexationist rearguard during the Spanish "invasion" of the country and the initial crisis with Haiti and its local allies during the spring and summer of 1861 (Rodríguez Demorizi 1955, 194; De Jesús Domínguez 1979, 1:169).

The Havana in which Francisco Fort arrived in the fall of 1860 had not ceased to celebrate the African War. Prim, Fort, and his Catalan Volunteers in Morocco were familiar, and thus accessible, images for the more than ten thousand Catalans then resident in Cuba, and for many of the thousands of other peninsulares settled on the island. There is abundant evidence in this regard.

In May 1861 the newspaper *Eco de Euterpe*, published in Barcelona by Josep A. Clavé, announced that "lately a philharmonic academy has been established in Havana, under the name *Orfeón*, and directed by Don Felipe Grau," in all probability a Catalan emigrant.[13] We know that during the following months the choral societies inspired and recognized by Clavé in Catalonia set down new roots in the urban areas of Cuba with Catalan communities, with an impetus and political blessing that was in part provided by the Guerra de África. In 1863 Clavé himself sent his congratulations to the by then well-established Sociedad Coral de Euterpe of Havana, a list of whose members was published by the Havana weekly *Don Junípero* in June of the same year, with the names of around twenty "young Catalans."[14] This same society or other "Choirs of Euterpe" formed the group that the Havana-based paper *El Moro Muza* heard sing "compositions by the highly regarded Sr. Clavé of Barcelona" during summer 1863, under the direction of one Juan Gelabert.[15] Ironically, the Clavé choirs that had come to Cuba in the atmosphere of celebration of the African War of 1860 would eventually lend their name—and their "civilizing" reputation—to the *cabildos de nación* or Afro-Cuban ethnic associations, which were partially reinvented as the Coros de Clave (without the accent on the e) in the last two decades of the century after the prohibition of their parades and drums in the years that followed the end of the first Cuban war in 1877–78 (Sublette 2004, 262–63; Miller 2009, 160–61).

Alongside the choral societies and the songs by Clavé that celebrated the war in Morocco, several other manifestations of Spanish patriotism aimed at a wide audience were in circulation in urban Cuba. In March 1860 "a leaflet that contains the celebrated proclamation by General Prim, in the Catalan language, which is, in addition, illustrated with characteristic images and uniforms of the Catalan Volunteers who undertook so many feats in the campaign in Africa" was distributed in Havana.[16] In October the "public" continued to visit, in the same Havana bookshop and print workshop El Iris that had produced this leaflet, a "panorama" that had as its principal attraction "a most beautiful collection of views of Spain's recent war against Morocco."[17] The owner of El Iris was Magín Pujolá, who by his name was also very probably Catalan, whose bookshop also published the annual reports of the Society for the Welfare of the Natives of Catalonia. The satirical Havana weekly *El Moro Muza*, the first issue of which appeared on October 16, 1859 and whose title was inspired by the very recent declaration of war on the empire of Morocco, also came from Pujolá's press.

It is notably revealing that a publication such as *El Moro Muza*, born in Havana invoking a popular anti-African stereotype and amid the excitement of the African War, should have been the personal project of a figure such as Juan Martínez Villergas, "the great satirist" of radical and democratizing liberalism in the Spain of 1850. A writer and agitator who had been very active in the radical and democratic circles of 1840s Madrid, a fierce critic of the Moderate Party and its leader and prime minister Ramón María Narváez ("the Spanish Caligula"), Martínez Villergas consequently ended up in prison, in 1851, and shortly afterward in exile. He was compensated by the brief Progressive revolution of 1854–56 with modest consular appointments, the last of which he had scarcely completed as Spanish consul-general in Haiti when the Moderate counterrevolution of 1856–58 drove him to seek refuge in Spain's Caribbean colonies (Gil Novales 1992). Of particular interest here are two central features of the combative literature of Martínez Villergas and others like him in the Madrid of democratic radicalism, as Xavier Andreu Miralles has pointed out: populism and nationalism (Andreu Miralles 2011). Shortly after disembarking in Havana Martínez Villergas provoked a tussle with the established press that culminated in his producing a public and inflammatory defense of "my readers," "a class who have been branded in a shocking manner," so that "I have come to speak out in defence of my friends, the employees in shops and in commerce (*dependientes del comercio*)," the great majority of whom were peninsulares of humble origins.[18] Exaltations of the "people" abound in the Havana projects of Martínez Villergas of the early 1860s.[19] They were a "people" whose customs and virtues were the "authentic expression of *lo español*" (Spanish-ness), as Andreu Miralles has traced, in opposition to the "oligarchies" subject to foreign influences and therefore "alien to the national body" (Andreu Miralles 2011, 77–84). This populist nationalism, forged in the political radicalism of metropolitan Spain, would be further nourished in Cuba, and would be a mark of the Caribbean years of Martínez Villergas. It was a populist nationalism that did not just come to him in Havana, and which throws new light, for example, on the series that *El Moro Muza* published in October 1860 on Haiti, associating political despotism of an orientalist, African kind with "a country in which the love of work has been completely lost."[20] It equally throws a fresh light on the verses with which Martínez Villergas sought to bury the Cuban rebellion of 1868, very shortly after it had broken out: *"Déjala [la insurrección de Yara], caminante, en esta fosa, / que indigna es de compasión siquiera, / que no la vean más eternos soles; / que fugitiva, hambrienta y harapposa, / escribió –¡miserable!– en su bandera / ¡ANTES SER AFRICANOS QUE ESPAÑOLES!"* (Leave it [the Yara insurrection of October 1868], to go on its way, in this abyss, / unworthy even of compassion, / let the eternal sun see it no more; / [The rising that] as a fugitive, ragged and starving, / wrote — how wretched! — on its banner, / BETTER AFRICANS THAN SPANIARDS!)"[21]

It was against this background of celebration of and a popular appetite for the Moroccan war in urban Cuba, chiefly among its communities of peninsular-Spanish origin, that Francisco Fort y Segura, celebrated as "late commander of the Catalan Volunteers," landed in Havana in the fall of 1860 "en route to Santo Domingo." A point to be highlighted is the insistence that was made in the press on the "civilian"—and also "civilizing"—mythology of the Catalan Volunteers in Morocco in order to endorse, or at least encourage acceptance of, Fort's new and uncertain mission in Santo Domingo.[22] Most relevant to the Cuban experience of thousands of ordinary peninsulares, and their capacity for perceiving the African War as an episode with resonances and continuities in the Caribbean, were two central aspects of Fort's mission in Dominican territory.

In the first place there was the project already mentioned to form a militia of "Spanish Volunteers." Francisco Fort organized his "corps of militia" in Santo Domingo when "the annexation [by Spain] had still not been made public" by President Santana, that is, before March 18, 1861 (González Tablas 1870, 40). By the time that Spain accepted and ratified the annexation, on May 19, there were "two companies of Spanish Volunteers in Santo Domingo, captained by the Catalan Colonel Fort" (De Jesús Domínguez 1979, 1:169). These companies each consisted of "more than two hundred individuals." They were also a force that, "when the Haitians invaded [Dominican] territory in the last days of May," went into action.

The first antiannexationist uprising had taken place in Moca, in the north of the country, at the beginning of May, and was revived very soon afterward by the eruption across the border of the anti-Santana Dominicans Francisco del Rosario Sánchez and José María Cabral in Las Matas, with support from Haiti. The press in Spain that had links with communities in Cuba and Puerto Rico then reported that "Colonel Fort is one of the leaders who marched forth to combat the Haitians as soon as he knew of their entry into the Spanish dominions." The Haitians were referred to as the *negros vecinos* (neighboring blacks), "savage and tireless enemies," and "disorderly hordes."[23] Having subdued the "almost black" "Moors" in Morocco, Fort was the right man to confront—once again with civilian volunteers—a colored rebellion that obscured the new frontier of Spanish territory and drew it, implicitly and politically, in racial terms. The Haitian president, Fabre Geffrard, had also just reminded "our brothers in the East," in his anti-Spanish proclamation in April, that "the Spanish flag authorizes and protects the enslavement of all the children of Africa."[24] "Colonel Fort, as a consequence of the displeasure caused him by the latest Haitian outrage," crowed *El Mallorquín* on July 22, 1861, "has departed for the border with the intention of giving a lesson to M. Geffrard and his troupe, which we believe he will achieve without great effort."[25] Anne Eller has shown in detail the manner in which the new Spanish authorities used the shadow of Haiti to discredit, belittle, and crush these first uprisings, all of which were "clearly Dominican-led," which did no more than intensify—and confirm—the "native Dominican anxiety over Spanish racism" that had fueled them at the outset (Eller 2011, 245 and 244–55).

The continuities between the Catalan Volunteers of the Moroccan war of 1860 and the "Spanish Volunteers" in the Dominican annexation of 1861 are obvious. The continuities included the encouragement of national feeling, and potential political inclusion, through experiences and languages based in an opposition of civilizations and races. There were also continuities in the promotion and extra visibility given to a civilian militia separate from the conventional army recruited by conscription, given the resonance that this could have in the Spain of 1860–61, when the National Militia had been disarmed by the Moderates in 1856, but still figured among the goals of the most cross-class and democratizing elements among liberals. The much-missed National Militia played an influence in the image of the Catalan Volunteers in the Moroccan war, and was one of the reasons for their success among the popular classes of Barcelona in 1859–60 (Garcia-Balañà 2002, 30–48). Francisco Fort came precisely from this largely civilian, militia-based milieu, as had Victoriano Sugrañes, his predecessor at the head of the Volunteers in Morocco, who had died at Tetuan. A captain of the National Militia in his hometown of Tortosa during the wars against Carlism, Fort had transferred to the regular army thanks to the ability he had shown in the Militia, before being "retired"—purged—by a Moderate government. Prim had then cleverly reclaimed him, with clearly political intent, for his Volunteers in Africa in 1859.[26]

No less obvious are the affinities between Fort's mission with the militia in Santo Domingo and the recently created Instituto de Voluntarios or Institute of Volunteers in Spanish Cuba. Established in 1855–56 to confront the threat of armed "annexationist" incursions against Cuba, the Institute of Volunteers represented the transfer to the Caribbean of the model of a civilian irregular militia seen in the Milicia Nacional, at a point when the latter had just been dismantled in metropolitan Spain. Its numbers were rapidly filled with poorer-class peninsulares, shop-workers and tradesmen. Despite the fact that it reproduced in its ranks the social and community hierarchies seen among the peninsular Spaniards on the island, the volunteer corps in Cuba was not experienced by the shop clerks and artisans as a passive obligation, or merely a favor granted from above. With a new position of relative strength, its members soon obtained from the captain-general's office freedom to enter new work contracts without the need for official authorization, removing a restriction on *peninsular* employees that associated them with the controls exerted on slaves, and in 1857 they secured the first permission to found local mutual aid societies (Casanovas Codina 2000, 78–80). The Havana Volunteers celebrated the Spanish victory in Morocco en masse with "great spectacles" held in the city's bullring in May and June 1860.[27] The Institute of Volunteers was full of Catalans, amid groups from other parts of Spain, when the Cuban rebellion broke out in 1868. Of the nearly three thousand armed Volunteers in the district of Matanzas in the early months of 1869, 464 (or 16 percent) had been born in Catalonia or the Balearic Islands, a representation that was only exceeded by those born in Cuba itself (710) and by Canary Islanders (555), and all but equal to the numbers from Asturias (466).[28]

The first reports we have of Francisco Fort's mission with the militia in Santo Domingo were also intermixed with information on schemes for emigration from the home country to the new Spanish province. This was the second element that had unquestionable resonance among the communities of peninsular origin in the Spanish Caribbean. The Madrid newspaper *La Correspondencia de España* of August 10, 1860 reported that "Sr. Fort, Colonel of the valiant Catalan Volunteers . . . has been in Madrid, and left here his friend Don Pedro Carreras, charged with the task of exploring the determination of those who request to travel as colonists to the island of Santo Domingo, and [whose names] he has noted in a register open to families and laborers so that they may proceed there as colonists."[29]

Thanks to the researches of Magdalena Guerrero we know that this was not a matter simply of castles in the air. A few weeks earlier, in July 1860, the first expedition had left from Cádiz for the Dominican Republic, with armaments, military instructors, and around a hundred colonists, an initiative instigated by Santana with the full collaboration of O'Donnell. Prior to the official annexation a second expedition sailed with civilian colonists, on the vessel *Santa María* in January 1861, with nearly 150 colonists on board and the entire support of the Spanish Ministry of War. By then the "register" that had been opened of Spaniards ready to emigrate to Santo Domingo amounted to some twenty-five hundred names (compared to a total Dominican population at the time of approximately 185,000, eight thousand of them in the city of Santo Domingo). Between the summer of 1860 and that of 1862 at least seven expeditions arrived in Santo Domingo from Spain, bringing around five hundred "colonists," mainly artisans, laborers, and their families (Guerrero Cano 2002–03). In addition, the Army of Santo Domingo would also become a notable channel for the migration of peninsular Spaniards to the Spanish Caribbean, above all during the initial, quieter years of the annexation (1861–63). Catalans in particular continued to be overrepresented among these troops by comparison with their presence among the *quintos* or military conscripts in mainland Spain (Moreno Fraginals and Moreno Masó 1993, 69–90). O'Donnell summarized his initial expectations for the colonization and "whitening" of the territory—since over 80 percent of the Dominican population "was of African origin"—in a letter to Serrano of August 1, 1861. "If the great elements of wealth that the island of Santo Domingo contains are to be developed, an increase in population is indispensable," the prime minister wrote, "fortunately, the conditions of the country permit us to expect that the *white race* may fill this immediate need."[30]

The outbreak of the Dominican war against annexation or the Restoration War, as it is known, during the winter and spring of 1863 (Eller 2011, 336–61) brought a definitive end to this first episode of imitation of militia recruitment and modest-scale white immigration, with its resonances among the peninsular Spaniards in Cuba. On January 6, 1862, *La Época* in Madrid reported that "at the request of Colonel Don Francisco Fort, who commanded the force of Catalan

Volunteers in Africa, permission has been granted for him to withdraw to this city [Madrid], and the commission with which he had been charged on the island of Santo Domingo is declared to be concluded."[31] Exactly two years had gone by since the enlistment in Barcelona of the Catalan Volunteers for the war in Morocco. For Fort, the African-based militia had opened the doors to a leading role in the attempt at outward expansionism onto the "very African" island of Hispaniola.

Creole Patriotisms: Antonio Serret, from Santiago de Cuba to Matanzas via Barcelona and Wad-Ras

On the night of June 25, 1860 the recently established Liceo Artístico y Literario or Artistic and Literary Society of Matanzas in western Cuba celebrated, in a suitably literary manner, Spain's already-concluded military campaign in Morocco. The evening's events were opened by society member Casimiro del Monte (or Delmonte) y Portillo with his ode to the "valiant Cuban Don Antonio Serret," who was "declared an 'eminent hero of the fatherland' (*benemérito de la Patria en grado heroico*) for the valour he demonstrated in the African War," according to the notes in the record of the night's contributions published by the society.[32] This was not the first public celebration of the Guerra de África undertaken by the Matanzas Liceo, which was itself a product of the political and institutional liberalization permitted in Cuba by Serrano from late 1859.[33] However, Casimiro del Monte's ode in honor of the "valiant Cuban" Antonio Serret is notable for the two epic story lines that combine within it. First is the acclaimed status as a "Cuban hero" of Serret for having fought in Africa. With Serret, Cuba had contributed to a European war beyond the frontiers of liberal Europe: "*Oh héroe sin segundo: / Tu has hecho ver al mundo / Que esas flores eternas que en la Antilla / Ostenta Primavera, / Más son para corona a la guerrera*" (O Hero without equal, / You have made the world see / That these eternal flowers that in the Antilles / Reveal the spring, / Also serve as a crown for warriors). This was a European war, because the word "Spain"—or the adjective Spanish—does not appear in any of the poem's seventy-seven verses. It was a European war also, and above all—and herein appears the second theme of the narrative—because the classical model that Del Monte employed to laud Serret was none other than Leonidas, the Spartan who had confronted the oriental and therefore "barbarian" armies of the Persian Xerxes. "*Tu [Serret], sin que el riesgo y la distancia midas / Empuñas el acero sin tardanza, / Bravo como Leónidas, / Y lleno el pecho noble de esperanza, / Vuelas a la batalla, y a la venganza*" (You [Serret], without measuring the danger or distance / Take up the sword of steel without delay / Brave as Leonidas, / With your noble breast full of hope, / You fly into battle, and to take vengeance).[34]

Civic and public celebrations of the "valiant Cuban" Antonio Serret were not limited to this one episode in Matanzas. According to the *Crónicas* of the history of Santiago de Cuba compiled by Emilio Bacardí, Serret was a "son of Santiago [de Cuba]" who had served as a "second lieutenant in the regiment of Catalan Volunteers in Africa" and was "gravely wounded in the battle known as Wad-Ras," on March 23, 1860, and the municipality of Santiago also celebrated his being declared a "eminent hero of the fatherland" in May of the same year (Bacardí Moreau 1925, 3:298–99). The archival records of the Catalan Volunteers of 1860 confirm the information published by Bacardí. Antonio Serret y Capello, born in Santiago de Cuba, is listed as a second lieutenant in the first of the four companies of the Volunteers of Catalonia, and as having enlisted in December 1859 and taken part in three battles in Morocco, being wounded and subsequently decorated for his actions in the last of them, at Wad-Ras.[35]

Serret remembered his own war in Africa in a text he wrote in 1861 but published some years later in a collection titled *Prosa Perdida*, with an appendix in which he included a list of the Volunteers who had been beneficiaries of the "donation from the Island of Cuba" raised by the Catalan community. His account presents a complete panorama of the factors and elements that explain the success of the Volunteers in the popular and lower-class Catalonia of 1860, from their embarcation in the Andalusian port of Tarifa to the accompaniment of songs "by Maestro Clavé" to an atmosphere of camaraderie that was more civilian than military; from the liberal militia tradition represented by those among the Volunteers who had "taken part in all the struggles that have left our homeland desolate ever since the last war of succession" to the eulogy for the first commander of the Volunteers who had died at Tetuan, Victoriano Sugrañes, Francisco Fort's predecessor and a Democrat who had been subjected to reprisals by the Narváez government prior to 1859 (Serret y Capello 1871, 15–26). Much earlier, in a speech he gave in Madrid in the summer of 1860, Serret had already justified "the war that Spain has sustained against the Empire of Morocco" by maintaining that this battle—and his own personal involvement—had been undertaken "in the name of civilization."[36]

The fundamental question here is that of what led the men of the Matanzas Liceo, the educated creole elite of the city, to celebrate the African War publicly in the figure of the "Cuban"—meaning creole—Volunteer Antonio Serret y Capello. Which leads on to the question whether, among these reasons, we can discern any kind of connection with the misgivings that were being expressed among creoles around the same time regarding the continued existence of the Milicias Disciplinadas de Color and, in particular, the proposal to arm a battalion of pardos and morenos libres as volunteers to be sent to Morocco. What exactly had been the transoceanic life story of Antonio Serret y Capello by 1860? And who exactly were the men who acclaimed him in Matanzas as a Cuban "Leonidas"?

Antonio Serret y Capello was born in Santiago de Cuba in 1834 or 1835—since, according to a sworn statement by his brother Francisco, he was "five or six years old" in 1840—and was the son of Francisco Serret, "a native of Catalonia," and María Dolores Capello, "from Gibraltar." Although there is evidence that the older Francisco Serret had spent some time in Cádiz on the way to Cuba, his family roots point to his having come originally from the Catalan coastal district of Garraf, south of Barcelona. After a first visit back to Barcelona alone, in 1848 Francisco senior "proposed to move his entire family from this city [Santiago de Cuba] to Barcelona," including Antonio, "whom he proposed to educate and provide with a profession in that city."[37] Hence, Antonio studied at the Law Faculty of the University of Barcelona, where he gained a degree in jurisprudence in 1856. He then went on to the Central University in Madrid, where he obtained a doctorate in 1858–59 with a thesis titled "The Administration of Justice in the Overseas Provinces."[38] It seems highly likely that when Antonio enlisted in the Catalan Volunteers destined for Morocco, in December 1859, he already had in mind a return to Santiago de Cuba. In January 1861, only a few months after the end of the Moroccan campaign, the recently created Ministerio de Ultramar (Ministry for Overseas Territories) appointed him to the post of junior prosecutor in the *alcaldía mayor* or district courts of Santiago de Cuba. Serret never ceased to mention, on this and subsequent occasions, the respect he was due as an "officer of the Catalan Volunteers in the African War." After fourteen years of childhood and early adolescence in Cuba, thirteen years of adult life in mainland Spain, and three months of fighting in Africa, Serret sailed from Barcelona to cross the Atlantic once again on March 31, 1861. He took up his post in Santiago, in the lower levels of the colonial legal administration, on June 1, 1861, aged twenty-six or twenty-seven.[39]

When he enlisted in the Catalan Volunteers on their way to fight in Morocco Antonio Serret may have been hoping simply to accelerate his entry into and promotion in the judicial hierarchy. He may perhaps also have wished to qualify or mitigate his status as "Cuban," which in this context may have been more counterproductive than favorable for his ambitions. However, it cannot fail to catch our attention that his first posting in 1861 was to his birthplace of Santiago de Cuba, and that, shortly before embarking for Morocco, he had publicly demonstrated his interest in Spanish colonial policy and particular concern, and hopes, for the course this might take in Cuba.

I am referring here to the speech he delivered during the ceremony in which he was awarded his law doctorate, which he gave in Madrid in the spring of 1859, and which was published shortly afterward. Serret spoke on the royal decree of January 1855 "for the administration of justice in the overseas provinces," an important milestone in the reform of the system of overseas *audiencias* or courts that had as its goal the final definition of the areas of judicial competence of these courts and the progressive clearing away of the political and consultational attributes and jurisdictions that they had inherited from the old Leyes de Indias (Laws of the Indies) of the sixteenth century (as well as dealing with the singular continuity of these historic laws as a consequence of the exclusion of Spain's overseas territories from the country's constitutional settlements since 1837). Although in the short term this decree might have strengthened the "supreme command" of the captain-general in Cuba, Serret emphasized, very significantly, its potential consequences in a different direction. "The Royal Decree mentioned," Serret suggested, "by establishing *alcaldes mayores*, district judges who can replace the political and military governors and lieutenant-governors in the exercise of the ordinary Royal Jurisdiction in the Island of Cuba, notably neutralizes the effects of the now-debased original form of organization" (Serret y Capello 1859, 9–10). Serret also applauded the extension to the overseas colonies of the right of appeal to a higher court, though not without lamenting that "only civil matters are comprehended within it, with criminal [cases] specifically excluded." Consistently prudent in tone, on this point he argued in his speech for an early "modification of the primitive rigor [of the decree], and hence the immediate extension [of the right of appeal in criminal cases] to Overseas affairs" (Serret y Capello 1859, 10–12). The centralizing logic that underlay the reform of 1855 was presented by Serret in 1859—when Francisco Serrano was on his way to Havana to build bridges with the island's creole elites—as a hypothetical guarantee against the habitual and still recent interference by the Cuban captain-general's office in judicial matters and other spheres of jurisdiction, despite these areas being supposedly distinct from the executive power.

Here one can see a connection between the men of the Matanzas Liceo and the figure of Serret in 1860, a man who was "Cuban" at the same time as "Catalan," and who had returned rapidly to Cuba under the auspices of an administration of justice influenced by the attempts at overseas reform of Serrano and O'Donnell. The Matanzas Liceo would play a significant role on the island as a platform in favor of colonial liberalization, a meeting point, during the early 1860s, for the creole elites most wary of any radical break with the past and those groups from metropolitan Spain who were most open to colonial reform. This connection does not contradict the possibility of some sort of tactical calculation in the eulogizing of Serret in Matanzas—on the contrary, it reinforces it—nor that there may have been personal contacts and friendships involved as well. Casimiro Del Monte y Portillo, author of the ode to Serret in Africa, had been born in Cimarrones, in Matanzas Province, in 1838, and so was scarcely three or four years younger than Serret. Around 1860 Casimiro was taking his first steps as a "public author," in the wake of his brother Domingo, secretary of the literature section of the Matanzas Liceo in the first year of its existence. Both literary careers, both relatively discreet, would develop within the characteristics of the school of creole fiction preoccupied with Cubanidad or "Cuban-ness," the idea of a Cuban creole identity. The two brothers would be obliged to go into exile when the first Cuban war of independence broke out in 1868–69, both of them in Santo Domingo, where from 1870 Domingo Del Monte y Portillo would edit *El Laborante*, a "newspaper published by Cuban immigrants," whose "principles will be those of liberty, and whose aim will be to inform [readers] about the Cuban Revolution" (Calcagno 1878, 239–40).

It is advisable here to warn against looking at these events with excessive hindsight; that is, to avoid regarding the men of the Matanzas Liceo in 1860 as a function essentially of their respective fates after 1868. Political and community-based radicalism was never among the aims of the associations founded among white, educated creoles during the reign of Queen Isabel II prior to 1868, as Alfonso W. Quiroz has reminded us (Quiroz 2011, 52 and 62). The example of Emilio Blanchet, general secretary of the Liceo at the time of the honoring of Serret in June 1860, demonstrates both aspects, his Cubanidad in negotiations with Madrid during the reformist 1860s and his forced radicalization following the outbreak of civil war on the island in 1868–69. Blanchet, a professor at Matanzas's high school or *instituto* and guiding spirit of the Liceo from the moment of its foundation, was the author of a *Manual de Historia de España* (1865) that was used as a school textbook in Cuba from 1865 to 1868. The war would change everything. In summer 1869, a year after the official prohibition of Blanchet's 1865 *Manual*, the director of the Matanzas Institute announced that "Don Emilio Blanchet, Professor of French, had taken absence abroad." Shortly afterward, the higher authorities in Cuba included Blanchet on the list of individuals in Matanzas whose possessions were to be confiscated due to their being considered *infidente* (disloyal), one of the many victims of the indiscriminate wave of anticreole confiscations and seizures unleashed from July 1869.[40]

Ten years earlier, however, in 1859, the position of Emilio Blanchet had been very different, as an influential citizen of Matanzas who also played a part in public life across Cuba. In the same period, prior to the creation of the Liceo, Blanchet and the Del Monte y Portillo brothers had founded *El Eco de Matanzas*, a weekly newspaper that aspired to recoup the prestige of the historic *La Aurora de Matanzas*, founded in 1828. Domingo Del Monte y Portillo was the first editor of *El Eco* in summer 1859, when favorable winds seemed to be blowing thanks to the political changes in Madrid and in the captaincy-general in Havana. The local creole elite thus regained a tribune from which to proclaim their hopes and expectations, and share their doubts and fears, in a kind of collective exorcism. Among these expressions of malaise was one that was repeated a number of times in the pages of *El Eco* during the second half of 1859: the excessive and, for the newspapers' writers, discomfiting presence of gente de color (people of color) in the public life of Matanzas, reflected in particular in the warnings that appeared in the newspaper regarding the supposedly growing facility with which certain highly racialized sociocultural barriers were being crossed.

One example will be enough to capture the extent and level of the state of alarm. In September 1859 *El Eco* published an extensive letter signed by someone using the name "Otelo," with an ironic commentary that focused chiefly, though not solely, on the "comedies presented by *gente de color*." The writer said that he had attended, in "an old warehouse in the Calle del Sol," a performance of two comedies by the local author Rafael Otero presented by "amateur actors" who "belong to that class of society that has in its veins 50 per cent of northern blood and another 50 of southern blood," all before a "most numerous audience graded into as many colors as are employed in the human epidermis." The color of the nonprofessional actors, all people of different degrees of African descent, was a perfect metaphor for their cultural incapacity, and not for nothing was the element of blackness, for "Otelo," the root cause of this inability. "It seemed to me that the comedies were being presented in the dark," he went on, "not because of a lack of candles, but because the color of the actors made you think it was dark. Watching them I understood for the first time that celebrated expression of Milton, 'darkness visible.' The performance was sublimely bad."[41] For this correspondent of *El Eco*, the solution did not lie in education, but in the definition of racially separate cultural territories. Such a solution would be based upon a "black" re-creation of "white" culture that, if it were suitably differentiated and deferential, would avoid any possibility of assimilation or imitation on a level of equality. "I don't see anything bad in the *gente de color* performing comedies," he conceded condescendingly, "at the end of the day it's better for them to amuse themselves like this than in some other ways . . . but if they want their theatre to acquire some credit, they should imitate the companies of American *negrito* minstrels who parody dramas, operas and comedies, adapting the parody to their own language and customs." He closed his letter with an ironic comment not without malice, writing, "Our comedies in the mouths of *gente de color* can only be casual parodies, and the element that the performance has of the ridiculous will count against the actors."[42]

A glance at the dozen or so issues that *El Eco de Matanzas* produced in 1859 demonstrates how indicative was this incident with the "gente de color" who sought to perform cultured theater. In August of that year *El Eco* lamented the recent debasement of "our celebrated national dance," the Cuban *danza*; "today's *danza*," asserted a writer who went by the pseudonym *El Matancero*, was a "monstrous amalgam of the old [*danza*] and the 'African tango.'" Revealingly, this "monstrous amalgam" was portrayed as the product of a political erosion of particular social boundaries—an observation that was also very common in Europe at that time in relation to dancing—boundaries that in a place like Matanzas in 1860 were also, and above all, racial. "Instead of moving towards social equality by raising up to the heights of the enlightened classes those others who seethe together in the slime of ignorance," bemoaned *El Matancero*, "those amongst us who have adopted the idea of equality . . . have lowered the rungs that separated them from the most abject classes. Hence we have seen young gentlemen express themselves with the abrasive nonchalance of the *negro curro* [free blacks long established in Cuba, associated particularly with the slums around the port of Havana], we have seen modest young beauties dance like a *mulata* and we have seen things that the pen refuses to inscribe on this white sheet of paper."[43] Unease at the possibility of a renewed advance of processes of "Africanization" in the social life of Matanzas and its province constituted a kind of continuous undertone in the pages of *El Eco* in 1859. The following year the Matanzas Liceo inherited all these concerns.[44]

The population of pardos and morenos libres in the city of Matanzas had grown by some 70 percent between 1841 and 1862, from scarcely three thousand to a little more than five thousand, approaching the much more stable number of slaves. Together, free people of color and slaves formed over 40 percent of the urban residents of Matanzas in 1862. Fertility rates and so population growth rates among free people of color were easily more than double those of whites (and of slaves) during the 1860s (Bergad 1990, 34 and 101–5). This process reflected demographic, economic, and socio-racial dynamics that were in operation all across the island: when Antonio Serret returned to Santiago de Cuba in 1861, for example, its more than fifteen thousand libres de color already constituted the largest single group in the census of the city, 42 percent of its population of over thirty-six thousand. It was no accident that the years around 1860 saw a second upsurge in the African cultural fraternities or *cabildos de nación* in colonial Cuba, inspiring the formation of new nonwhite mutual aid societies in which Africans of different ethnic and territorial origins mixed with Afro-Cubans already born on the island. After a first, supervised expansion of African associationism during the first decades of the century, and then the severe repression imposed after the supposed attempt at a slave revolt known as the Conspiración de la Escalera in 1844 and the subsequent persecution of hundreds of free people of color, the policy of deploying a veiled threat of "Africanization" against the Cuban creoles introduced by Captain-General De la Concha had permitted a monitored revival of black mutual-aid organizations between 1855 and 1860 (Howard 1998, 97–99). With the rebirth of the *cabildos de africanos* there also came a reemergence of spaces for socializing shared by libres de color and urban slaves, and of the practice whereby these associations used their funds to buy the freedom of individual slaves. There was also a return of certain other potentially political phenomena that were very familiar and in no way comforting for the elites of Matanzas, such as the traditional closeness between the leaders of the cabildos and those of the armed battalions of pardos and morenos (Howard 1998, 31–36 and 84–96).

We know, also, of the significant contribution that was made by free people of color who had been exiled from Cuba following the Escalera conspiracy and the persecutions of the mid-1840s—in exile communities based mainly in the United States and Mexico—to the formation of a first Cuban political culture that was explicitly interracial, abolitionist, and republican, and so also Afro-Cuban, during the 1850s. Michele Reid-Vazquez has confirmed that many of the at least twenty-two hundred libres de color exiled from the island after 1844–45 came from the province of Matanzas. She has also pointed out that a considerable number of them tried to take advantage of the amnesty of 1857 to return, and that it was precisely the experience of dispossession and exile that made them ready, well before 1868, to pursue "a variety of methods to reclaim their lives in Cuba" and proclaim "Cuba as home" (Reid-Vazquez 2011, 97 and 68–97). A new concept of Cubanidad thus began to take shape, one very different from the white, creole image of the reformist elites. It was a new moral and political community, openly antislavery and republican, with aspirations to interracial democracy of the kind that David Luis-Brown has traced in the pages of the newspaper *El Mulato* and the "Cuban novel" *El Negro Mártir*, published by Francisco Agüero Estrada in New York in 1854 (Luis-Brown 2009).

This early and incipient Afro-Cuban politicization questioned, within its modest capacities, the elitist creole "annexationism" of 1845–55, and contributed to exposing the tactical nature and extremely restrictive political, social, and racial boundaries of the latter. It contributed, no less than the Spanish policy of "Africanization" and the changing geopolitics of the triangle between Madrid, Washington, and London, to the rapid cooling in interest in the idea of a revolution with annexation (to the United States) and the rhetoric associated with it among the creole planters and their spokesmen in the late 1850s. As a result it also contributed to the vigorous revival in discussion of the desirability of a "whitening" of the island that accompanied the rebirth in creole reformism around 1860. The emblematic motto of the leading Cuban liberal of an earlier generation José Antonio Saco, *blanquear, blanquear, y después hacerse respetar* ("whiten, whiten, and then make yourself respected"), reappeared. Projects proliferated for white peasant immigration and reform to make agriculture more productive, and for the definitive termination of trading in and further arrivals of Africans, but with only a very gradual emancipation of existing slaves, with compensation paid to their owners (in 1860 slaves formed the principal fixed asset of plantation owners, many of whom were heavily mortgaged). Christopher Schmidt-Nowara threw considerable light on this period (Schmidt-Nowara 1999, 102–8 and 116–22). During the same weeks in which the Liceo in Matanzas was celebrating Serret's exploits in Africa and censuring the daring of the gente de color, Francisco Frías y Jacott, Count of Pozos Dulces and a leader of the emerging creole reform movement, gathered together and published his letters from Paris on "the important question of the employment and increase of the white race in Cuba," a milestone in the elaboration of the reformist program of the 1860s (Naranjo Orovio and García González 1996, 94–96).

The language of "whitening" and the racialization of the level of political equality that could be demanded between (white) creoles and peninsular Spaniards were entirely familiar—in all senses of the word—to the two members of the literary section who presided over the session on June 25, 1860 in which the Matanzas Liceo celebrated the "Volunteer" Antonio Serret and his battle, "standing firm on the sun-browned sand," against an African army.

These men were the brothers Antonio (1819–1901) and Eusebio (1823–93) Guiteras y Font, born in Matanzas to Catalan parents who had settled and made themselves rich in Cuba at the beginning of the century. Family tradition and the time they had spent in the Havana school of the distinguished liberal scholar José de la Luz Caballero inclined them both to cultivate literature, and to found and maintain the demanding La Impresa school in Matanzas in the 1850s, and subsequently make significant contributions to the foundation of the local Liceo, of which Eusebio Guiteras would be president in 1861.[45] Previously, between 1843 and 1845, both brothers had undertaken an exceptional and quite particular "grand tour" through mainland Spain, France, the main Italian cities, Greece, "Constantinople," and Jerusalem, a journey that reaffirmed their sense of European identity and civilization and contributed to their political education. This political education was no doubt guided by their elder brother (since their father had died in 1829, and their mother in 1833), Pedro José Guiteras y Font (1814–90), author of the most ambitious *Historia de la Isla de Cuba* (published 1865–66) to emerge from creole circles prior to 1868 (Guiteras 1865–66). In the words of David Sartorius, who has recently analyzed the text, "in that history, Spanish policies attempting to manage racial difference placed in relief the fractures and fissures Guiteras observed in the pact between Spain and some of its colonial subjects" (Sartorius 2012, 176). When he wrote his *Historia* of Cuba in the early 1860s, Pedro J. Guiteras was searching, again in the words of Sartorius, for "a model for reform that would give white Cubans a louder voice in colonial politics and keep Cubans of African descent on the margins" (Sartorius 2012, 180).

A Reencounter and Two Conclusions

On September 17, 1863 Joaquín Martí y Moner, a Catalan who had arrived in freshly annexed Santo Domingo two years earlier, wrote to his father in Mataró, near Barcelona, from the Dominican town of Puerto Plata. "Since I wrote my last letter to you dated 31 of August, extraordinary things have happened. In that letter I told you," Martí recalled, "that we were in a revolution, and a big revolution, and today I can add that it is a horrific revolution. It is a race war, a war of extermination, and if God does not help us here we must all perish."[46] Joaquín Martí had predicted the Dominican revolution in a previous letter in December 1862, in which he told his father that "every day posters appear threatening that all the Spaniards have to have their throats cut," and that the Spaniards had gone back to the system of "companies or patrols [of Volunteers] for mutual defence" that Francisco Fort had instituted during the first months of the annexation.[47]

A lawyer who had emigrated to Cuba in 1861 and had soon afterwards been posted to by-then Spanish Santo Domingo, Martí had rapidly assimilated the new Caribbean world in terms unequivocally of race and civilization, to the point of making use, from the first moment, of images and vocabularies of racial defamation that were entirely Spanish or European in origin. Immediately after he arrived in Santo Domingo in the summer of 1861, Martí had described Santana—despite his being an ally—as "a very stubborn, malicious man; he is a *mulato*, a *verdadero gitano* [real gypsy]. . . . He is a rogue in disguise, and nothing will come of this island while he is Captain-General."[48] Santana, as a "mulatto, a real gypsy," was for this same reason incapable of becoming a Spaniard. The war with its enormous racial intensity and dysentery would eventually confirm Martí's worst forebodings. He left Santo Domingo already gravely ill in November 1863, and died in Santiago de Cuba in January 1864. News of his death reached his family in Catalonia by means of one last letter signed by a new young leader of the community in Santiago. In this last letter Antonio Serret y Capello attributed the death of Joaquín Martí not just to "the prostration and devastation of his body" but also, and no less decisively, to the "desolation of his spirit as a consequence of the terrible scenes that he had witnessed in Santo Domingo."[49]

This coincidental reencounter of the transatlantic biographies of Antonio Serret and Francisco Fort in the winter of 1863–64, via the intermediary presence of a third individual, the dying Joaquín Martí, brings us back to the principal argument of this study: the existence of a significant transatlantic circulation of imperialist experiences, patriotic languages, and ideas of the nation in the Spain of the Unión Liberal around 1860, and the notable contribution made to these ideas by the Guerra de África of 1859–60. Without the war in Morocco, Francisco Fort would not have "progressed" to Santo Domingo in the winter of 1860–61 in the way that he did, amid publicity and celebrations in Barcelona and Madrid,

Havana and San Juan de Puerto Rico. In 1861 Fort personified, in a Spanish Cuba that in no way stood apart from the African War, the living image of a body of civilian volunteers, originating simultaneously from peninsular Spain and "from the people," that had just demonstrated its national virtue, its political merit, by subjugating—"in the name of civilization," according to Serret—an African "race of slaves." These were battles and merits that could not fail to reverberate in colonial Cuba and throughout the Spanish Caribbean.

From this one can draw a second conclusion. A key factor in the transfer of these forms of patriotic language was their definition of the national community in increasingly racial terms. The Guerra de África emphasized a reliance on phenotypic genetic characteristics as thermometers of civilization and value, confirming their power and multiple political meanings in European Spain. The voyage across the Atlantic reinforced them, given their potential significance and role as a focus of identification in Caribbean Spain. Fort was the natural candidate to halt the Haitian "neighboring blacks" in 1861 because he had just defeated, with his fellow volunteers, the "almost black" Moroccans. Serret could symbolize a certain Cuban creole pride because in combating an African Xerxes he dispelled, tacitly, any ideas of a more prominent role for free people of color—and slaves with them—in the Cuba that was looking for reform in 1860. For this white creole world the exploits of Serret were, at the very least, a Cuban contribution to the Moroccan war that was far more innocent than the dispatch of a battalion of pardos and morenos.

These transatlantic borrowings were possible thanks to the greater integration and ambition of Spanish overseas policy around 1860, albeit that this would soon falter. They developed thanks, too, to the greater potential for collective evocation generated by new and more frequent life experiences of transoceanic return journeys; and thanks, above all, to the power of inclusion (and its opposite, the power of exclusion) of racially based language in defining the nation—without doubt an "imperial" one[50]—as a political community of equals.

Notes

1. Christopher Schmidt-Nowara (1966–2015) was one of the first friends who was kind enough to read an earlier and longer version of this text in Spanish, in the winter of 2014–15. I hope that the publication of this version in English may serve as a modest tribute to the intellectual stimulation he gave and his personal generosity, and to pay respect to his memory.

A shorter version of the Spanish text appeared in *Ayer*, review of the Asociación de Historia Contemporánea (Spain). Albert Garcia-Balañà, "Patriotismos trasatlánticos: Raza y nación en el impacto de la Guerra de África en el Caribe español de 1860," *Ayer, Revista de Historia Contemporánea* 106, no. 2 (2017): 207–37. I wish to thank the editor of *Ayer*, Juan Pan-Montojo, for facilitating the publication of this longer version in English.

I am also thankful to Nick Rider for his careful English translation of the original Spanish text.

2. See Reid-Vazquez (2011, 140–42) and Sartorius (2013, 90–91). The original document is in the Archivo Nacional de Cuba (La Habana), Asuntos Políticos, 53, 1: "Documento acerca del proyecto de D. Martín de Arredondo y Oléa de formar un batallón de Voluntarios de pardos y morenos libres que pasasen a tomar parte en la Guerra de África . . ." (1860).

3. Archivo Histórico Nacional (Madrid) [hereafter AHN], Ultramar, 5176, 27, "Celebraciones en Manila por la toma de Tetuán" (1860); 5081, 4: "Felicitaciones por la toma de Tetuán" (Government of Puerto Rico) (1860).

4. The quotations are from Clavé and Torres (1860, 44–49) and the chapbook novel *Cruel e inicua venganza llevada a cabo en la ciudad de Cádiz en el mes de junio de este presente año por un moro . . . casi negro . . .* (Barcelona, 1860). For more detail, see Garcia-Balañà 2002, 59–62 and 20–21.

5. Arxiu Històric de la Diputació de Barcelona (Barcelona) [hereafter AHDB], 1.006, 8 ("Donativo de Cuba"): letter from Francisco Milá and Emilio Roig to the Diputación de Barcelona (Havana, December 12, 1860).

6. *Memoria de los donativos de la provincia de Barcelona con motivo de la Guerra de África en 1859* (Barcelona: Narciso Ramírez, 1861), 40–42.

7. AHDB, 1.004, 4: letter from the Diputación de Barcelona to the Caja de Ahorros de Barcelona (May 4, 1860).

8. AHDB, 1.004, 11: "Estado de fuerza presente que tienen hoy estas compañías . . . durante la campaña de Marruecos" (Francisco Fort, May 1860); 1.004, 12: letter from Francisco Fort to the Diputación de Barcelona (Wad-Ras, March 24, 1860).

9. AHDB, 1.006, 8: letter from Francisco Milá and Emilio Roig to la Diputación de Barcelona (Havana, December 12, 1860).

10. *La Discusión* (Madrid), May 11, 1860, 2; *La Iberia* (Madrid), May 26, 1860, 3.

11. *La Discusión* (Madrid), May 11, 1860, 2; *La Iberia* (Madrid), May 26, 1860, 3.

12. *La Iberia* (Madrid), December 7, 1860, 3 ("Ultramar").

13. *Eco de Euterpe* (Barcelona), May 5, 1861, 7–8 ("Sociedades Corales en América").

14. *El Metrónomo* (Barcelona), October 10, 1863; *Don Junípero* (Havana), June 28, 1863, 307.

15. *El Moro Muza* (Havana), June 28, 1863, 312.

16. *El Moro Muza* (Havana), March 18, 1860, 184.

17. *El Moro Muza* (Havana), October 28, 1860, 67.

18. *El Moro Muza* (Havana), September 16, 1860, 19–20 ("Mi escribanía").

19. *El Moro Muza* (Havana), September 9, 1860, 9–10; *Don Junípero* (Havana), November 16, 1862, 55.

20. "De Jacmel a Port-au-Prince" (I–II), *El Moro Muza* (Havana), October 21, 1860, 57–58, and October 28, 1860, 65–66.

21. Quoted in Gil Novales (1992, 130); capitalization as in the original.

22. *La Iberia* (Madrid), August 10, 1860, 2; *La Correspondencia de España* (Madrid), August 10, 1860, 3.

23. *El Diario de Menorca* (Maó), July 14, 1861, 2; *El Mallorquín* (Palma de Mallorca), July 22, 1861, 1.

24. Quoted in Robles Muñoz (1987, 121, note 31).

25. *El Mallorquín* (Palma de Mallorca), July 22, 1861, 1.

26. AHN, Estado, 6320, 87: "Nombramiento de Caballero de la Orden de Isabel la Católica a Francisco María Fort, capitán de la Milicia Nacional Movilizada de Tortosa" (1838); "D. Francisco Fort," in *Heraldo de Tortosa* (Tortosa), December 1, 1928, 4.

27. *El Moro Muza* (Havana), May 20, 1860, 256; June 17, 1860, 288.

28. *Estadística de los Voluntarios existentes en 31 de Julio de 1869 en Matanzas, Cabezas, Ceiba-Mocha, Corral-Nuevo* . . . (La Habana, 1869), 130.

29. *La Correspondencia de España* (Madrid), August 10, 1860, 3.

30. Quoted in Robles Muñoz (1987, 128, note 5).

31. *La Época* (Madrid), January 6, 1862, 3; *La España* (Madrid), March 14, 1862, 3.

32. "Al valiente cubano Don Antonio Serret . . . Oda del Sr. D. C. Delmonte," in *Liceo de Matanzas* (Matanzas), July 1, 1860, 35–36.

33. For the first celebration, see "Triunfo de España," *Liceo de Matanzas* (Matanzas), June 17, 1860, 19–20.

34. All quotes from "Al valiente cubano Don Antonio Serret . . . ," 35–36.

35. AHDB, 1.004: "Listas de los individuos que componían el cuerpo de Voluntarios Catalanes (1860)."

36. *El Faro Nacional* (Madrid), July 24, 1860, 88 ("Las letras y las armas").

37. AHN, Ultramar, 2067, 4: "Expediente personal de don Antonio Serret y Capello" (1860–77), fols. 139–42.

38. AHN, Universidades, 4768, 10: "Expediente académico de Antonio Serret y Capello, alumno de la Facultad de Derecho de la Universidad Central" (1856–59).

39. AHN, Ultramar, 2067, 4: "Expediente personal de don Antonio Serret y Capello" (1860–77).

40. AHN, Ultramar, 147, 16: "D. Emilio Blanchet, Catedrático del Instituto de Matanzas" (1865–69); Ultramar, 4447, 25: "Insurrectos comprendidos en circular de 20 de abril de 1869" (1870).

41. "Comedias representadas por gente de color," in *El Eco de Matanzas* (Matanzas), September 18, 1859, 206–7.

42. "Comedias representadas por gente de color," in *El Eco de Matanzas* (Matanzas), September 18, 1859, 206–7.

43. "La danza cubana," in *El Eco de Matanzas*, August 7, 1859, 57–59.

44. Other examples include "División del trabajo en los ingenios," *El Eco de Matanzas*, August 7, 1859, 41–43; "Horas de trabajo," August 14, 1859, 67–69; "Los blancos y los negros," in *Liceo de Matanzas*, August 12, 1860, 89.

45. *Liceo de Matanzas*, July 1, 1860, 33 ("Sección de Literatura"); AHN, Ultramar, 30, 30: "Establecen 2ª Enseñanza en el Colegio La Empresa de Matanzas" (1855).

46. Letter from Joaquín Martí y Moner to his father Joaquín Martí y Andreu (Puerto Plata, September 17, 1863), in Martí Coll (1961, 44–46).

47. Letter from Joaquín Martí y Moner to his father (Puerto Plata, December 5, 1862), in Martí Coll (1961, 40–41).

48. Quoted in Martí Coll (1961, 23) (highlight by the author).

49. Letter from Antonio Serret to Joaquín Martí y Andreu (Santiago de Cuba, January 22, 1864), in Martí Coll (1961, 47).

50. On the concept of "imperial nation," see Fradera 2015.

Works Cited

Andreu Miralles, Xavier. 2011. " 'El Pueblo y sus opresores': Populismo y nacionalismo en la cultura política del radicalismo democrático, 1844–1848." *Historia y Política* 25: 65–91.

Bacardí Moreau, Emilio. (1908) 1925. *Crónicas de Santiago de Cuba*. Santiago de Cuba: Arroyo Hermanos.

Bergad, Laird W. 1990. *Cuban Rural Society in the Nineteenth Century: The Social and Economic History of Monoculture in Matanzas*. Princeton: Princeton University Press.

Calcagno, Francisco. 1878. *Diccionario Biográfico Cubano*. New York: Imprenta-Librería de Ponce de León.

Casanovas Codina, Joan. 2000. *¡O pan, o plomo! Los trabajadores urbanos y el colonialismo español en Cuba, 1850–1898*. Madrid: Siglo XXI.

Clavé, José A., and José M. Torres. 1860. *El Carnaval de Barcelona en 1860*. Barcelona: Librería Española.

De Jesús Domínguez, Jaime. 1979. *La anexión de la República Dominicana a España*. Santo Domingo: Editora de la Universidad Autónoma de Santo Domingo (USAD).

Eller, Anne E. 2011. "Let's Show the World We Are Brothers: The Dominican Guerra de Restauración and the Nineteenth-Century Caribbean." PhD diss., New York University.

Fradera, Josep M. 2005. *Colonias para después de un imperio*. Barcelona: Edicions Bellaterra.
Fradera, Josep M. 2015. *La nación imperial: Derechos, representación y ciudadanía en los imperios de Gran Bretaña, Francia, España y Estados Unidos (1750–1918)*. 2 vols. Barcelona: Edhasa.
Garcia-Balañà, Albert. 2002. "Patria, plebe y política en la España isabelina: La Guerra de África en Cataluña (1859–1860)." In *Marruecos y el colonialismo español (1859–1912): De la Guerra de África a la "penetración pacífica,"* edited by Eloy Martín Corrales, 13–77. Barcelona: Edicions Bellaterra.
Garcia-Balañà, Albert. 2008. "'El comercio español en África' en la Barcelona de 1858, entre el Caribe y el Mar de China, entre Londres y París." *Illes i Imperis*, nos. 10–11: 167–86.
Garcia-Balañà, Albert. 2012. "'The Empire Is No Longer a Social Unit': Declining Imperial Expectations and Transatlantic Crises in Metropolitan Spain, 1859–1909." In *Endless Empire: Spain's Retreat, Europe's Eclipse, America's Decline*, edited by Alfred W. McCoy, Josep M. Fradera, and Stephen Jacobson, 92–103. Madison: University of Wisconsin Press.
García Cantús, Dolores. 2004. "Fernando Poo: Una aventura colonial española en el África Occidental (1778–1900)." PhD diss., Universitat de València.
Gil Novales, Alberto. 1992. "Martínez Villergas, el gran satírico." *Trienio. Ilustración y Liberalismo*, no. 20: 101–36.
González Tablas, Ramón. 1870. *Historia de la dominación y última guerra de España en Santo Domingo, por D.-----, capitán de infantería, oficial que ha sido del ejército de operaciones de dicha isla*. Madrid: Fernando Cao Vidal.
Guerrero Cano, Magdalena. 2002–03. "Expediciones a Santo Domingo: El fracaso de un proyecto de colonización (1860–1862)." *Trocadero*, nos. 14–15: 63–92.
Guiteras, Pedro J. 1865–66. *Historia de la Isla de Cuba (con notas e ilustraciones)*. New York: Jorje R. Lockwood.
Howard, Philip A. 1998. *Changing History: Afro-Cuban Cabildos and Societies of Color in the Nineteenth Century*. Baton Rouge: Louisiana State University Press.
Luis-Brown, David. 2009. "An 1848 for the Americas: The Black Atlantic, 'El Negro Mártir,' and Cuban Exile Anticolonialism in New York City." *American Literary History* 21, no. 3 (Fall): 431–63.
Martí Coll, Antonio. 1961. *Don Joaquín Martí y Moner (1828–1864): Cartas de Ultramar*. Mataró: Caja de Ahorros de Mataró.
Miller, Ivor L. 2009. *Voice of the Leopard: African Secret Societies and Cuba*. Jackson: University Press of Mississippi.
Moreno Fraginals, Manuel, and José J. Moreno Masó. 1993. *Guerra, migración y muerte (El ejército español en Cuba como vía migratoria)*. Colombres: Archivo de Indianos / Ediciones Júcar.

Naranjo Orovio, Consuelo, and Armando García González. 1996. *Racismo e inmigración en Cuba en el siglo XIX*. Madrid: Doce Calles.

Quiroz, Alfonso W. 2011. "Free Association and Civil Society in Cuba, 1787–1895." *Journal of Latin American Studies* 43, no. 1: 33–64.

Reid-Vazquez, Michele. 2011. *The Year of the Lash: Free People of Color in Cuba and the Nineteenth-Century Atlantic World*. Athens: University of Georgia Press.

Robles Muñoz, Cristóbal. 1987. *Paz en Santo Domingo (1854–1865): El fracaso de la anexión a España*. Madrid: Consejo Superior de Investigaciones Científicas (CSIC).

Rodríguez Demorizi, Emilio. 1955. *Antecedentes de la Anexión a España*. Ciudad-Trujillo: Editora Montalvo.

Roldán de Montaud, Inés. 2011. "En los borrosos confines de la libertad: El caso de los negros emancipados en Cuba, 1817–1870." *Revista de Indias*, no. 251: 159–92.

Sartorius, David. 2012. "Race in Retrospect: Thinking with History in Nineteenth-Century Cuba." In *Race and Blood in the Iberian World*, edited by Max Hering Torres, Maria Elena Martinez, and David Nirenberg, 169–89. Berlin: LIT Verlag.

Sartorius, David. 2013. *Ever Faithful: Race, Loyalty, and the Ends of Empire in Spanish Cuba*. Durham, NC: Duke University Press.

Schmidt-Nowara, Christopher. 1999. *Empire and Antislavery: Spain, Cuba, and Puerto Rico, 1833–1874*. Pittsburgh: University of Pittsburgh Press.

Serret y Capello, Antonio. 1859. *Consideraciones sobre el Real Decreto de 23 de Enero de 1855 para la administración de justicia en las provincias de Ultramar*. Madrid: Tomás Fortanet.

Serret y Capello, Antonio. 1871. *Prosa perdida*. Barcelona: Juan Oliveres.

Sublette, Ned. 2004. *Cuba and Its Music: From the First Drums to the Mambo*. Chicago: Chicago Review Press.

Yáñez Gallardo, César. 1996. *Saltar con red: La temprana emigración catalana a América, ca. 1830–1870*. Madrid: Alianza Editorial.

Archival Materials

Archivo Histórico Nacional (Madrid) [AHN]:
  Fondo de Estado
  Fondo de Ultramar
  Fondo de Universidades
Archivo Nacional de Cuba (La Habana):
  Fondo Asuntos Políticos
  Arxiu Històric de la Diputació de Barcelona (Barcelona) [AHDB]
Arxiu de Revistes Catalanes Antigues (Barcelona) / Newspapers Collections:
  El Eco de Euterpe (Barcelona)
  El Metrónomo (Barcelona)

Other Newspaper Collections:
- *Don Junípero* (La Habana)
- *El Eco de Matanzas* (Matanzas)
- *El Mallorquín* (Palma de Mallorca)
- *El Moro Muza* (La Habana)
- *La Correspondencia de España* (Madrid)
- *La Discusión* (Madrid)
- *La España* (Madrid)
- *La Iberia* (Madrid)
- *Liceo de Matanzas. Órgano oficial del Instituto de su nombre* (Matanzas)

The End of the Legal Slave Trade to Cuba and the Second Slavery

José Antonio Piqueras

One of the most widely circulated misconceptions about the process that brought the African slave trade to an end is the unfounded belief that the Congress of Vienna, and the treaty approved at the end of the sessions attended by the foreign powers, was a decisive step toward the abolition of the transatlantic slave trade. From the nineteenth century onward a fair number of authors have claimed that, on February 8, 1815, eight European powers agreed to "the universal and definitive abolition of the slave trade," the declaration being considered "an imperishable monument to equity and wisdom," as *abbé* Castelli, the prefect apostolic of the Catholic Church in Martinique between 1834 and 1841,wrote in 1844 (Castelli 1844, 75). The claim has been repeated down to the present day, even though the declaration signed in Vienna only expressed a desire to adopt measures tending toward abolition. Mark Jarrett reproduces the misconception in considering that England managed to turn this issue into a problem of general interest and succeeded in getting the Congress to approve the condemnation of the slave trade as repugnant to the "spirit of the times," thus marking a milestone that would later lead to diplomatic actions. In January 1815, Jarrett continues, the British reached an agreement with Portugal and a short time after that signed an agreement with Spain on the abolition of the slave trade, supposedly based on the Vienna resolution (Jarrett 2013, 145–46). In the same line, Keith Hamilton and Farida Shaikh state that the Vienna declaration set a precedent in humanitarian diplomacy: the slave trade was condemned and considered a matter of international interest. Although the abolitionists made some progress at the Congress, the ensuing bilateral agreement and declarations marked a change in the attitudes of nations. However, as the authors add, the Royal Navy needed a defined body of law allowing it to seek out and detain ships used for the trafficking of slaves (Hamilton and Skaikh 2009, 6–7). Other historians consider the signature of the representatives who participated in the Congress as having legal effect, although the Declaration Relative to the Universal Abolition of the Slave Trade lacked any normative power because it was an additional act to the treaty (Chew 1997, 1:673–74).

The declaration condemning the transatlantic slave trade has also been seen as having a great impact on public opinion, but regarding Europe it did not go much further than Great Britain, which was the only country at that time with political freedom. The classic study by Charles Webster stated that the British posture was determined by "an almost fanatical public opinion in England," whereas the view of the French, who opposed the prohibition, was based on the advantage England gained from the condemnation. This advantage consisted in the fact that, before addressing the abolition of the transatlantic slave trade, it had already stocked sufficient manpower in its colonies. This was especially true during the five years prior to the measure, that is, as of the moment in which the abolitionist principle had been grasped by the majority in the parliament at Westminster (Webster 1919, 41–42). Webster also remarked that the affairs concerning the colonial possessions were excluded from the debates and deliberations of the Congress upon the decision of the United Kingdom, with the exception of the matter of the slave trade (Webster 1919, 127). It is obvious that this power was not interested in discussing the surrendering of islands that it had obtained from France in previous agreements, in giving any explanations regarding the temporary annexation it had carried out of Dutch possessions, and, far less, in listening to the opinion of the absolutist powers regarding Spanish America. The continental balance of power, laboriously put together with British consent, excluded the Atlantic world in which Great Britain stood as a single power upon which it established its naval, military, and trading hegemony. The principle of legitimacy (a principle used by the absolutists) on which the Restoration was based in Europe would not be in force in the American world, and Spain, which, albeit for other reasons, also avoided taking the affair to the Congress, had to resolve the rebellion with its own means.

In his book Webster stated what would later be repeated over and over again: Lord Castlereagh, secretary of the Foreign Office and plenipotentiary in Vienna, "succeeded . . . in obtaining a declaration condemning the practice of the slave trade, which was annexed to the Final Act." But he also achieved more than that, he claims, as he simultaneously negotiated with Portugal to abolish the trade north of the equator in exchange for monetary compensation, thereby beginning a procedure that was to continue in the following years (Webster 1919, 135). It is thus clear that the matter was included in the discussions held at the highest level within the multilateral diplomatic forum, marking the beginning of a new phase in international diplomacy.

In his review of the topic carried out at a later time, Harold Nicolson claimed that Great Britain sought the total abolition of the slave trade at the Congress of Vienna and "it was only after many years, and at the cost of serious sacrifices and gross misrepresentations, that her efforts were successful." Nicolson rejected the idea that Castlereagh acted only under pressure exerted by left-wing agitators or sentimental idealists. Castlereagh was convinced that the trade was a terrible evil in itself and after Napoleon's defeat he directed Great Britain's "missionary spirit" toward that achieving that aim (Nicolson 2000, 210). Nevertheless, the same author recalls that the memorandum Castlereagh delivered to the Cabinet on December 26, 1813, in anticipation of setting Britain's objectives in the future reconstruction of Europe, included the withholding of several French colonies as compensation, but no mention was made of abolishing the slave trade, which sparked an angry protest from abolitionist William Wilberforce (Nicolson 2000, 69).

Other historians have pointed out that the "humanitarian liberalism" opposed to the slave trade, which characterized the British position, was seen with suspicion by the other powers, who feared that it would be followed by a political and economic liberalism (constitutions and free trade, respectively) (Chapman 1998, 20–23).

The first question to be answered is the following: What was decided in Vienna with regard to the slave trade and how did it affect the Spanish colonies in the Caribbean?

Vienna and Bilateral Diplomacy

Between October 1814 and June 1815, the plenipotentiary ministers of the main European powers gathered in Vienna discussed a wide range of affairs concerning the international political order and signed a treaty that committed the countries with representation there. The labor issue had been in the air since the beginning of the meetings in the Austrian capital at the end of 1814. In 1807 England had put an end to the African slave trade in its dominions and for its subjects, and in

1814 it called for the abolition to be made universal. "The first work undertaken by the Congress was aimed at achieving the abolition of the black slave trade," Pedro Gómez Labrador, the Spanish plenipotentiary ambassador, wrote in his memoirs. In this diplomat's opinion, the English representative, Lord Castlereagh, was very interested in getting the Congress to view abolition favorably (Labrador 1849, 36). All the diplomats present in Vienna were previously aware of this aspiration, but most of them did not share the same understanding of this important matter with the English.

In early 1815, over a period of three weeks, the plenipotentiary ministers held five conferences—one general and four specific—on the abolition of the black slave trade. But finally the subject was excluded from the international treaty and its promoters had to reluctantly accept a simple "Additional Declaration to the Treaty of Vienna," which lacked any legal effect in the law of peoples (*ius gentium*).

The Declaration included four aspects: (a) the slave trade was condemned as being "repugnant to the principles of humanity and universal morality"; (b) the difficulty involved in abruptly arresting that commerce was acknowledged despite the fact that several governments had resolved to put a stop to it, as they had to pay "due regard to the interest, the habits, and even the prejudices of their subjects"; (c) each country could decide on the period it considered most advisable for the definitive abolition in each case; and (d) the powers were urged to negotiate with one another in order to attain this goal.

The last three points, that is, everything unrelated to the moral declaration and that had practical consequences, reflected the posture taken by the representatives from Spain and Portugal, since both countries were opposed to the matter being discussed by powers that had no colonies, declared themselves opposed to an immediate end of the slave trade, and refused to act against the interests of their American colonists, who considered that the end of the trade could never come into force within a period of at least eight years so as to allow them time to stock a sufficient number of slaves (minutes of the meetings, Schoell 1816).

Despite the foregoing, the Anglo-Spanish Treaty to abolish the practice of the black slave trade by Spain in all its territories was signed on September 23, 1817. Yet the 1817 treaty was not really a consequence of the Congress of Vienna but rather of the bilateral diplomacy that had been set in motion before the meeting was held in the Austrian capital; it was, to a certain extent, the continuation of the alliances established between Spain and Great Britain from 1808 onward. In fact, it was not until June 1817 that Spain officially ratified the Final Act of the

Congress of Vienna, where Castlereagh had not managed to obtain any concession from the Spanish representative (Brennecke 2010, 64–66).

These considerations force us to look back to a previous date. On May 4, 1814, Ferdinand VII, after being handed over by the French, abolished the constitutional government and recovered absolute power, surrounding himself with civil servants who were in line with these ideas. On July 5, the minister of state, the Duke of San Carlos, and the British ambassador in Madrid, Henry Wellesley, signed a treaty of peace, friendship, and alliance between the two countries. The treaty has been proposed by the regency of the constitutional regime, in March of that same year, and ratified the "strict and intimate alliance" agreed between the two countries in January 1809. It must be noted that Henry Wellesley was the British envoy in Spain from May 1809, when he took up the position held until then by his brother Richard, who had been named Marques of Wellesley and was appointed secretary of the Foreign Office. Both of them were brothers of Arthur, commander-in-chief of the Anglo-Spanish army during the war against the French, first Duke of Wellington and, by agreement with the Spanish Cortes, Duke of Ciudad Rodrigo and Grandee of Spain, a title of nobility confirmed by Ferdinand VII. Henry Wellesley held the position in Madrid until 1821, and was therefore a privileged witness to all the negotiations between the two countries, especially in matters concerning the slave trade. His correspondence and his diary, however, shed little light on the matter (Wellesley 1930).

On August 28, 1814, several additional articles were incorporated into the Anglo-Spanish Treaty of July 5, and on being ratified, on October 19, 1814, these additions became secret articles. One of the most important articles was the one that reflected England's commitment not to furnish the "revolted in America" with arms and to do whatever it could to ensure they returned to their obedience to the King of Spain. In another article, His Catholic Majesty, "with respect to the injustice and inhumanity of the traffic in slaves," said that he "will take into consideration, with the deliberation which the state of his possessions in America demands, the means of acting in conformity with those sentiments"; as a gesture of goodwill, the king of Spain promised to prevent foreigners from engaging in this traffic in ships under the protection of the Spanish flag ("Treaty of peace, friendship and alliance constituted and signed at Madrid, the 5th day of July, 1814, by the plenipotentiaries of Spain and England, and ratified by his Catholic Majesty, the 28th day of August of the same year." In Cantillo 1843, 732–33). The secret articles of the treaty were obviously not made public but were binding for the signing parties.

The Anglo-Spanish Treaty of 1814 made no reference to any deadlines by which the abolition of the transatlantic slave trade with the Spanish dominions should be negotiated or terminated. However, in documents from 1815 and 1816 mention is made of the commitment undertaken by Ferdinand VII that trafficking would not be outlawed until eight years later, that is to say, not until 1822. In a report drawn up by the Council of the Indies, it was stated that "when [King Ferdinand VII] offered to ban the slave trade within eight years, he demanded certain conditions that are unknown to us," thus insinuating that that clause had been included within the secret articles of the agreement, which was totally inaccurate, but shows that the councilors were unaware of the existence of the 1814 agreement, although they did have knowledge of a royal commitment to study the abolition of the slave trade (in Arango 2005, 2:128).

The 1814 treaty made the negotiations carried out in the summer of 1817 unavoidable. The Spanish Crown, in contrast, was not willing to offer any facilities, as it was fully aware of the importance of the slave trade for the growing economy of the Spanish Antilles. This therefore accounted for the attitude of the Spanish plenipotentiary Pedro Gómez Labrador in Vienna, who was opposed to any resolution that set dates for the abolition and was even against the idea of incorporating the matter within the articles of the Final Act. Meanwhile, between October 1814 and the middle of 1815 the government in Madrid gathered the reports available on the abolition of the slave trade and on the antecedents of the issue, and on June 14, 1815 the king ordered that the documents should be submitted to the Council of the Indies for study and for a decision to be made accordingly.

The Council of the Indies delivered its answer on February 15, 1816. Note that this occurred eighteen months before the final negotiations were conducted with the British. Nevertheless, according to the *Memorias* written by José García de León y Pizarro, who was appointed to the Ministry of State at the end of 1816, the English "always presented this matter as an obstacle to all the other negotiations that were pending" (García de León y Pizarro 1999, 260).

The Spanish Crown delayed its decision while at the same time, by taking the matter to the Council of the Indies, sending out a message to the colonies and letting the British agents in the Corte know that the issue was being studied. By so doing it was of course buying time and was also able to continue and to increase the trading of slaves. Finding a solution to the issue required reconciling the opinions of its councilors and the interests of the *hacendados* overseas, and more especially the planters in Cuba. This last point can be confirmed by examining the treaty agreed to in 1817, the essence of which did not match the recommendations of the majority of the members of the Council of the Indies but instead those of the dissenting votes of seven of its members, among whom the Cuban minister Francisco Arango y Parreño played a key role.

The Treaty and the Interest of Havana

The dissenting vote of the minority who disagreed with the majority vote was subscribed by Francisco Requena, Francisco Ibáñez Leyva, the Dominican Francisco Caro de Torquemada, José Navia y Bolaños, Bruno Vallarino, Mariano González de Merchante, and the above-mentioned Francisco Arango.[1] Most of them were modest magistrates who had held positions in *audiencias*. The *oidor* Ibáñez Leyva had been a judge commissioned by the king in 1814 to order the capture of the liberal members of the Cortes; Requena was a military engineer who had lived in America for thirty years (Panama, New Granada, Peru); Caro de Torquemada had been the royal delegate in Santo Domingo in 1810 and member of the Cortes for the island in 1813. The last two were therefore familiar with the reality of colonial slavery.

As stated by Pizarro, who was to be appointed secretary of state a short time later, "The councillor of the Indies Arango, a wealthy man from Havana, was opposed to abolition and said to [Secretary of State] Cevallos that the Havanans would give the king more than that offered by England, provided that he did not forbid the trade" (García de León y Pizarro 1999, 259). The British ambassador, in a letter to Lord Castlereagh, mentioned this offer: "Mr. Pizarro . . . assured me that the capitalists of the island of Cuba had offered the King $20 million" on the condition that the slave trade continue (Wellesley 1930, 84). Arango's resistance to the abolition of the transatlantic trade, on behalf of the Cuban planters, was not new. As *síndico* of the Royal Consulate of Agriculture and Commerce of Havana, *regidor perpetuo* and *alférez mayor* of the City Council of Havana, former representative of the council of this city in the Corte of Madrid, in 1811 he had drafted a representation on behalf of the main Cuban corporations in which they opposed the end of the slave trade, the possible gradual abolition of slavery, and any debates on this issue in public sessions in Parliament. A member of the Spanish Cortes in 1813–14 and an effective member of the Council of the Indies from 1814 onward, Arango appears not only as the main author of the political economics of the second slavery (Tomich 2005, 55–85), but also as a decisive player in the diplomatic strategy followed by Spain to obstruct and delay the ban on the transatlantic trafficking of Africans.

In July 1814, Arango was appointed, by royal decree, deputy in the reestablished Council of the Indies. He immediately traveled to France, however, and did not take up the post until he returned, on March 7, 1815 (Ponte Domínguez 1937, 137), one month after he had agreed to the declaration on the African slave trade, in Vienna. The plenipotentiary Pedro Gómez Labrador was in Paris during the summer of 1814, engaged in negotiations with the French government over the bilateral treaty of July 20, 1814, and preparing his participation at the Congress. Labrador set off for the capital of the Habsburg Empire in the second week of September. This coincidence therefore leads us to speculate on the intervention of Arango y Parreño in informing and indoctrinating the ambassador.

The arguments taken up by the dissenting vote of the Council of the Indies in 1816 coincide with those expressed in one of the *Notas escritas* (a mode of diplomatic proposal) that the ambassador Labrador submitted in Vienna in January 1815 for them to be attached to the protocol of the sessions of the commission in the Congress that dealt with the subject of the abolition of the slave trade. More specifically, the note from the ambassador in 1815 and the vote of the minority of the Council of the Indies in 1816 coincided in highlighting the unequal preparation with which the powers involved found themselves when faced with the abolition of the slave trade, as Great Britain had stocked up with slaves in its colonies over the previous years. They also highlighted the fact that the wars had made it impossible for the Spanish colonies to trade with Africa in the previous years, to the point, it is said in both documents, where they could not have replaced the deceased. Lastly, they recalled the great capital investments made to set up this business, which for the Spanish was a recent occurrence. The coincidences reinforce the hypothesis of both documents being inspired by a single person: Francisco Arango.

The majority opinion of the Council of the Indies opted for the immediate abolition of the slave trade in 1816. It based this criterion on the fear that the horrors of Haiti would be reproduced in the Spanish dominions. The Council, however, also took the liberty of denouncing the iniquity of trafficking that fed off an unfair enslavement of Africans, which was the first time that an opinion had been expressed in those terms in a high body of the monarchy, although it had been pronounced by liberal voices in the Cortes in 1811 and 1813.

In contrast to what was stated by the majority, the dissenting vote held that the slave revolt had been possible in Saint-Domingue due to a set of blunders ranging from taking a political revolution that had started in Paris to the island, and declaring equality, to arming the negroes, a measure that Spain had also participated in. In the Spanish dominions, they added, the number of slaves was not so large and there was a racial balance that was not going to be altered because of the addition of a few Africans. Although they did not see the need to put an end to the slave trade, the seven dissenting members of the Council of the Indies somewhat reluctantly accepted the ban on slave trading. They did not let themselves be carried away by humanitarian feelings, however, but instead acknowledged the fact that its abolition was unavoidable as the whole of Europe had decided that it was to be and Spain was not in a position to oppose the measure, as England had "extremely powerful means of accomplishing its wishes at all costs."

The councilors admitted the political and military hegemony that the United Kingdom had secured as a result of the Napoleonic Wars. Consequently, the dissenting vote focused on ensuring that the trade was not "suddenly" banned, claiming that no other country had proceeded in that way. The United States had had twenty-one years to deliberate on the abolition of that trade, and in Great Britain they had been debating the matter for nineteen years before it was finally abolished in 1807. England had given Portugal five years to study the matter before obtaining the prohibition of the slave trade to the north of the equator in 1815, leaving for a later date the drawing up of a new treaty that would permanently resolve the issue.

In short, the recommendations of the influential minority members of the Council of the Indies were focused on four points: (1) agreeing to the English request and banning the slave trade to the north of the equinoctial circle, and in the rest of the world as of April 22, 1821; (2) getting the British to pay compensation to the owners of the Spanish expeditions that had been detained, as the consulate in Havana and the intendancy of Puerto Rico had been calling for; (3) obtaining assurances from the English that they would stop the searches carried out on ships dedicated to trafficking below the equator until 1821; and (4) taking into account the losses that the *hacendados* in America would suffer, the king should take steps to increase the white population, especially in Cuba, "where the lack of manpower must be greater," and once this point, and the trafficking business in general, had been resolved, the freedom to trade with friendly and neutral foreigners would not be touched as far as this island was concerned ("Voto particular de varios consejeros de Indias," 131).

The Anglo-Spanish Treaty for the abolition of the black slave trade of 1817 established the abolition of trafficking in all the Spanish territories as of May 30, 1820. However, five additional months were granted so that the trading ships that had begun their crossing to Africa prior to that date would have time to return to the American ports with their cargo. As a result, the ban on allowing slaves to disembark was postponed until October 30, 1820. The prohibition on the African coasts to the north of the equator would come into effect immediately, with a delay of six months to allow them to complete their voyages under the abovementioned terms, that is to say, as of May 21, 1818. The trading of African slaves that continued until 1820 would be regulated by means of passports signed by the king and countersigned by his minister of the navy. Searches by the English were authorized only if there was reliable evidence of any illegal cargo of slaves. Great Britain committed itself to pay the sum of £400,000 on February 20, 1818 as compensation to the subjects engaged in this trafficking, whose expeditions have been captured under the application of these stipulations, but prior to the exchange of ratifications, which took place on November 21, 1817 for Spain. In the same way as in the agreements signed with the Kingdom of Portugal and Brazil, mixed commissions were established to judge the lawfulness of the boats that were captured.[2]

In accordance with the Treaty of 1817, Fernando VII issued the Real Cédula of December 19 by which he ordered the publication in America and the Philippines of the ban on the black slave trade in the Spanish dominions, with the abovementioned deadlines, to allow any ships that had already begun their expedition time to complete it. The *cédula* announced that Negroes who were transported in breach of the prohibition would be declared free on disembarking at a Spanish port, and buyers and captains, boatswains and pilots of the slave ships were to be sentenced to ten years' confinement in exile in the Philippines. According to the treaty, ships that obtained permission to continue trading until 1820 would not be able to carry more than five slaves for every two tons of deadweight, in order to avoid overcrowding, but that number did not include any children born on board during the voyage or any slaves employed as domestics on the ship. The Real Cédula included a description of the motives that justified the royal measures that had favored the introduction of black slaves into America since the sixteenth century, the Indians being disqualified from engaging in various "useful, though laborious occupations," it said. This measure did not create slavery, it hastened to add, but only took advantage of the slavery that already existed in Africa, and "far from being prejudicial to the negroes . . . transferred to America, afforded them, not only the incomparable benefit of being instructed in the knowledge of the true God, and of the only Religion through which that Supreme Being is desirous that His creatures should adore Him, but also the advantages attending a state of civilisation, without, however, subjecting them in their slavery to hardships more intolerable than those they had endured when free in their own country." This is the case of a measure that put an end to the transatlantic slave trade—by indicating the benevolent nature of slavery and the advantages the Africans themselves had gained from the transatlantic slave trade!

The introduction of slaves into America had always been carried out with a great deal of circumspection and with the granting of particular permissions, the royal description continued, until the Real Cédulas of September 28, 1789, April 12, 1798, and April 22, 1804 authorized their free introduction within the times stipulated in each of them. Restored to the throne amid commotions and differences in the American dominions, the monarch had noticed that the circumstances that gave rise to the previous provisions had varied, it was said. And thus, by means of this narrative, the king announced the measure as though it were of his own initiative and not in response to pressure from the British and the negotiations that had been conducted.

The king went on: the number of indigenous Negroes, that is, black creoles, was now greatly increased, as was the number of whites, who were now better adapted to the climate for farm work than before. At the same time, the task of civilizing the Africans was no longer as urgent since the moment in which a powerful nation (Great Britain) had undertaken "the glorious task of civilising them in their own native land." The Congress of Vienna, finally, had expressed the humanitarian sentiment that was driving the major powers of Europe.[3]

The Trafficking of Africans Preceding the End of the Legal Slave Trade

In the six years that elapsed between the Congress of Vienna and the coming into effect of the prohibition, the trafficking of slaves in Cuba and Puerto Rico multiplied as never before, and the economic power conditions were created in Cuba that led to the breach of the abolition of the trade after 1821. After the year 1814, all the accumulation of capital, investment, and organization of the large new plantations, the commercial circuit fostered since 1796 by means of neutral trade, was to be translated into a forward-looking measure that led to the implementation of the technical advances that had been developed and tried and tested in the previous twenty years: from steam-powered machinery to horizontal mills with three iron rollers (both around 1817) or the generalization of the "Jamaican train" (around 1820) in the middle of an expanding sugar cycle that was for the first time based on an "industrial" conception (Piqueras 2016, 49–75).

Between the Anglo-Spanish Agreement of July 1814—with its secret article—and the end of legal trading in October 1820, the pressure to advance the trafficking business before its prohibition increased, and this attracted a whole generation of high speculators without any experience in the field, including traders, usurers, sailors, royal officials, and planters. A handful of peninsular Spaniards who arrived in Cuba after 1808, fleeing from the war and seeking their fortune, rushed into the slave trade adventure, declaring themselves willing to enroll in expeditions to Africa or to set them up in association with traders established on the island. Some traders from the island sought capital through external partners, either from the Peninsula after 1814 or in the main business centers of Great Britain and the United States. It was in 1815, as Eric Williams reminded us, that a bill was presented in the British Parliament "to proscribe the slave trade as an investment for British capital." In 1807 Britain had banned the transatlantic trafficking of slaves in its dominions and also forbidden all its subjects from practicing this trade, regardless of the destination of the cargo of African slaves. In 1815 they sought to extend the prohibition to capital participation. As Williams goes on to say, "Baring, of the great banking house which was to have such intimate relations with independent Spanish America, issued a solemn warning that every commercial organisation in Britain would petition against it, and the House of Lords threw it out" (Williams 2011, 247).

This race against the clock to incorporate Africans into Cuba, to gather a stock of as many slaves as possible before an agreement was reached on the prohibition of the trade, began in 1814. It was further spurred on by the information that Francisco Arango conveyed to his friends in Havana, in which he warned them about the abolitionary measure that was being studied, while the Spanish participation in the Congress of Vienna was being prepared.

This urgent *stockpiling* of human beings, which began in late 1814, displayed a set of particular characteristics. I will highlight nine aspects.

First, the sudden rise in demand for slaves in Cuba, resulting from the announcement that the supply would soon be brought to an end, multiplied the number of voyages (Figure 2). This movement of ships undoubtedly required a greater business capacity, better equipment, the availability of ships' crews, provisioning, and the means of payment to settle the price to be paid in Africa. In 1816 the port of Matanzas was authorized for the black slave trade.

The increased cargo of African slaves in each *armazón* (group) meant using vessels with a greater tonnage. This necessarily involved provisioning oneself with new ships, normally ones that were already registered and only in the later years with vessels that were built *ex profeso* (on purpose).

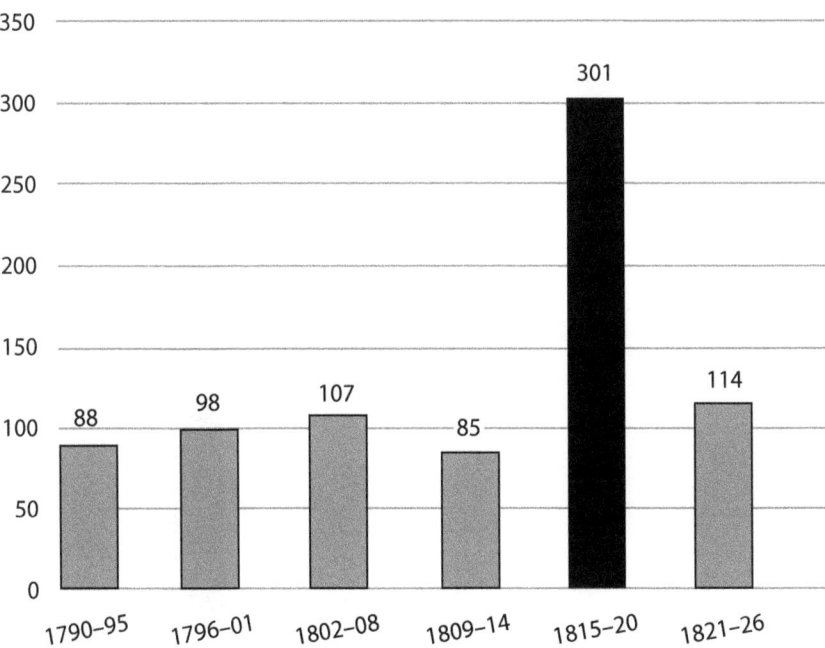

Source: Voyages Database. 2016. Voyages: The Trans-Atlantic Slave Trade Database. http://www.slavevoyages.org.

Figure 2. Number of voyages in the slave trade between Africa and Cuba (1790–1826).

Second, the number of slaves that were transported and disembarked in Cuba over the six-year period 1815–20 increased fivefold with respect to the previous six years (Figure 3).

It should be noted that the figures we are dealing with here continue to indicate minimum numbers. A comparison of the data in the Registry books in the Archivo Nacional de Cuba (Cuban National Archive) for the years 1802 to 1807 shows figures for the voyages to Africa that are much higher than those registered by *The Trans-Atlantic Slave Trade Database*. It also reflects a proportion of slaves that, in three of the years, was up to 30 percent higher than that noted in the valuable database on which our study is based (Joda Esteve 2014, 111–12). That deviation was not likely to continue over time, before or after the samples analyzed, but the evidence points to an underestimation of the number of slaves taken to Cuba during the time in which the trade was legal and free, that is, from 1789 to 1820.

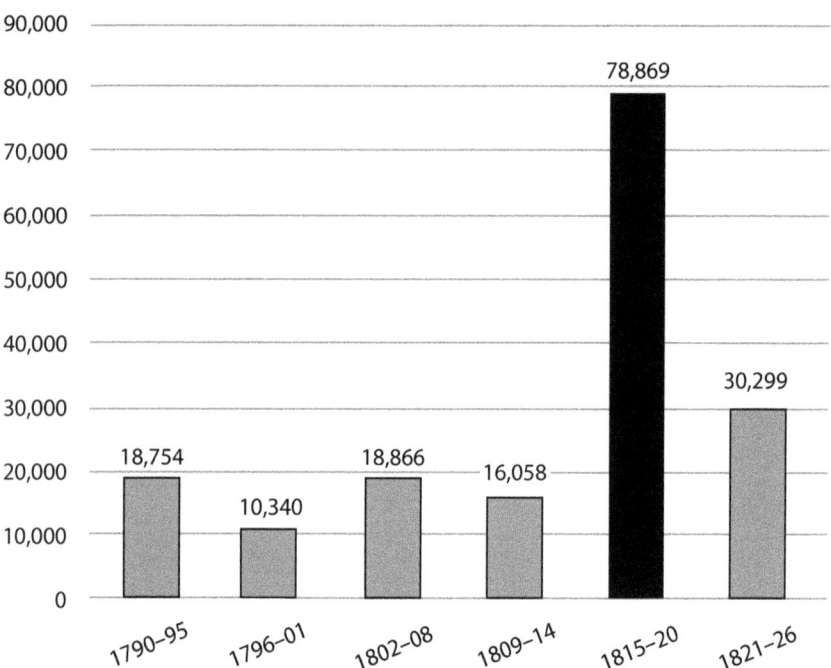

Source: Voyages Database. 2016. Voyages: The Trans-Atlantic Slave Trade Database. http://www.slavevoyages.org.

Figure 3. African slaves disembarked in Cuba (1790–1820).

As the average ship over the period 1815–20 carried a cargo of 120 Africans on disembarking, if the deviation observed for the years 1802 to 1804 had continued, the figure of almost seventy-nine thousand Africans who disembarked according to *The Transatlantic Slavery Database* would have risen by 6,680.

It can be supposed that the urgency with which exhibitions were put together and the increased tonnage and cargo would give rise to greater overcrowding in the holds of the ships. However, instead of increasing the number of deaths during the intermediate crossing, a lower mortality rate was recorded on such voyages with respect to the previous and ensuing periods (Figure 4). From this we can deduce that there was a greater interest in preserving the cargo than usual, which also shows that the traffickers knew how to do things better in this sense if they put their mind to it.

Fourth, the announcement of a forthcoming end to the transatlantic African slave trade led to an increase in the number of women transported each year, the aim being to facilitate the natural capacity for reproduction on the island in the future. Until then, the number of women transported to Cuba was less than a third of the total number of slaves, a proportion recommended by Spanish law

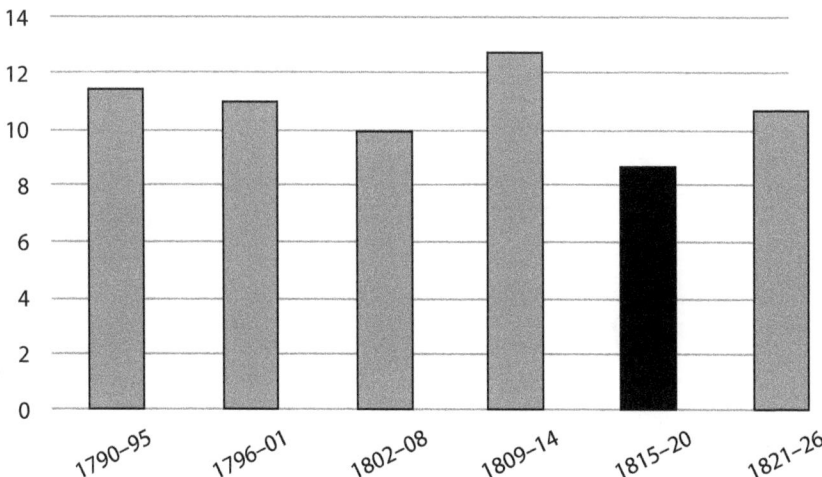

Source: Voyages Database. 2016. Voyages: The Trans-Atlantic Slave Trade Database. http://www.slavevoyages.org.

Figure 4. Deaths of African slaves during the transatlantic crossing (1790–1820) (percentage of the number of slaves embarked).

since the sixteenth century and which had become mandatory in 1789 and 1804 (Joda Esteve 2014, 107–30).

Fifth, the demand for manpower in Cuba had had a characteristic that distinguished it from its immediate antecedents in the rest of the Caribbean and which consisted in its specialization in young males who were in possession of a maximum labor potential. From 1815 onward, that demand became more diversified with the incorporation of a proportion of women, whereas the proportion in the younger age brackets was not only confirmed but in fact higher.

We do not have access to reliable series on the ages of the slaves taken to Cuba, but we do have a series of the prices of African slaves in Havana, drawn up by Laird W. Bergad, María del Carmen Barcia, and Fe Iglesias, in which the slaves are differentiated by age and sex (Figure 5).

The figure above shows a relative correspondence between the prices of the Africans of all ages sold in Cuba and the price of the slaves included in the main age cohort, from fifteen to forty years. It must be noted, however, that the range with the greatest demand was that from fifteen to thirty years old. The increases in the price of slaves aged 15–40 years to values above the average price of Afri-

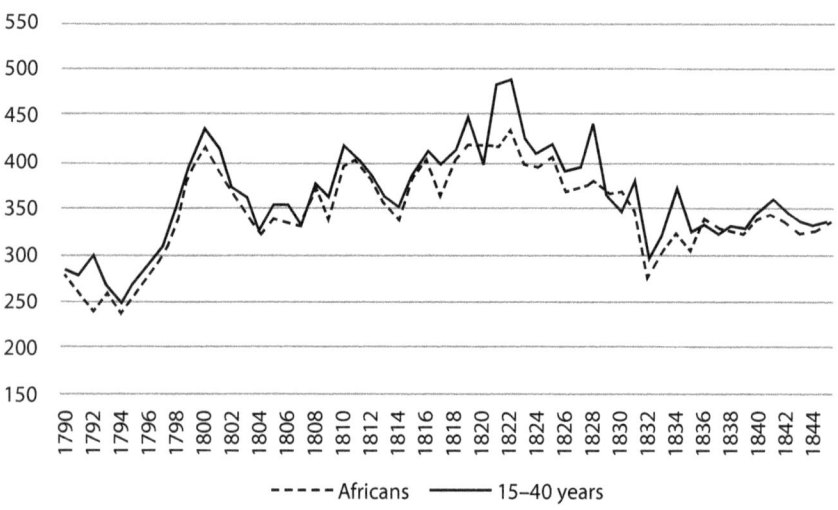

Source: Laird W. Bergad, María del Carmen Barcia, and Fe Iglesias, *The Cuban Slave Market, 1790–1880* (New York: Cambridge University Press, 1995). (Compiled by the author.)

Figure 5. Prices of African slaves (in pesos) sold in Havana (1790–1844).

cans can be taken as an indicator of a greater demand for slaves with full labor potential, rather than children and other adults.

The price of slaves aged 15–40 years was nearly always a little higher than the average, but within the series we find two significant temporal deviations: at the beginning of the free trade, during only two years (1791 and 1792), and in the years between 1816 and 1835, when, with only two exceptions (1820 and 1830), the prices paid within the range of ages between fifteen and forty years is always higher. This tendency can also be observed in the years 1815–20, which was the cycle of "hasty" transatlantic trade. The highest price paid for a particular age bracket is a good indicator of the increase in demand for that same segment.

Sixth, the annual number of transatlantic voyages in the period 1816–20 increased by 254 percent with respect to the period 1811–15. That fleet, as we have pointed out above, could not be improvized and neither could the capital needed to undertake business on that scale. Between 1790 and 1795, the vessels devoted to the African slave trade that supplied the Cuban market sailed under the flags of Great Britain, the United States, France, Portugal, and Spain. Some of the Portuguese ships were registered in Brazilian ports and a number of ships sailing under the Spanish flag were registered in Montevideo, a port that facilitated trading between Buenos Aires and Alto Peru by supplying slaves while it continued to trade with Cádiz and which benefited from carrying out smuggling activities with Brazil and supplying the Caribbean with jerky.

When the war between Spain and Britain broke out in 1796, the ships under the British flag left the scene and the transportation of African slaves was largely carried out by ships from the United States, although there were also a number of English ships among them that changed flag so as to be able to continue in business. They were also joined by several Danish ships. The new slave fleet hastily put together by Spanish and creole traders from Havana, Matanzas, and Santiago, often with ties with traders from Cádiz, Santander, and La Coruña, also made its first appearance. During the Napoleonic Wars, the links of the Spanish and Creole shipowners extended to New Orleans, Baltimore, Philadelphia, New York, and Boston. From 1809 onward, nearly all the ships dedicated to the transatlantic slave trade sailing to Cuba operated under the Spanish flag, with a few exceptions from the United States, Portugal, and France (the French ships were more frequent in 1820 and after the beginning of clandestine trading).

We have a wealth of information available to us, although it needs to be completed and refined far more than it has been to date. There were undoubtedly changes of ensign due to interests, together with the fraudulent nationalization of ships. That was one of the lines followed by the British Admiralty in order to pursue and capture, from 1809 onward, ships bearing the Spanish flag that docked in British ports before beginning their crossings, without revealing the fact that they were sailing to Africa or the cargo they hoped to pick up there. The fact that the Spanish vessel had been purchased by its current owner for a price that was much lower than that of the naval market was also interpreted by the English Admiralty as an indicator of its possibly being used for the African slave trade. This gave rise to speculations about the concealment of the true ownership of the vessel, which could continue to be English or maintain the participation of British partners in the expedition, or the captain having a share in the ownership of the vessel, which made him one of its operators.

From 1809 onward, a year after the British ban on the slave trade and its abolition came into force in the United States, the ownership of the slave ships practically disappeared from the registers, at least in the wide array of sources used to create *The Trans-Atlantic Slave Trade Database*. At the same time, the captains of the ships were all Spanish. We know, however, that for some time part of the crew and even most of the sailors on many expeditions continued to come from the United States. It was not uncommon for the true captain of the ship to be of this same nationality although a Spaniard, who was in fact the pilot of the other, was registered as such. The transatlantic trade preserved its international nature after 1809, but the identity of the participants was camouflaged. As of 1814, with the important growth in the slave trade to Cuba, these two characteristics became more pronounced.

Seventh, from 1790, the traders established in Havana, Matanzas, Trinidad, and Santiago, moneylenders, and some plantation owners became interested in the transatlantic slave trade and consigned the shipments (*armazones*). The most noteworthy of them between 1790 and 1810 were Santiago Drake, the three Poey Lacase brothers (Simón, Juan Bautista, and Juan Andrés), Bonifacio González Larrinaga, Juan Luis and Santiago Cuesta, Antonio and Nicolás Frías, the four Hernández brothers (Gaspar, José, Francisco, and Sebastián), and Juan Magín Tarafa. The traders were soon joined by peninsular traders and ships' captains from Cádiz, the Basque Country, Santander, Asturias, Galicia, and Catalonia. In the first decade of the nineteenth century, together with those cited above, we also find Sebastián Lasa, Ramón Marcial, Francisco de Navia, Juan Villavicencio, Benito Patrón, and Francisco Antonio Zequeira, among others. As of 1808, a small but constant stream of Spaniards fleeing from the war being fought on the Peninsula also began to arrive. They were to be found piloting the ships that plied the route from Africa. Vicente Alfonso was particularly active in 1810, 1811, and the years that followed; Joaquín Zorrilla was in charge of slave ships in 1809, 1818, and 1819, and very possibly on a regular basis throughout the second decade of the nineteenth century; others who appeared at that time were Ignacio de Azcárate and Domingo Aldama Arechaga, who were soon to climb to the top positions among the companies dedicated to the slave trade. There were also the shipping agents of foreign firms devoted to the slave trade, who, in view of the opportunities that were emerging, became directly involved in the business, as is the case of Martin Madan, an agent of the London firm Thomas Comyn, who around 1807 set up business in Matanzas by himself, or perhaps not entirely by himself.

With the end of the French occupation of Spain, around 1814–15, another stream of emigrants left for Cuba, all of whom were devoted to African slave trading. Jaime Pinto captained his ship in 1814, and José Antonio Suárez Argudín did the same in 1815, 1816, and 1818, before entering in partnership with Gabriel Lombillo in 1820. Pedro Blanco, from Malaga, embarked in 1816, at least, and in 1819 his nephews Fernando and Julio settled in Havana to work in the loan business and to insure their uncle's expeditions. Around that time, Joaquín Gómez did the same and captained a ship in 1819. The trading house Zangronis, Hermanos y Cía. prospered in the years 1817 and 1818, when it put together three voyages. Francisco Marty y Torrens had arrived in Havana in 1809 after being discharged from the Marquis de La Romana's army; in 1816 year he appeared as the captain of a slave ship although he supposedly covered the crossing to Matanzas. Even the son of a hero from the War of Independence, Francisco Romeu, appeared as the owner of a small vessel used for trafficking slaves in 1817. In 1816, Juan de Carredano possessed two ships and that year he dispatched 536 slaves. It became increasingly more frequent for slave traders to then invest in founding sugar plantations. After 1820–23, with their sights set on the clandestine slave trade, the Spaniards José Manuel Manzanedo, Pedro Juan de Zulueta (the latter granted loans in Havana and Santiago without leaving his London residence), Salvador Samá, and others settled in Cuba.[4]

The profits from each expedition to the African coasts yielded high returns on the capital invested and allowed assets to be set aside to finance the next voyage. With average profits ranging from 100 percent to 150 percent, very often a loan to cover the expenses of the first crossing was enough to get such a lucrative business underway. Nevertheless, the cost of the slaves transported over the period 1815–21, according to their prices on embarking in Africa, required an outlay of around fifteen million pesos. Such a figure was beyond the capacity of the Spanish trading houses located in Cuba, despite their growth since 1796 under the protection of free trade with neutral countries, or of the trading houses of the Peninsula at a time when they were emerging from a long devastating war.

Eighth, with the end of the Napoleonic Wars important changes began to take place in the world's productive structure. The stagnation of production in the British West Indies forced the United Kingdom to begin to open itself up to sugars from elsewhere for the European refineries. The capture of French and Dutch colonies by the English during the previous wars and the strengthening of the relationships with India and the Pacific, with which Britain sought to offset the effects of the continental blockade decreed by Napoleon against British industry and commerce, anticipated the new trend.

The recovery of the transatlantic trade in 1815 and the new influx of half-finished material—muscovado sugar—had two consecutive effects on the structure of the world sugar industry: a continued decline in sugar prices on the London market, which had been the international reference since the previous century (Figure 6),

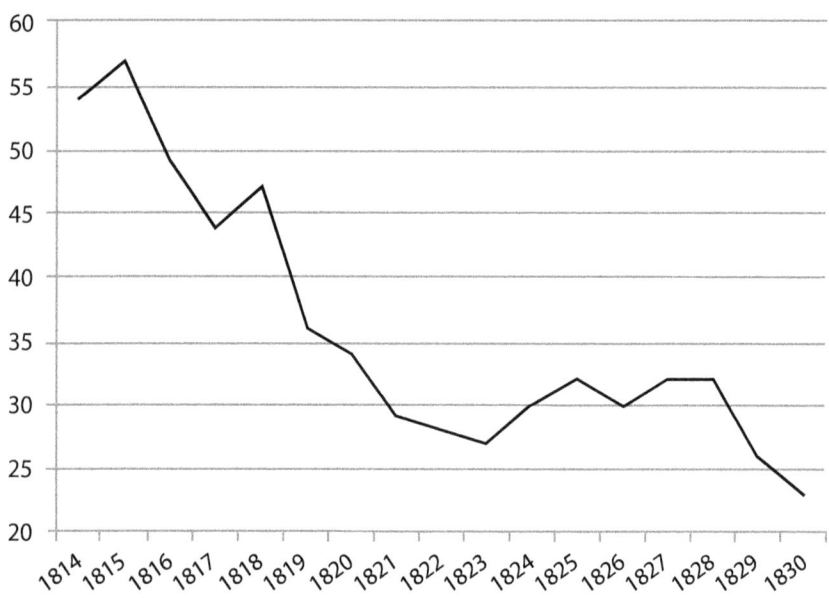

Source: N. Deer, *The History of Sugar* (London: Chapman and Hall, 1949), 1:531. (Compiled by the author.)

Figure 6. Evolution of the price of sugar on the London market (1814–1830) (sh/cwt).

and as a consequence of this, its consumption became widely popular, as it was now far more affordable. The combined effect of these two factors gave rise to a sustained increase in demand for the half-finished material. This in turn called for the creation of a commercial supply circuit that was stable and not dependent on one's own colonies, the productive capacity of which was becoming increasingly lower than the refining capacity in the mother country and the market that the British and other competitors hoped to supply.

The continued decline in sugar prices reduced the plantations' profits and made the plants more dependent on external, insular, or international funding. Moreover, the combination of the foreseeable forthcoming closure of the market for supplying African manpower, which would increase the production costs as it meant that the process of replacing labor had to include the time spent waiting until creoles became adults, and not having any control over the proportion of males (the ideal worker on the plantation) forced the great transformation that took place in Cuba. This shift consisted in the expansion of the average surface area of the sugar *ingenios*, the definitive conquest of natural spaces, the adoption of mechanical means in the manufacturing phase, the use of large gangs of slave workers, and the search for solutions to the internal transportation of the sugar cane to the factory and the external transportation from the *ingenio* to the port of embarkation, which was to be resolved in the 1830s with the arrival of the railway.

The prospect of a rising and sustained demand for sugar by the international markets and large-scale production offset the decrease in the rate of return on investment; the increased productivity achieved by the means mentioned above had the same result. The large-scale illegal trafficking of African slaves after 1820 guaranteed the process and corrected some of the deficiencies highlighted earlier by providing manpower that was well suited to the model at a favorable price.

Ninth, during the Napoleonic Wars, the British banking houses did not cease in their quest to seek out business that offered returns on their loans, including the purveyance of sugars. "Purveyance of sugars" is a fairly technical term that can include several facets: financing the purchase and preparation of land, financing the construction of the buildings needed in the *ingenio* and the warehouses in port cities, financing the acquisition of machinery, participating in the commercialization operations of sugar exportation, financing the annual support of the workers until the sale of the harvest, and financing the provisioning and replacement of workers, that is, of slaves. This last activity was carried out with the greatest possible discretion as of 1808 while doing everything they could to prevent the British Parliament from forbidding its subjects to participate financially in the transatlantic trafficking of slaves. Commercial and banking houses in New York, Boston, Philadelphia, and New Orleans followed the same modus operandi in Cuba.

In 1814, the trading house Baring Brothers Co. Ltd., which was so interested in sugar that it focused its operations in the British West Indies, recorded in its ledgers "its dealings with Cuban exporters," in particular with James Drake, a British merchant established in Havana who specialized in the exportation and importation of goods (Roldán de Montaud 2015, 240–41). Drake soon became the owner of a plantation and an investor in the slave trade. In the text we have just cited, Inés Roldán has illustrated the participation of Baring Brothers in the expansion of the Cuban sugar trade in the following decades. Some time ago, Ángel Bahamonde and José Cayuela noted that the first economic contacts between Baring Brothers and the Cuban houses were made in 1812, when they were established with José Luis Alfonso, Domingo Aldama, and the Fesser family. The contacts with these and other families became more frequent between the 1820s and the 1840s (Bahamonde and Cayuela 1992, 303–5). The early years, however, from 1812 onward, correspond to the period in which these names—Aldama, Alfonso, Fesser—were not yet linked to the plantation and to the great sugar trade, but instead their core activity was in the transatlantic slave trade. Loans for slave trading, in this and in later periods, were camouflaged as credit operations related to the exportation of sugar and to mortgages, which allowed them to devote their own capital to the slave trade while outside funding was used to cover the expenses arising from production.

The prospect of the end of the African slave trade, evidenced in 1814 and agreed to in 1817, rather than imposing the humanitarian criteria that seemed bound to succeed due to the force of the pressure from the world hegemonic power and its diplomatic efforts, actually increased that trade until it reached figures that were previously undreamed of. Likewise, it hurriedly set in motion an enormous international mechanism centered on Cuba for the purveyance of slaves and the enhancement of sugar production. This resulted in the creation of a set of conditions that allowed the business to continue for another forty-five years after the slave trade was banned. The second slavery found the most favorable conditions in Cuba precisely in the moment in which the forthcoming abolition of the transatlantic trade was made known and when there was an intensification of all the processes that would end up enhancing the plantation and the sugar business instead of alleviating the scarcity of manpower. In 1818, in acknowledgment of the difficulty involved in reestablishing Spain's trade monopoly, which had been interrupted in Cuba in 1796, and largely as compensation for the possible effects of the Anglo-Spanish Treaty of 1817, King Ferdinand VII granted the island what the Spanish American continent had been denied in war, namely, free commerce with the world.

As had occurred since the mid-eighteenth century, the Atlantic appears as a whole in the Braudelian sense: it is a Mediterranean that is far more extensive than the Mediterranean, in which a number of players are involved. From 1814 onward, after spending two decades preparing itself, Cuba took over as the epicenter of the world sugar plantation, which in the past had been Saint-Domingue and Jamaica.

Notes

This text has been researched and written within the framework of project HAR2016-78910-P (AEI, FEDER-EU) and the Prometeo Program 2013/023 of the Generalitat Valenciana for Groups of Excellence. Translated by Mark Andrews.

1. Francisco Arango, "Dissenting Vote of Several Councillors of the Indies on the Abolition of the Slave Trade," in Francisco Arango y Parreño, *Obras* (La Habana: Imagen Contemporánea-Ciencias Sociales, 2005), 2:126–32.

2. *Tratado entre S.M. el Rey de España y de las Indias, y S.M. el Rey del Reino Unido de Gran Bretaña e Irlanda para la abolición del tráfico de negros, concluido y firmado en Madrid a 23 de septiembre de 1817* [Treaty between His Majesty the King of Spain and of the Indies and His Majesty the King of the United Kingdom of Great Britain and Ireland for the Abolition of the Black Slave Trade, signed at Madrid the 23rd of September 1817].

3. *Real Cédula*, in *Tratado . . . para la abolición del tráfico de negros*, 75–81. Published in Cuba in the *Memorias de la Real Sociedad Económica de La Habana*, no. 15, "distributed on 31st March 1818," 97–102.

4. The slave trader clans are in Moreno Fraginals (1978, 1:265–69). Ships' captains and shipowners are in Voyages Database. 2016. *Voyages: The Trans-Atlantic Slave Trade Database.*

Works Cited

Arango y Parreño, Francisco. 2005. *Obras*. La Habana: Imagen Contemporánea-Ciencias Sociales.

Bahamonde, Ángel, and José Cayuela. 1992. *Hacer las Américas: Las elites coloniales españolas en el siglo XIX*. Madrid: Alianza Editorial.

Bergad, Laird W., María del Carmen Barcia, and Fe Iglesias. 1995. *The Cuban Slave Market, 1790–1880*. New York: Cambridge University Press.

Brennecke, Christiana. 2010. *¿De ejemplo a 'mancha' de Europa? La Guerra de independencia española y sus efectos sobe la imagen oficial de España durante el Congreso de Viena (1814–1815)*. Madrid: CSIC-Ediciones Doce Calles.

Cantillo, Alejandro del, comp. 1843. *Tratados, convenios y declaraciones de paz y de comercio que han hecho con las potencias extranjeras los monarcas españoles de la Casa de Borbón desde el año de 1700 hasta el día*. Madrid: Impr. de Alegría y Charlain.

Castelli, [Pierre-Paul]. 1844. *De l'esclavage en général, et de l'émancipation des noirs, avec un projet de réorganisation de l'action religieuse*. Paris: Comptoir des Imprimeurs-Unis.

Chapman, Tim. 1998. *The Congress of Vienna, 1814–1815: Origins, processes and results*. London: Routledge.

Chew, William L., III. 1997. "Vienna, Congress of." In *The Historical Encyclopedia of World Slavery*, vol. 1, edited by Junius P. Rodriguez, 673–74. Santa Barbara, CA: ABC-CLIO.

Deer, N. 1949. *The History of Sugar*. London: Chapman and Hall.

García de León y Pizarro, José. 1999. *Memorias (1770–1835)*. Edited by Álvaro Alonso-Castrillo. Madrid: Centro de Estudios Políticos y Constitucionales.

Hamilton, Keith, and Farida Shaikh. 2009. Introduction to *Slavery, Diplomacy and Empire: Britain and the Suppression of the Slave Trade, 1807–1975*, edited by Keith Hamilton and Patrick Salmon, 1–18. Brighton: Sussex Academic Press.

Jarrett, Mark. 2013. *The Congress of Vienna and Its Legacy: War and Great Power Diplomacy after Napoleon*. London: I.B. Tauris.

Joda Esteve, Beatriz. 2014. "El comercio de esclavos a Cuba (1790–1840): Una proporción femenina." *Anuario Colombiano de Historia Social y de la Cultura* 41, no. 2: 111–12.

Labrador, Marquis de. 1849. *Mélanges sur la vie privée et publique du marquis de Labrador, écrits par lui-même*. Paris: Impr. Thunot et Cie.

Moreno Fraginals, Manuel. 1978. *El ingenio: Complejo económico social cubano del azúcar*. La Habana: Ciencias Sociales.

Nicolson, Harold. (1946) 2000. *The Congress of Vienna: A Study in Allied Unity, 1812–1822*. London: Grove Press.

Piqueras, José Antonio. 2016. "The Discovery of Progress in Cuba: Machines, Slaves, Businesses." In *New Frontiers of Slavery*, edited by Dale Tomich, 49–75. New York: State University of New York Press.

Ponte Domínguez, Francisco J. 1937. *Arango Parreño, estadista colonial cubano*. La Habana: Sociedad Económica de Amigos del País.

Roldán de Montaud, Inés. 2015. "Baring Brothers and the Cuban Plantation Economy, 1814–1870." In *The Caribbean and the Atlantic World Economy: Circuits of Trade, Money and Knowledge, 1650–1914*, edited by Adrian Leonard and David Pretel, 238–62. London: Palgrave Macmillan.

Schoell, Federico. 1816. *Documentos del Congreso de Viena, en que tiene particular interés España, sacados de la colección pública en París por el Sr* . . . Madrid: Imprenta Real.

Tomich, Dale. 2005. "The Wealth of Empire: Francisco Arango y Parreño, Political Economy, and the Second Slavery in Cuba." In *Interpreting Spanish Colonialism: Empires, Nations, and Legends*, edited by Christopher Schmidt-Nowara and John Nieto-Phillips, 55–85. Albuquerque: University of New Mexico Press.

Tratado entre S.M. el Rey de España y de las Indias, y S.M. el Rey del Reino Unido de Gran Bretaña e Irlanda para la abolición del tráfico de negros, concluido y firmado en Madrid a 23 de septiembre de 1817. Madrid: Impr. Real, 1817.

Webster, Charles K. 1919. *The Congress of Vienna, 1814–1815*. London: Humphrey Milford / Oxford University Press.

Wellesley, H. 1930. *The Diary and Correspondence of Henry Wellesley, First Lord Cowley, 1790–1846*. Edited by F. A. Wellesley. London: Hutchinson & Company.

Williams, Eric. 2011. *Capitalismo y esclavitud*. Madrid: Traficantes de sueños.

From Cotton to Camels

Plantation Ambitions in Midcentury Hispaniola

Anne Eller

When Spanish authorities annexed the Dominican Republic in 1861, they and Dominican collaborators planned to remake the territory's landscape and to reorder the way its rural residents labored and lived.[1] These authorities intended to make Dominicans—who lived overwhelmingly in dispersed, subsistence communities—into "productive" subjects, to formalize and commercialize peasant labor, and to bring them under the authority of an expanded colonial state. Newly arriving Spanish officials focused on investment in new industries and public works, and individual capitalists approached them with numerous concession petitions for cotton plantations, railroads, indentured labor, and a series of other projects, which ranged from the mundane to the outlandish. One US merchant even proposed camel transport (May 1979, 406). Although the territory had been separated from Spain for nearly forty years, Dominican president Pedro Santana insisted that the cession was voluntary. The Spanish official with whom the Dominican president had been most closely in collusion—the activist governor of Cuba, Captain-General Francisco Serrano—emphasized his agreement and support. Only after annexation ceremonies did both officials send word to the governor of neighboring Puerto Rico and to Queen Isabel II and her ministers. However, preparations had been the talk of Havana for months. A Havana resident bragged, "Spain should not limit her aims to the Dominican Republic; it needs the whole island, and the Haitian Republic will be invaded before long." He urged Spanish authorities to be inspired by Spain's recent victory in Ceuta toward more conquest. Given the distraction of the United States by the Civil War, the man predicted more Spanish expansion in the Gulf of Mexico imminently, boasting, "soon it will be Mexico's turn" (Rodríguez Demorizi 1955, 157).

Like supporters of French intervention in Mexico, which unfolded almost simultaneously, Dominican annexationists were a small, mainly conservative elite who were tired of political fighting, wary of the populace, and eager for outside military resources to secure order, just as the Cuban governor was eager to provide them. The Dominican annexationists shared ready economic extroversion, but also strong local political commitments. They were nationalists after a fashion, believing that political stability, under a foreign monarch, might create more local meritocratic government appointments than successive fractious administrations (Pani 2002, 28). Dominican politicians' strategy of asking for a protectorate in exchange for limited territorial concessions was nothing unusual; it was an emergency recourse for embattled leaders throughout the hemisphere. The heightened political chaos of the Gulf of Mexico, however—where US interests loomed—made the annexation projects real. Although Spanish authorities had rejected Dominican entreaties for several decades, deeming the risk of failure or conflict with the US and other European powers too great, the Spanish governor of Cuba, Francisco Serrano, saw the dawn of the 1860s as a moment of opportunity. By annexing a free-soil territory, the Cuban governor hoped force new debates about legal questions of representation and inclusion that would resolve decades of constitutional uncertainty in Cuba and Puerto Rico as well.[2] Like his Dominican collaborators, Serrano hoped reoccupation would also bring imperial profits.

Authorities maintained that Dominican annexation presented a new direction in Spanish Caribbean rule: a jurisdiction without slavery or legislative distinctions of race that might become a profitable export territory. They intended the reestablished project to be a free-labor "experiment"—and to be ruled by Spanish law. As Christopher Schmidt-Nowara observes, the midcentury moment represented the apex of debates over the centrality and governance of "overseas Spain" (Schmidt-Nowara 2006). The newly arrived authorities reveled at the prospect of the "inexhaustible riches" from the "virgin land," but Dominican coffers, which had been in a state of more or less permanent economic crisis for decades, offered no immediate help.[3] In effect, the Spanish sought to jump-start cash-crop production where there was almost none; their endeavor amounted to an early effort at "hegemony on a shoestring" (Barry 1992). In a territory with very little commercial export other than tobacco and wood exports, officials soon floundered for means to make it profitable, or at least less of a drain on Cuba's coffers, whose authorities sent 150,000 pesos in July 1861 alone. After his brief stay in the Dominican capital and several hours in a north-coast port, the Cuban governor ordered a "complete reorganization of a tattered [*desquiciado*] . . . administration" and left.[4] This chapter details some of the profit-making schemes of the early days of Spanish reoccupation that followed. Although the Dominican Republic rarely figures into histories of midcentury plantation production, an important group of Dominican elites shared aspirations of a new day of tropical prosperity with arriving Spanish officials, foreign industrialists, and authors of postemancipation schemes elsewhere. Just as in other sites, too, their cash-crop aspirations were in direct and urgent conflict with those of the Dominican majority.

Tropical Exuberance: New Dreams for Caribbean Labor Control

Forced labor, transformed once by the Haitian Revolution and the expansion of the second slavery, was on the precipice of another fulcrum: an expanding market for tropical goods and new international projects of migration and labor control, occurring simultaneously with a sudden interruption of production in the United States. As secession and warfare suspended US cotton exports, international industrialists schemed for new sites—and new modes of labor control—to fill the market void.[5] Well before wartime disruption, in fact, cotton's high prices made Manchester merchants impatient to foment production in more territories, an ambition that neatly reinforced imperial expansion.[6] British joint-stock cotton companies in the Caribbean proliferated overnight, including an Anglo-Spanish company in Cuba (Watts 1871, 93–94). This vision was shared by Haiti's new president, Fabre Nicholas Geffrard, who committed to cotton production plans, sending officials to conduct a vast survey of potential production sites (Joseph 1860). The Haitian government facilitated credit to private buyers to purchase cotton and sugar machinery and offered bounties for production.[7] Cotton was highly sought after, could be planted on all types of terrain, could be produced with reasonable start-up capital, and would improve the country's trade balance, Geffrard urged (Geffrard 1861, 1; 1860, 1). High wartime prices made cotton bounties unnecessary; Haiti's production soared from less than seven hundred thousand pounds in 1860 to more than twice that by 1862, and samples were displayed at the Great Exhibition in London that year (St. John 1884, 367). Meanwhile, Manchester capitalists sent cottonseed to Trinidad, Tobago, Antigua, British Guiana, Barbados, Dominica, Tortola, and a plethora of other semitropical sites (Watts 1871, 96; Calhoun 2012). Investors and authorities embraced a "myth of tropical exuberance," eager and confident that they could profit in new locations (Ratcliffe 1982, 87).

Postemancipation programs of cash-crop export and labor control, rather than being a departure from slavery and plantation production, were eminently legible to local elites. In conjunction with imperial offices across the Atlantic, Caribbean officials mobilized new programs of indenture. Beginning in the 1820s, more than 430,000 predominantly young men and women arrived as contract laborers in the British Caribbean, more than 76,000 to the French Caribbean, and more than 125,000 to Cuba (Kale 1998, 1; López 2013, 22; Northrup 2000; Renault 1976).[8] They arrived from different sites in Africa, only just released from having been kidnapped onto illegal slave ships, and by contract from different Indian states, China, and Madeira. Britain occasionally jealously opposed the importation projects of other empires, but programs thrived (Marsh 2012, 225). Across the islands, in Brazil, Peru, and elsewhere, the men and women were bound to an individual employer, faced criminal charges for civil offenses (including labor discipline), and had to labor for as long as ten years to earn return passage (Schuler 1980; Rodney 1981; Jung 2006; López 2013). Planters intentionally tried to isolate the newly arrived into a "cycle of coercion" (Jung 2006, 17). The very language of labor scarcity was one of division and control, of course, directed as a weapon against the independence of the emancipated. On islands where land was available, the formerly enslaved had tenaciously carved out small plots, despite all manner of restrictions, forging internal markets for crops like ginger, arrowroot, and bananas (Thompson 1997, 122). Low wages, surveillance, intolerable discipline, and an aversion to economic dependence—not any sort of absolute demographic shortage—had hastened freed peoples' exodus and planters' ire simultaneously. On smaller islands with no available land, the balance of power tipped hard to planters (or, in the case of Turks and Caicos Islands, salt mine owners). Here, elites colluded with authorities to try to prevent the formerly enslaved from leaving the island at all.[9] Dominican elites would have observed these contests with interest in the 1840s and 1850s, even as no such projects were yet operative on Dominican soil.

Even authorities who promoted cotton explicitly as a crop that might "vindicate" free labor looked to immigration projects and to expand labor surveillance. Haiti's secretary of state, François Jean-Joseph, concluded that both state and private plantations needed foreign agricultural laborers, in areas of Haiti not subdivided into small family plots. He proposed immigration bureaus domestically and in the United States with the supposition that prospective immigrants would work in agriculture (Joseph 1860, 1–4). President Geffrard invited African Americans to immigrate; US-based abolitionists James Redpath and James Theodore Holly served as formidable allies who promoted the plan widely.[10] The administration awarded free passage to those who would settle on larger plantations as sharecroppers; artisans were to repay travel costs in three months' time. About two thousand African Americans arrived, but the program dwindled after 1862; the families reported poor conditions, unsatisfactory land distribution, and other conflicts. As many as a third quickly bought return passage (Alexander 2010, 75). An isolated scheme to populate Île-à-Vache quickly collapsed not long after.[11] Disappointed but not deterred, Geffrard hoped Haitian peasants would themselves flock to the cotton industry, out of personal interest and an abstract patriotism. "Rural populations, I like to think, will not remain deaf to these exhortations," he remarked, "and will know to enter in a path which, while taking them individually to well-being, will bring the country to an elevated position . . . , through their industriousness and the importance of their production, . . . [and will] make them indispensable." Authorities urged district generals to encourage, without requiring, cotton production, and to submit regular reports (Geffrard 1861, 1). Wealthy Haitians approved of these measures and called for sugar production, too, and even suggested seeking contract laborers from India (Nicholls 1974, 15; Monfleury 1862, 1). Surrounding both Haiti and the Dominican Republic, an elaborate geography of labor restrictions, contract labor, and other restraints emerged alongside emancipation and slavery, a map that was well known to Caribbean residents.[12]

In the pre-occupation Dominican Republic and Haiti, as elsewhere, discourses about free peasant labor ranged from paternalism to outright moral panic. Authorities harbored didactic fantasies that "instruction" would make emancipated or peasant individuals behave as was economically and politically convenient; they were particularly obsessed with the inculcation—or performance of respect—for the rule of law (Paton 2004, 149). In Haiti, authorities codified an archetype of the rural agricultural worker (*habitant agriculteur*) as a national symbol, unequally integrated into the state. They celebrated May 1 as "la fête de l'agriculture," with equal parts pomp and moralizing. "Fathers and mothers, prepare your children from their youth for the love of work, the submission they owe the law, and the respect they owe to the authorities of the Empire!," Haitian president Faustin

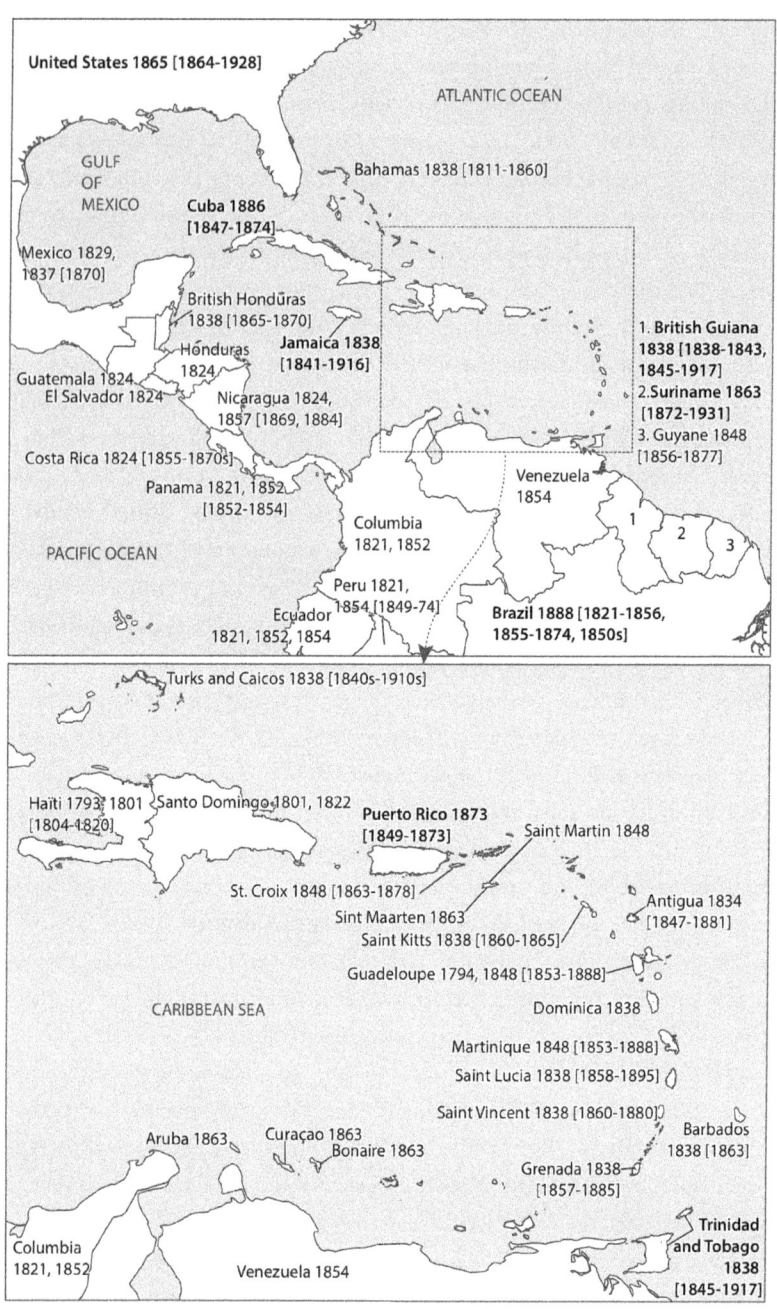

Figure 7. Map showing emancipation dates, with major projects of indenture, labor control, or indenture emigration in brackets. Map by Annelieke Vries. For clarifications, see note 12.

Soulouque exhorted.[13] Geffrard's first promises were to amend the Rural Code to create a stronger rural police, local inspectors, and stronger antivagrancy strictures (Geffrard 1859, 1). Authorities fretted about labor control through the lens of moral formation. "In [Puerto Rico and Santo Domingo] immorality and the lack of religious education deprive men of the essential bases to keep them in line with their duties," Puerto Rico's governor asserted (Febres-Cordero Carrillo 2008, 83). White island residents fantasized that German, Irish, French, and other white laborers might "model" agricultural wage work; it was a common enough reverie that combined the preservation of a white plurality and the dream of a subordinate and docile sector, all at once (Breen 1844, 306; Schmidt-Nowara 1999, 42). As coercive reform "experiments" eroded in some islands, moral panic grew, about sexuality, marriage practices, religion, medicine, and all manner of imagined deviance (Dalby 2015, 136–59; Fryar 2013, 598–618). Geffrard directed his attentions to vodou, making it a central legal target (Ramsey 2011, 83–90). His minister proclaimed that "idleness and vagabondage are a leprosy" that authorities would "work tirelessly to repress."[14] Later, his opponents would say he did not go far enough. "Surely what they are wanting then is the reestablishment of forced labor for the benefit of aristocracy, as with during Christophe," the president retorted, in frustration (Geffrard 1865, 1).

Among the small southern Dominican elite coauthors of annexation—and the commercial class in the Cibao Valley—a significant sector entered eager to benefit from Spanish plans for investment and labor control.[15] Dominican politicians had long argued that the country's raw potential was undeniable, a "hidden mine . . . an earthly paradise."[16] A small but enthusiastic group of elites in the Cibao mentioned development in their annexation manifesto, hoping for an end to the inflation that had crippled the tobacco exports of the region for so long (and forced the trade into the hand of Danish and German banks). Financial reform, the idea of "sacred property," and the military tools to control unrest appealed to them greatly.[17] From the capital, elites wrote enthusiastically that reunification should henceforth "never be erased in the minds of Spaniards," and they joined authorities in celebrating Spanish arrival with ceremony and pageantry.[18] But they also ascribed, enthusiastically, to indenture schemes, including involving "*emancipados*," people freed from the illegal slave trade but not repatriated to the site of their kidnapping and sale across the Atlantic. These captures might have taken place nearby, in Cuban waters. When a cotton capitalist wrote asking for "ten *emancipados* per *caballería* [about thirty-three acres]," Manuel de Jesús Galván and other town council members endorsed the proposal. "It is certain that [cotton] will soon thrive in Santo Domingo," Galván wrote.[19] Prominent capital residents urged cash-crop development as a means of vindicating the occupied territory from its subsistence past. "The Dominican people are victims of calumny when they are supposed to be lazier than other people," Pedro Valverde explained to Spanish administrators. "Augment [their needs], as one would expect in the course of good government . . . , and their productivity will grow proportionately."[20] Valverde was eager to discipline rural Dominicans. His antivagrancy proposals were so stringent, in fact, that incoming Spanish administrators thought them too harsh to implement.[21]

The Crown supported Dominican elites' labor proposals, ordering land surveys and abrogating tariffs on the import of machinery. Authorities daydreamed—against all regional evidence—that Dominicans might be willing to grow export crops for low wages.[22] Confidentially, the Crown suggested that Dominicans might be impressed into public works projects for a small wage, too, as they had "been obliged to live arms in hand and ready to serve for so long." Additionally, the administration should pay for, or at least promote, projects of Spanish migration, early edicts determined.[23] A handful of established planters asked for liberated Africans or other foreign indentured laborers instead. Meanwhile, the queen approved a royal order in June 1861 that banned free people of color from traveling to the island, intending to prevent enslaved people from Cuba and Puerto Rico from escaping to freedom. Santo Domingo, as a province of Spain, had a different status than its neighbors—with the Dominican civil code and Spanish criminal codes intended to govern—but separation from the neighboring plantation states proved immediately troublesome. Before the end of 1861, major economic obstacles also became obvious. The lack of commercial endeavors was "incredible . . . in a country where sugar cane grows by itself, where coffee growers just have to plant the seed and then harvest . . . , [and] where corn grows wild," a Spanish official remarked in disbelief.[24] Still, loyalists rallied, with new proannexation newspapers and new project proposals. Spanish journalists entered the debates, arguing for open ports like that of Singapore to stimulate free trade.[25] Annexation supporters wrote to the queen with breathless optimism, describing "the vehement desire . . . to equal, and even to exceed if possible, the progress made in neighboring Puerto Rico and Cuba."[26] "The Spanish government knows perfectly well that European immigration will not come to fertilize this fertile but hot soil," an anonymous French observer countered, and predicted slavery would soon arrive in Santo Domingo.[27]

Assembling the Spanish Colonial State

Spanish troops disembarked quickly in Dominican ports. Two thousand from Havana and eight hundred from Puerto Rico arrived in the capital within three weeks. Nearly a thousand of them moved from the capital to Puerto Plata by steamship. A few hundred continued on to the nearby southern town of Azua.[28] The next real order of occupation was to set up a new bureaucracy. Colonial governments in Cuba and Puerto Rico had multiplied many times in size since the 1830s; colonial subjects paid taxes at higher rates than those on the peninsula.[29] Famously, infrastructure was so advanced in the plantation centers of eastern and central Cuba that the capitalists had begun a railroad system there years before construction began in the metropole itself. Frequent steam communication connected the islands to their own coastal extremities, to each other, and to the Spanish peninsula. Troops were everywhere; there were more than twenty thousand infantry in Cuba and about four thousand in Puerto Rico. The mandate for governing, however, resided in Spain. The centralization of power was so extreme that one political aspirant in Cuba complained, "Cuba went from being an integral part of the monarchy to . . . an enslaved colony" (quoted in Martínez-Fernández 1994, 61). "To be born in Cuba is a crime," complained another would-be delegate (Martínez-Fernández 1994, 63). The colonial governments in both Cuba and Puerto Rico were large, professionalized, and overwhelmingly Spanish.

The informality of law and government, particularly the lack of records, in Dominican territory shocked Spanish authorities who were arriving from Cuba. "The Government has not provided me with the data for which I have asked and which are indispensable, public archives have not been at my disposition, no collection of laws exists, nor even historical books . . . , [and there] are no statistics, not even approximated ones," José Malo de Molina complained. He could not procure court records, either. Even the Catholic Church's archive was "nothing more than a few Council books, almost all illegible, and a few boxes in really poor condition," another concerned Spanish official wrote.[30] The existing laws, based on the more recent Bourbon restoration codes, had been only inconsistently translated and applied; it was "almost always an imaginary thing, and administration is more often through common sense or custom," Malo de Molina sniffed.[31] "Laws are absolutely lacking," Governor Serrano echoed, calling the overlapping legal codes an "unintelligible chaos."[32] Malo de Molina continued, "For all its written laws, the Government nonetheless has been really just verbal, and the highest-ranking officials condescend to dictating the smallest details. . . . The four Ministers of State have just one [assistant] of whom they can't even ask very much, given the stingy and insufficient state salaries. The employees are such just to avoid military service, and even high dignitaries had to dedicate themselves to commerce or another occupation to provide them with subsistence."[33] Malo de Molina fretted at the lack of credentials required to preside over the courts and other irregularities. Serrano hastily appointed the archivist of public works in Cuba to a new secretarial post in the capital.[34]

Royal decrees established Santo Domingo's Real Audiencia and other parts of the administration in October 1861. As promised, the civil code of Spain ruled, replacing the French-Haitian civil code that had technically been in place since 1822 (Spanish authorities first translated it into Spanish, but they repressed the publication of articles about civil marriage).[35] Municipal juntas were to govern in the small cities of the island, with five civilians and three military officials (although just six had been established by early 1862).[36] Law divided Dominican territory into six military districts; neighboring Cuba had more than thirty.[37] The island was linked by weekly steamship service to Puerto Rico and Cuba, but the ferrying of internal mail was another matter entirely. The roads throughout the republic, which were in poor condition often to the point of being impassable where they existed, presented a significant challenge. Expanding the mail system generated a tremendous paper trail in Spanish correspondence, and the budget for mail services quickly rose above ten thousand pesos annually.[38]

General Pedro Santana, former president of the independent territory, continued as head of state, and Spanish officials explicitly agreed that other Dominican officials would be integrated into the new colonial administration. In the first months of the occupation, it was so.[39] Malo de Molina made recommendations for two Supreme Court judges (both Dominicans of "notorious integrity"); in his report, Governor Serrano named nineteen more officials, just five of them from Havana.[40] Santana's former vice president became a field marshal, and a handful of former ministers from the independence period joined the Real Audiencia.[41] Two prominent Dominicans held high civil governor positions in the capital and in Santiago de los Caballeros. Still others remained in provisional posts closely linked with Santana.[42] Appointments were contingent on a number of measures to professionalize the positions. Dominican ministers, at least in theory, were to be paid more, and they were no longer to engage in other professions while in office. Commissioner Malo de Molina drafted salaries for Real Audiencia legislators and other governors at levels significantly higher than their current pay; eventually, the salaries were fixed to be comparable to those of Puerto Rico.[43] Judges were to serve and be housed in the same building as the Audiencia because in so doing they would "be more respectable, avoid the trouble of having to find them in their homes . . . and keep them from [undesirable living conditions] and inconvenient favors."[44]

The loyalist response to annexation, particularly in the capital, was effusive. Ten prominent Dominican residents of the capital formed an ad hoc Economic Committee to advise treasury officials. Their acceptance letters were effusive. Pedro Ricart y Torres wrote enthusiastically:

> As a loyal servant of my country and the Queen; as an enthusiastic co-participant in the political transformation that has just taken place and that opens to Santo Domingo a vast opportunity to better its luck and change the sad situation . . . It will be my true pleasure to cooperate with my small component of insight and experience in the noble and difficult enterprise. . . . I cannot go without mentioning my feelings of gratitude that I, as a son of this soil, feel at hearing the praise you have for its inhabitants, whose self-denial, loyalty, and sacrifice ought to earn that estimation from all patriotic and educated Spaniards.[45]

Incorporation represented a "mission . . . as grave as it was delicate," admonished Ricart y Torres, himself a prominent landowner and former minister during the ex-republic. "The transition from one system of government to another by the offspring of the same mother must be conducted as smoothly as possible, in the family," he wrote. Electing the right high officials demanded care, he continued, but it ought to be done "without losing sight of public opinion or of honorable men who have made great sacrifices over many years to regain the autonomy of this brave pueblo that owes its name, religion, language and civilization to the same raza in whose arms they return."[46]

An expeditionary brigade had gathered on the island by late spring 1861, which included Spanish soldiers from the peninsula, Cuba, and Puerto Rico; there was also a Militia of Color, origin not recorded. Spanish troops arrived in the capital, San Cristobal, Azua, Samaná, Puerto Plata, and Santiago de los Caballeros, soon constituting a standing force of ten thousand. Even the capital, however, offered gravely insufficient housing. Soldiers were forced to split off into the convent, the basements of the courthouse, fort, and palace, and other temporary shelter. In

Samaná they stayed in seventeen huts (*bohíos*); in Puerto Plata, they took refuge in two government houses and another rented one.[47] In territory with difficult and minimal infrastructure for wheeled transport and an overwhelmingly subsistence economy, provisions were no easier to procure. "They are forced to import everything, even bricks," one diplomat reported. Flour was imported from the United States, "all manner of merchandise" arrived from Europe, and medicines were exceedingly difficult to obtain. Prices were high; a saddle cost 150 *pesos fuertes*, "even as the fields are full of cattle," he observed grimly.[48] "The people of the country maintain themselves generally on wild plants [*viandas*] and free-range pigs," an officer explained, and "articles of primary necessity are not just in shortage, but the few that are around are sold at really outrageous prices." The corps sought additional supplies from Cuba, Puerto Rico, and Saint Thomas, but the official asserted that "the troops and even the Commanders and Officers have suffered hunger and privation without measure from this matter."[49] Incoming administrators were generally unimpressed with the capital. Even the archbishop's house and the Convent of Santa Clara were in ruins, and the government buildings were little better.[50] Few houses had much furniture at all (Dhormoys 1859, 90). Coconut-oil lighting had only barely been introduced the year before; outside of the capital, most of the rest of the cities and towns probably went dark at sundown (Landolfi 1981, 93).

Labor, Capital, and Profit

"There is no country where nature offers more resources, nor where the inhabitants are in a worse state," one Spanish official mused, one year before annexation.[51] When the Cuban governor, Francisco Serrano, arrived from Havana in the summer of 1861, he agreed. "The people are living in such a way that it can even be called miraculous," he marveled. "Uncultivated lands, virgin forests with plants still just as the explorers found them, sparse population, barely any production, industry dead, commerce almost unknown . . . [and] miserable paper money"[52] (Serrano quoted in Rodríguez Demorizi 1955, 245). The governor's parting recommendations—fortification of the Samaná Peninsula, regularization of the government, and economic reform—signaled a fairly ambitious plan for state reorganization of the former republic intended to orient it toward commercial agriculture. "It pains me to see such magnificent terrain, much more fertile than those rightly praised in the Island of Cuba . . . without one generous heart to rebuke the unhappy

Dominicans," wrote another Havana official paternally.[53] Authorities began a flurry of small projects in early months, including new wooden houses in Monte Cristí, a new dock in Santo Domingo, and the groundwork for more infrastructure projects (Bosch 1998, 84).

Officials implemented a mixture of Cuban and Puerto Rican legislation. They decided that direct taxation of residents would be too onerous, opting for sales and other indirect taxes instead, including the lottery, which they noted was popular.[54] Dominican goods became "national" products, along with goods from the rest of the empire.[55] Serrano and other officials urged the regularization of rural landownership, creating registries where possible.[56] Officials looked into the idea of cargo shipments between Cuba, Santo Domingo, and Puerto Rico, and special attention was given to plans for strengthening the defenses of Samaná, which was to be a free port.[57] A steamship connected Santo Domingo to Saint Thomas twice a month; Samaná was linked into a Veracruz–Puerto Rico–Havana route by early fall.[58] Twice-monthly service was supposed to connect the island to Cuba and Cádiz.[59] Travel to Havana on the *Pájaro del Océano* or *Cuba* was available to all those who could buy a ticket on their biweekly voyages. While the lack of pharmacies meant that prohibitively high prices for medicine persisted, military health officials offered civilians basic medical training.[59] Joaquín Manuel del Alba, *intendente* of Puerto Rico, assumed the position of *comisario regio*, where he would serve for the next two years, charged with assessing the financial status of the island and the extent of paper money.[61]

News of the annexation caused a relative stir of excitement among residents in other Spanish territories, mostly over the idea of new investments, large and small, that might be made in the colony. Even as Serrano, Santana, and Molina waited for approval from Spain, news of annexation produced immediate interest. A handful of priests requested transfer to Santo Domingo from Sevilla, Puerto Rico, and Santiago de Cuba, and at least several individuals requested that their pensions be transferred to Santo Domingo.[62] A handful of wealthy Venezuelans, fleeing political unrest, set up plantations on the Ozama River.[63] A British subject sought to profit off of "abandoned" lumber in the center-island region.[64] Others proposed canals, lighthouses, a bridge over the Ozama River in the capital, and gas lighting for all the towns of the island.[65] One wealthy man proposed building a café in the ruins of the capital city theater, another proposed a submarine telegraph cable, Don Vidal from Santiago de Cuba proposed a covered market, and various British capitalists proposed different railroad developments (at least one of which was approved).[66]

Some small-business owners applied for licenses that were already running—suggesting perhaps greater official scrutiny—as Dr. Guillermo Gothburg did for his small pharmacy in Puerto Plata.[67] Other small-scale plans abounded: fabric making, an icehouse (*nevería*), printing presses, and so on. Not every small project gained approval; officials denied a rum maker a license on moral grounds, for example, despite the "extremely backward" state of distillery in the newly annexed territory.[68]

Large-scale projects like coal mining, cotton production, and the fomenting of tobacco cultivation generated huge amounts of official documentation as officials responded to the proposals of interested capitalists and directed their own surveys.[69] Spanish authorities were very interested in Samaná's coal, and they sent teams of military engineers to inspect possible mining sites. The standards and licenses were to mirror Cuban legislation, but experts arrived from Puerto Rico and Spain as well.[70] Several financiers competed for rights to introduce new cotton-processing technology, and the Cotton Association of Manchester offered to send numerous

Figure 8. Coffee bean sheller. (Source: Catálogo Ilustrado de Tredwell y Jones. AGN-RD.)

informational leaflets, translated into Spanish.[71] Another individual requested reimbursement for importing strains of tobacco into Puerto Plata, as had been requested by royal order.[72] Repeated royal orders directed officials to explore the possibility of cotton cultivation, compared agricultural conditions with those in Puerto Rico, and so on.[73] Enthusiastic planters recopied and sent Cuban edicts back to Spanish authorities, asking for the same concessions and promising future profits for Cataluña's cotton mills.[74] Well into the thick of conflict in 1864, mining development efforts and other fomentation schemes, particularly cotton, never ceased.

Immigration and Indenture

Most export agriculture proposals to the Crown involved the prospect of immigration. These plans often detailed schemes of semifree contract labor, moralization schema, and, invariably, white supervision. The Spanish media wrote approvingly of such proposals, suggesting that "freed blacks, African prisoners, Chinese coolies, and Irish settlers" would all be ideal laborers for the colony, under the watchful eyes of Spaniards.[75] Specifics varied. A cotton capitalist sought tools and the importation of *emancipados* to labor on his land; he deferred to the "wisdom of the government" on how to proceed. His own land, already planted, could be "a small example of the richness and fertility of this virgin land," he urged, adding that "with a little manpower, the land could produce torrents of richness."[76] The proposal of another cotton planters association urged, "the island was a source of inexhaustible riches that only needed the strength of . . . colonization based on the principles of morality, police, and order" to thrive.[77] The proposal suggested that black laborers were adapted to the hot climate and that, under watchful white discipline, they would bring the province prosperity. "One thousand or more apprentices of the African nation . . . are the only race who can make Antillean soil productive," the letter writer argued. These "apprentices" would be signed "of their own spontaneous will" to ten- to fifteen-year contracts cultivating cotton and tobacco, "under the same conditions and regulation that Asian colonization has taken place in the neighboring island of Cuba." To oversee the African indentured, the company promised to bring in one "Spanish head of family . . . individuals of good customs, morality, and intelligence" for every ten contract laborers. The association could pay for machinery and nominal taxes for each Spanish colonist, he boasted, as long as land was provided for ten years for free.

The details of one individual's ambitious railroad proposal to connect the Cibao Valley forty miles to the northern coast exemplifies the "racial knowledge" that typified the proposals Spanish authorities received. The railroad industrialist effused antiblack sentiment and fantasies of "coolie" docility. For the hard labor of construction, he called for ten thousand indentured men and women "from Calcutta, Hong Kong, or Cuba," specifically because of the perception that Asian laborers would stay separate from black Dominicans and would also thus serve as a racial bulwark against Haiti.[78] He maintained that these subjects would be more adapted than European emigrants to the climate, and that they might have "convincing moral and political influence" for the entirety of the colonial endeavor, not just the proposed regional railroad. In Cuba, these laborers had "consistently demonstrated that they are not to be confused with the enslaved African race," one high official insisted, concurring.[79]

From the very first days of the reoccupation, Spanish officials and private white industrialists called for large-scale white immigration, too, most often to oversee indentured nonwhite laborers. Authorities liked the idea of Spanish immigration particularly. Individual Spanish settlers might apply for support, and authorities passed laws welcoming white settlers identical to Cuba's.[80] The Spanish consul to Haiti proposed a project of immigration of two to three thousand white individuals from within the "Spanish" community of the US South, especially Florida and Louisiana. He suggested that the government award each family a substantial plot of two to three hundred *caballerías* of land—ostensibly vacant—along with materials to build houses, the state honors afforded to colonizers, and a ten-year reprieve from any kind of tax. The government should also furnish Asian contract laborers as aides, "given that they are already acclimated."[81] The Overseas Ministry quizzed Santana on which professions might be the most useful for potential Spanish émigrés. Authorities felt no compunction telling Santana, himself a man of color, that they envisioned the white race as the motor of the colony's progress. It was "of utmost necessity that the population be increased: luckily, the conditions of the country allow that the white race fulfill this most important need," one official informed him.[82]

Outside capitalists proposed similar schemes of white immigration. William Cazneau, the US agent, proposed a colonization plan of one thousand white families under ten to fifteen years of indenture. "Under the direction of proper superintendents," they would cultivate sugar, cotton, tobacco, and rice, "those species of tropical products for which the fertile soil of Santo Domingo appears so remarkably adapted."[83] The laborers—to "be of an orderly and well-disciplined class"—would follow Spanish law, Cazneau assured his readers. The settlers should be housed on "unappropriated public lands" near the capital, with one square league afforded to each one hundred male laborers between the ages of sixteen and fifty. The advantages of such a project were not just economic, Cazneau wrote, "but also a wholesome example to the existing population of the province . . . able, industrious, and well disciplined." López and Company was one of the companies that sought compensation from the Crown for individual passengers, although they were remonstrated to seek individual approval first.[84] Spanish authorities expressed suspicion about US-led projects, however, and it does not seem that any came to fruition.[85]

Discipline and Leisure

In addition to immigration and indenture schemes, authorities were centrally concerned with inducing Dominicans to labor. Vagrancy preoccupied Spanish authorities and their loyalist allies. In a letter to the arriving authorities, Pedro Valverde described the "drunken scandal and disorder" caused by male vagrants and of "prostitutes and corrupt women whose licentious life significantly affects . . . public morale."[86] Vagrant men eluded prosecution by citing their occasional (weekly or monthly) day labor gigs; the women usually hid behind claims of being washerwomen, pastry sellers, cooks, or servants, Valverde complained. Under the existing laws, vagrants spent a few days in jail in lieu of the fine (that they could not pay); then they returned to the streets once more. New laws proposed that all vagrants be presented to the police, where they would be given work, provided they were of age, and beggars were to seek a license proving disability.[87] Valverde sought harsher sentences still. He wanted three-time vagrants to be deported to Samaná for one year. Valverde also argued that foreigners should have to have a guarantor vouch for them, just like in Puerto Rico, followed by steadily renewable provisional licenses—available at a small fee—for the first year of their residence. They should be deported entirely for vagrancy, he continued.[88] Valverde's zeal was praised by other authorities, if not the specifics of his plan. Sending vagrants to nearly deserted Samaná would "simply put them in a place where they could not work, rather than inculcate in them the desire to do so," one reply concluded, expressing caution about the rights of foreign residents who antedated Spanish reoccupation.[89]

In August 1861, Santana signed into law an extensive antigaming bill, which legislators borrowed directly from codes in the neighboring islands. "It has come to my attention . . . that there are frequent meetings of people of all classes to engage in the pernicious vice of game playing," the bill began. "I am responsible to Her Majesty Our Queen (God protect Her) . . . to repress and correct this vice." The ordinances banned all games, even legal ones, from most public businesses, imposing a stiff penalty of 250 pesos. Public officials, civic or military, faced the same fine; others owed sixty pesos, all doubled for repeat offenses. Loss of businesses and even exile loomed for three-time offenders. Finally, the bill laid out explicit instructions for registration of the offenders' names and steps to prosecution.[90] The fines had to be paid in pesos fuertes, not paper money, authorities emphasized. Other provisions extended the ban to all games of luck, *rayuela* (hopscotch), dog-fighting, gaming during work hours, prostitution, and even boisterous behavior during theater performances. Some new provisions, like the banning of clothing to impersonate public officials or of masks (outside of festivals), represented clear security concerns. Others strictures sought control of leisure, especially in public and semipublic spaces. Cockfights could only be held with a license. Dances, too, required licenses, and the *holandés, danois, tango,* and *tambulá* dances were of particular concern. Along with *jodú*, they caused "frequent scandal," authorities alleged, and were to be held by permission only.[91] *Jodú* remained totally prohibited. Some provisions, like Article 69—which banned "using dress that pertains to another sex, class, or category that is not one's own"—arguably implied legal distinctions that were not supposed to be operative in the colony at all.[92]

Other new statutes created new costs, supervision, and the threat of fines for Dominicans living in towns. School administrators, merchants, street vendors, and other small enterprises required licensing. Female cooks, washerwomen, and sweets and fruit sellers were to register with their local municipality.[93] Midwives who wanted to continue to practice their skill were to present themselves to the newly formed Medicine Committee, where they would pay twenty pesos for the title. In addition, the women were expected to report the sex of the baby, the address, and other details immediately or face a stiff fine.[94] Family heads were expected to independently report their household numbers as well. Even visiting sailors were expected to register with authorities.[95] Residents were further expected to adhere to a number of public health provisions (from dampening their stoops twice daily during dry spells to adhering to a ban on throwing laundry water into the street), and public nudity, even for small children or when bathing animals in the river, was explicitly prohibited. Architects were to vet blueprints with authorities. The new, albeit small, force of watchmen in Santo Domingo and other towns implemented these laws and increased state contact with town residents. In Santo Domingo, they enforced minor rules (such as one stating that doors to the street should open inward), announced the time hourly, and conducted a rudimentary census of the city center, counting 686 brick houses and 767 huts.[96]

Authorities intended to rebuild and expand the colony's prison system. The first change was literally nominal, as town jails across the island acquired names like the "Royal Prison of Azua." The conditions in the territory's few prisons were atrocious, reflecting an absolute lack of resources since the republican period; the arrival (and imprisonment) of Spanish soldiers exacerbated the problem of space, conditions, and supplies.[97] In Santo Domingo, prisoners complained of the rations, which were only a half pound of raw meat and five platanos a day amid gloomy, humid conditions and terrible smells. After repeated inquiries, authorities nominated a full-time commissioner to monitor the conditions.[98] In Santiago de los Caballeros, prisoners had survived during the period of the republic on fifty *papeletas* (the devalued paper currency) and family aid. After 1861, prisoners received one peseta daily, but the amount was wholly insufficient for imprisoned peninsular soldiers, who had no family to bring them meals. Officials observed that they were obliged to beg for money as they cleaned the streets and performed other menial tasks.[99] After months of delay, the allocation was increased.[100] Blueprints for new prisons, civil and military, arrived from Madrid for Samaná and other sites.[101] Still, officials continued to ask that money for prisoners' upkeep be paid in advance, so paltry were the rations and unhealthy the conditions of the jails, and complaints continued into 1863 and 1864.[102] Some individuals languished for a year or more in detention with no trial.[103]

Slowly, authorities' vision for prison reform transformed to include a segment of prisoners serving long sentences elsewhere in the Spanish Empire, as these prisoners were ideal candidates for the reintroduction of prison labor on public works projects. The Cuban governor ordered a brigade of a hundred prisoners to rebuild government buildings in the Dominican capital almost immediately.[104] The Samaná Peninsula in particular—strategic as it was for ships arriving from Spain and Havana—received prisoners from various corners of the Spanish Empire. The first East Asian prisoner ordered to Samaná was probably twenty-three-year-old "Antonio" from Macau, who had already begun to serve a ten-year sentence in Cuba for the murder of another man on a plantation. He was transferred to Santo

Domingo in the fall of 1861.[105] More Chinese prisoners arrived in groups of twenty or thirty.[106] The jail soon housed prisoners from Cádiz, Puerto Rico, and Cuba serving long sentences; they were destined to work in mines and the fortification of the bay itself.[107] The East Asian prisoners in Samaná did not have enough to eat, especially given the "rude" nature of their prison labor, Santana wrote.[108] A handful escaped immediately after they arrived, and their capture often entailed serious bodily harm.[109] In Azua, as in Samaná, sometimes foreign prisoners fled together with Dominican nationals, who likely were able to serve as guides for the group; Spanish officials gave pointed phenotypic descriptions of such escapees.[110] Documentation is sparse regarding the specific public works projects on which prisoners were made to work, but it is clear that officials in the capital, including the antivagrancy champion Pedro Valverde, quickly came to rely on prisoners' labor and even squabbled over their allocation to different projects.[111] More than six hundred prisoners crowded Samaná's prison by fall 1863.[112]

A Sacred Decree . . . a Categorical Prohibition

For all of the public proclamations about Santo Domingo as the "free" Spanish territory, not only was isolating the colony from slavery difficult, but the attitude of some Spanish authorities about legal freedom proved chillingly cavalier. For example, the Spanish consul in Haiti allegedly remarked to other diplomats not only that fugitive slaves from Cuba and Puerto Rico would be sought out and apprehended but that slavery would be reestablished, and even the descendants of slaves could be reenslaved. Although his statements flew in the face of the actual annexation statutes, they reflected the ease with which some Spanish authorities imagined such an eventuality.[113] Other Spanish authorities wrestled—often secretly, in classified documents—with the problem of unequal status between their three Caribbean colonies. They decided that Santo Domingo should be kept as separate as possible from its plantation neighbors. Meanwhile, repeated public decrees promised that abolition remained a "sacred guarantee . . . a categorical prohibition [against slavery]" on Dominican soil.[114]

In June 1861, fearing that enslaved men and women might flee to Santo Domingo, the queen issued a royal decree banning the entry into Santo Domingo of free people of color from Cuba and Puerto Rico. Such self-emancipation was a very reasonable fear for Spanish authorities, given the record of people doing just that from Puerto Rico, Martinique, British islands, and the US South during the previous several decades (Lora Hugi 2012, 127; Asaka 2012; Kerr-Ritchie 2013).[115] A local committee to verify a person's status would likely have been unpopular, impossible, or both. In fact, a secret edict insisted that under no circumstances could any search be conducted for escaped slaves who might have taken refuge in Santo Domingo, because it would stir tremendous panic among Dominicans.[116] Initially, Dominican authorities did not support the new prohibition of free travelers of color, arguing that the race-based prohibition was unnecessary and even alarming. Santana argued that the matter was "of utmost transcendence and offensive to public morality, [capable of] causing all manner of distrust."[117] Allowing free people of color to enter the colony would "give the men of color of this Province a better guarantee by calming the spirits of the suspicious," he urged, "whose fears, even if they stem from lamentable ignorance, were no less easy to spread by malevolent men among the simple masses of that part of the population." At the Dominican governor's insistence, it does seem that the travel ban was temporarily suspended in the fall of 1861.

Quickly, however, the prohibition proved necessary to prevent a practice that officials had not foreseen: the deception of wealthy colonists and authorities, arriving from Cuba and Puerto Rico, who were trying to sneak enslaved people into Santo Domingo, one by one. Government officials and Spanish officers often arrived with their families, and sometimes they brought domestic servants whose status was questionable.[118] One such case, of María Lucas Soto, reached the desk of authorities. Soto, abused by her female mistress after their arrival from Puerto Rico, fled and sought help. Upon examination of her case, authorities determined that "a number of other families have subsequently arrived in the capital with individuals of color as maids. . . . A [possible] pretext for better hiding slavery." Authorities averred that it was "essential that authorities redouble their zeal and adopt strict measures on a matter of so much transcendence."[119] Soto's abusive mistress managed to have her case dropped for lack of evidence, but Dominican officials observed that Soto was to "enjoy the full rights of liberty and the legal guarantees of all people *sui generis*" in Santo Domingo.[120] Authorities all over the island received a firm reminder that both men and women of color were strictly prohibited from entry and that all maids were to be presented to authorities as soon as they disembarked, so that officials could examine their passports. A royal order from Spain on December 4, 1861 reiterated the ban. Nevertheless, incidents continued in which slave owners employed "noticeably altered passports" in attempting to sneak in enslaved women as family members.[121] Dominican officials shared the concern. Sometime in the fall of 1861, Santana changed his position to support the ban himself; in fact, he even argued that it should be extended to include people of color arriving from Curaçao.

Violations, however, continued occurring at the very highest levels of the colonial administration. Malo de Molina himself—the same commissioner charged by the Cuban governor to study and ingratiate himself into the transitioning administration—flagrantly ignored the law. Civil governor Pedro Valverde, a Dominican of some standing, who had received royal honors for his role in the annexation, protested that Malo de Molina and another Cuban official had traveled with maids without notifying authorities.[122] When Valverde sent word to the two men to send the women to the government offices for paperwork inspection, Malo de Molina responded defiantly: if Valverde wanted to meet his maids, he retorted, he should come to his house personally.[123] Valverde, himself a prominent man, bristled at this hostile comportment. "I would have punished this discourtesy and the disrespect that it represents as it merits, if it had not fallen on no less than the Fiscal of Her Majesty," he protested. He was indignant of the challenge to his station. "I know how to fulfill the job with which Her Majesty the Queen (God protect her) has deigned to distinguish me, and I will execute it even at the price of my life, which I would happily sacrifice as long as it were in the fulfillment of my obligations and respecting the highest authority," he insisted. Santana delicately encouraged Valverde to persist in inspection, although the resolution is not clear. The matter was handled quietly, and the prohibition against free people of color definitively reinstated.

It is difficult to determine how the expanded travel ban was or was not enforced; probably, it was targeted primarily at white Spanish travelers arriving in the capital with an entourage, or at individual migrant travelers of color reaching the northern coast. Certainly, it could not have been directed at every Dominican of color who traveled to and from the island; it seems likely that the regular travelers to Saint Thomas and Curaçao must have been granted some sort of individual pass, for example, or were otherwise able to easily establish their residence and status. Poorer, more infrequent, and more inexperienced travelers must have had a more difficult time, however. In one such instance, Julieta Enriquez, described as a *parda* originally from Curaçao, discovered to her dismay that she could not return to her children in the fall of 1862. When attempting to return from a sojourn in Curaçao, she was detained upon arrival in Puerto Plata. Subsequently, she was sent to Mayagüez—a Puerto Rican town, where she likely knew no one, far from her family, and where slavery persisted—to wait for nearly a month for permission to reenter Santo Domingo, while officials verified the existence and whereabouts of her two children. Although she was finally allowed to reunite with them and return to her home, the ordeal must have been arduous and traumatizing for the entire family.[124] These conflicts, present from the earliest days of Spanish reoccupation, soon multiplied.

Conclusion

Because of the aborted early history of plantation slavery in colonial Santo Domingo, as well as the transient nature of Spanish reoccupation, few historians have grappled with Dominican elites' nineteenth-century development dreams, which remained largely unrealized. These dreams reflect a history of subjugation on Dominican soil that became easy to disavow in later decades. Dominican elites shared these aspirations with Haitian elites as well, another lesser-told narrative from Hispaniola in these decades, and their hunger for cash crops in these years represented a harbinger of the sugar investment that reached Dominican territory by the early 1870s (Nicholls 1974, 11). Just as most Haitians largely succeeded in defending rural autonomy in the west, however, so did rural Dominicans resist these potentially cataclysmic transformations. In the next months of occupation, Spanish authorities continued to privilege literate subjects and disenfranchise others, rigidify the laws in urban centers, rebuild and expand the prison system, tighten military discipline, foment immigration schemes, enforce strict religious reforms, and restrict the travel of free people of color to the territory. Compounding these restrictions and indignities were the often blundering, insensitive, and racist actions of Spanish authorities themselves, whose actions belied their experiences in the neighboring colonies and their fundamental unease with emancipated subjects. Soldiers and administrators were "accustomed" to these prejudices, one general observed, and they "did not hesitate to manifest as much" (de la Gándara y Navarro 1884, 238). In response, Dominicans mounted a monumental resistance, in steady collaboration with allies across the island. Spanish authorities considered the fields to be "abandoned," finding little other than "pure forests designated for cattle and pig raising."[125] After Spanish withdrawal in 1865, life in these rural expanses continued uninterrupted for decades more.

Notes

1. This chapter is excerpted and adapted from chapters 2 and 3 of *We Dream Together: Dominican Independence, Haiti, and the Fight for Caribbean Freedom* (Durham: Duke University Press, 2016). I am grateful to Gisèle Suzor-Morin for her help transforming the footnotes.

2. Spain's 1812 constitution proposed the transformation of the American colonies into representative provinces, albeit with unequal representation. Even though it excluded men of African ancestry from citizenship, Cuban planters had opposed it, associating constitutionalism with abolitionism. Implementation stalled, anyway, as independence vitiated the empire. In 1837, Caribbean representatives were expelled from Madrid's Cortes altogether. The overseas territories were ruled in a state of exception for the next several decades, despite the promise of "special laws" to bring the colonies back under constitutional rule: Josep M. Fradera, "Why Were Spain's Special Overseas Laws Never Enacted?," in *Spain, Europe, and the Atlantic: Essays in Honour of John H. Elliott*, ed. Richard L. Kagan and Geoffrey Parker (New York: Cambridge University Press, 1995), 334–49, 338, 348; Josep M. Fradera, "Reading Imperial Transitions: Spanish Contraction, British Expansion, and American Interruption," in *Colonial Crucible: Empire in the Making of the Modern American State*, ed. Alfred W. McCoy and Francisco Scarano (Madison: University of Wisconsin Press, 2009), 34–62, 57; Rafael Marquese and Tâmis Parron, "Atlantic Constitutionalism and the Ideology of Slavery: The Cádiz Experience in Comparative Perspective," in *The Rise of Constitutional Government in the Iberian Atlantic World*, ed. Scott Eastman et al. (Tuscaloosa: University of Alabama Press, 2015), 177–93, 184; Christopher Schmidt-Nowara, *Empire and Anti-slavery: Spain, Cuba, and Puerto Rico, 1833–1874* (Pittsburgh: University of Pittsburgh Press, 1999), 25.

3. Cruzat to Felipe Rivero, SD [Santo Domingo], August 15, 1862, Archivo Nacional de Cuba (hereafter, ANC): Audiencia de la Habana 245, Expte. 2.

4. Serrano to Min. de Guerra y Ultramar, Habana, September 5, 1861, Archivo Histórico Nacional (hereafter, AHN): Ultramar 5485, Expte. 16, doc. 1, 4.

5. In the first half of the nineteenth century, European markets were a "global cotton-growing countryside . . . grown by slave labor" (Beckert 2015, 226).

6. The doubling of the price of raw cotton from 1848 to 1857 had driven Manchester merchants to look to new supplies and become somewhat less enamored with laissez-faire dicta generally. Joint-stock companies to fund cotton in other parts of the empire sprang up. Ventures in West Africa included a failed cotton project in Senegal in earlier decades, an uptick of intervention in Dahomey and southwestern Nigeria, and other projects of so-called legitimate commerce, as missionaries and imperial adventurers bedecked their ventures with a cloying humanitarian veneer. Small-scale production of cotton in West Africa dated to antiquity, but the tide of imperial imports impeded proto-industrialization; by 1850, British merchants flooded West African markets with thirty times more finished

cotton goods than in previous decades (Ratcliffe 1982, 87, 91; Inikori 2009, 89; Hopkins [1973] 2014, 128, 137–38).

7. *Le Moniteur Haïtien*, no. 10 (February 9, 1861), 3.

8. My thanks to Kate Marsh for her clarification of French Caribbean statistics.

9. In 1863, nearly three thousand Barbadians left the island as indentured laborers to multiple sites; in an attempt to prevent future migrations, planters opposed political federation with the other British Islands in the next decade (Brown 2005, 44; Levy 1980). On the case of Antigua, see Lightfoot 2015.

10. Geffrard gave Redpath $20,000 to open an emigration bureau in Boston; it was decked with "mahogany splendor," probably from the island itself (Alexander 2010, 70–75; Dixon 2000).

11. Capitalist Bernard Kock, who had been leasing Ile-à-Vache, sought fifty dollars per person for up to fifty thousand émigrés. Privately, the Haitian minister in Washington, DC, was instructed to avoid any such massive-scale migration, although he need not have worried. Smallpox, mismanagement, and corruption crippled, then ended, the project (Logan 1941, 308–10).

12. Costa Rica and Nicaragua: Robinson, "The Chinese of Central America," 107, 113. Panama: Meagher, *The Coolie Trade*, 272. Although abolition legislation was passed in Colombia in 1851, the legislation took effect in early 1852; the *concierto* system of apprenticeship was abolished simultaneously (Jason McGraw, personal communication, November 7, 2015). Trinidad and Tobago: Roberts and Byrne, "Summary Statistics on Indenture," 127. The earliest contract schemes under British rule date to 1806 (Allen, "Slaves, Convicts, Abolitionism," 6). Jamaica: Roberts and Byrne, "Summary Statistics," 127; Schuler 1980; Anderson, "The Diaspora of Sierra Leone's Liberated Africans," 117–18. British Guiana: Roberts and Byrne, "Summary Statistics," 127. Some regional migrants arrived without contracts (pre-1846 and in 1864) (Richardson, "Freedom and Migration"; Brown, "Experiments in Indenture," 48). Barbados was a site of indenture emigration briefly (Brown, "Experiments in Indenture," 44). Saint Vincent, Grenada, Dominica, British Honduras: Roberts and Byrne, "Summary Statistics," 127; Robinson, "Chinese of Central America," 108. Antigua: the long dates reflect Madeiran migration more than smaller numbers from other places, which occurred in the early 1860s (Brown, "Experiments in Indenture," 42; Roberts and Byrne, "Summary Statistics," 127; Robinson, "Chinese of Central America," 108; Lightfoot 2015, 172). Saint Kitts: 1860–65 are the dates of Indian indentured migration (Steven Vertovek, "Indian Indentured Migration," 59); Madeira Island and African migration may have been longer (Roberts and Byrne, "Summary Statistics," 127). The Turks and Caicos: dates refer to changes in the salt rights system after emancipation that resulted in the predominance of truck system payments and bonded debt labor through the early twentieth century (*Laws of the Turks and Caicos Islands* [London: Saunders, Otley and Co., 1862)] 85–86, 415–16, 438; http://tcmuseum.org/slavery/emancipation-beyond/, accessed June 2015). Saint Croix,

indenture and Labour Act restrictions: Roopnarine, "The First and Only Crossing"; Roopnarine, "A Comparative Analysis of Two Failed Indenture Experiences," 207. Martinique and Guadeloupe: Marsh 2012; Saint Lucia, Guyane: Vertovek, "Indian Indentured Migration to the Caribbean," 59. Suriname: the 1931 date refers to the end of penal sanction (Hoefte, "Labour in the Caribbean," 259, 262; Hoefte, personal communication, January 3, 2016). Puerto Rico: dates refer to *libreta* controls; indenture projects were popular proposals in the 1860s but never materialized (Schmidt-Nowara 1999, 38; Figueroa, *Sugar, Slavery and Freedom*, 166–69). Brazil: the various dates refer to fragmented indenture schemes targeting liberated African and Chinese individuals (Mamigonian, "To Be a Liberated African in Brazil"). In 1855, Bahian sugar planters sent an emissary to China; one boatload of laborers arrived in 1855 (Meagher, *Coolie Trade*, 146, 266). In 1883, short-lived renewed Chinese indenture plans fizzled (Meagher, *Coolie Trade*, 269). United States: end dates refer to the end of the convict lease system in Alabama and may well be extended forward (for more on convict labor, see LeFlouria, *Chained in Silence*). Mexico: the 1870 date refers to debt labor in Yucatán, although there is considerable debate as to whether this constituted indenture (Levy, *The Making of a Market*, 48). Peru: Meagher, *Coolie Trade*, 40. Ecuador: Townsend, "In Search of Liberty," and Townsend, personal communication, January 3, 2016. Haiti's dates refer to the projects of *caporalisme agraire* of the earliest days of independence as well as to King Henri Christophe's militarized labor control in his northern kingdom, but they do not extend to subsequent rural codes, as land distribution and flight from plantations were extensive (see, e.g., Nicholls, *From Dessalines to Duvalier*, 68; González, *War on Sugar*).

13. *Le Moniteur Haïtien*, nos. 26–27, June 12, 1858, 2. Police were to verify the travel pass (*permis de route*) of any individual in the interior (*Le Moniteur Haïtien*, no. 24, May 21, 1859, 2).

14. "Le secretaire d'Etat au département de l'interieur et de l'agriculture, aux inspecteurs et sous-inspecteurs de culture de la République," *Le Moniteur Haïtien*, no. 27, June 11, 1859, 6.

15. Serrano to Min. de Guerra y Ultramar, Habana, August 16, 1861, AHN: Ultramar 5485, Expte. [Expediente, case file, hereafter Expte.] 14, Doc. 1, p. 4. "Every day they are happier to be part of the big Spanish family," he reported.

16. "Industria," *El Dominicano*, no. 1, June 29, 1855, 4; *El Oasis*, no. 2, December 4, 1854, 5.

17. Juan B. Zafra to Santana, November 17, 1862, Archivo General de la Nación–República Dominicana (hereafter, AGN-RD): Anexión 11 (DE/1800), Expte. 21. Land privatization support: "Artículo Primero," *El Dominicano*, no. 11, September 15, 1855, 41; "División de propriedad," *El Dominicano*, no. 13, September 29, 1855, 49.

18. Eduardo Alonso y Colmenares (Regente de la Real Audiencia de Santo Domingo) to Min. de Guerra y Ultramar, SD, January 8, 1862, AHN: Ultramar 3532, Expte. 8, doc. 2.

19. Manuel de Jesús Galván to Cap. Gen., January 20, 1862, AGN-RD: Anexión Leg. 11 (DE/1800), Expte. 40, doc. 2.

20. Pedro Valverde to Gob. Sup. Civil, February 8, 1864, AGN-RD: Anexión 26, Expte. 23.

21. Gob. Sup. Civil, to Pedro Valverde, September 5, 1863, AGN-RD: Anexión 23 (000149), Expte. 11.

22. Felipe Rivero to Min. de la Guerra y Ultramar, SD, February 2, 1863, AHN: Ultramar 3542, Expte. 1, Doc. 4.

23. Minuta de Real Orden (reservada), from Min. de la Guerra y Ultramar to Teniente Gral D. Felipe Rivero, June 19, 1862, AHN: Ultramar 3525, Expte. 14.

24. Mariano Álvarez, "Memoria: Santo Domingo o la República Dominicana." SD, April 20, 1860, AHN: Ultramar 2775, Expte. 16, p. 4. Henceforth Álvarez, *Memoria*.

25. Fontecha Pedraza and González Calleja, *Una cuestión de honor*, 75, 87.

26. Noel Henriquez to the Queen, London, November 9, 1862, AGN-RD: Anexión 25, 10.

27. *Les intérêts français et européens à Santo Domingo* (Paris: E. Dentu, 1861).

28. Consul Hood to Lord J. Russell, SD, April 8, 1861, AGN-RD: Anexión DE 000933, Expte. 5, p. 16; Consul Hood to Lord J. Russell, SD, April 21, 1861, AGN-RD: Anexión DE 000933, Expte. 9, p. 27.

29. The budget of the colonial state in Cuba and Puerto Rico "ballooned . . . to pay a bloated bureaucratic corps" from 1840 to 1860. Cuban and Puerto Rican taxes were high—in Cuba, as much as four times what the average peninsular resident paid (Martínez-Fernández 1994, 62).

30. Eduardo Alonso y Colmenares to Min. de Ultramar, SD, February 16, 1862, AHN: Ultramar 3545, Expte. 1, doc. 12.

31. Malo de Molina to Serrano, *Memoria*, 15. Henceforth Malo de Molina, *Memoria*. Interestingly, he suggests that the Dominican government might have chosen to continue with the French codes after separation from Haiti in 1844 because they were timorous of Spanish reoccupation and slavery (14), although just one page later, he suggests that the very reason for annexation was that the populace was eager to introduce the Spanish code in 1861.

32. Francisco Serrano to the Ministro de Guerra y Ultramar, 6 September 1861, AHN: Ultramar 3532, Expte. 2, doc. 2, 5. Henceforth Serrano, *Resultado*.

33. José Malo de Molina to Cap. Gen. Francisco Serrano, September 4, 1861 (July 15, 1861), AHN: Ultramar 3532, Expte. 1, doc. 2, 17. Hereafter cited as Malo de Molina, *Memoria*.

34. Real Orden de 7 de Oct. 1861, AHN: Ultramar 3531, Expte. 24.

35. Real Orden de 6 Oct. 1861, AHN: Ultramar 3532, Expte. 3; *Gaceta de Santo Domingo*, no. 92, June 12, 1862, 1; Alonso y Colmenares to Gob. Sub. Civil, SD, June 14, 1862, AGN-RD: Anexión Leg. 8, Expte. 29.

36. Expte. sobre organización y regimen municipals, September 1, 1861–November 14, 1863, AHN: Ultramar 3535, Expte. 3.

37. "Organización y planta de los gobiernos, comandancias militares y de armas de la Isla de Santo Domingo," Ministro de Guerra, 26 de Junio de 1862, AHN: Ultramar 3527,

Expte. 51, doc. 9. These were the five extant provinces (Santo Domingo, Santiago, Azua, la Vega, Seibo) and a new one, the commercial coast of Puerto Plata.

38. Felipe Rivero to Min. de Guerra y Ultramar, July 6, 1862. AHN: Ultramar 2785, Expte. 8, doc. 1.

39. Ministerio de Estado to Serrano, April 24, 1861, in Gaspar Núñez de Arce, *Santo Domingo* (Marrickville, NSW, Australia: Wentworth Press, 2019), 56–60.

40. Malo de Molina, *Memoria*, 64; Serrano, *Resultado*, 51–56.

41. Other founding members included José María Morilia, a lawyer (Spanish, practicing in Havana) and Ramón de la Torre Trassierra (ex-mayor in Philippines). Real Orden de 6 Octubre de 1861, in *Gaceta del Notoriado Español* (Madrid: Imprenta de D. Ramón Campuzano, 1861), 3:637.

42. Serrano to Min. de Guerra, Habana, September 1, 1861, AHN: Ultramar 3526, Expte. 3; Luis Álvarez López, *Dominación colonial y guerra popular, 1861–1865: La anexión y la restauración en la historia dominicana* (Santo Domingo: Editora de Universidad Autónoma de Santo Domingo), 78.

43. The mayor of Santo Domingo, making an estimated $20 a month at the time of annexation ($240 yearly), would have made $3,500 annually, according to his plan, for example. Serrano, *Memoria*, 17, 45–47, 50; Anexo 3 (3532.1 Expte. 1, doc. 5); Santana to Min. de Guerra, July 7, 1862, AHN: Ultramar 3540, Expte. 19.

44. Malo de Molina, *Memoria*, 51.

45. Pedro Ricart Torres to el Comisario (Joaquín Manuel de Alba), SD, November 20, 1861, quoted in Lugo Lovatón, "La junta económica anexionista de 1861," n.p.

46. Joaquín Manuel de Alba. Convocatoria del Comisario Regio Don Manuel Joaquín de Alba, Santo Domingo, November 19, 1861, quoted in Lugo Lovatón, "La junta económica anexionista de 1861," 111.

47. Ramón Blanco to Brig. Peláez (and to Cap. Gen. of Cuba), SD, April 1861, AGI: Cuba 1006B, in AGN-RD: Colección Herrera (hereafter CH), Leg. 21, Folder 172, May 1, 1861, p. 19.

48. Mariano Álvarez, "Memoria: Santo Domingo o la República Dominicana," SD, April 20, 1860, AHN: Ultramar 2775, Expte. 16, p. 4. (henceforth Álvarez, *Memoria*).

49. Ramón Blanco to Brig. Peláez (and to Cap. Gen. of Cuba), SD, April 861, AGI: Cuba 1006B, in AGN-RD: CH, Leg, 21, Folder 172, May 1, 1861, p. 20.

50. Expte. del Gobierno Político, September 1, 1861, AGN-RD: Anexión Leg. 1 (DE/1378), Expte. s/n (old #46).

51. Álvarez, *Memoria*, 4.

52. Serrano, *Informe de la visita a SD*, 245.

53. Memoria of Antonio Peláez y Campomanes to Gob. Serrano, Habana, November 8, 1860, AHN: Ultramar 3526: Expte. 2, doc. 2.

54. The customs rules were changed to Puerto Rican (from Cuban) standards, for example (Manuel de Alba to Min. de Guerra y Ultramar, January 9, 1862, AHN: Ultramar 3528.7; approved by royal order, March 12, 1862). While treasury oversight was delegated to Cuban officials, it was determined that merchants could pay in installments, as per Puerto Rican guidelines, for example (AHN: Ultramar 3528.6, 8). Taxes: Comisario Regio de Hacienda to Min. de Ultramar, February 19, 1862, AHN: Ultramar 3528, Expte. 30. The popular Cuban lottery was introduced as an additional revenue measure (Superintendente Delegado de Hacienda de SD to Serrano, October 16, 1861, AHN: Ultramar 3528, Expte. 2).

55. Cap. Gen. of PR to Min. de Ultramar, June 12, 1861, AHN: Ultramar 1128, Expte. 30.

56. Serrano to Santana, SD, August 8, 1861, AHN: Ultramar 3527, Expte. 4, doc. 3.

57. AHN: Ultramar online 1128:45.

58. Santana to Min. de Guerra, November 28, 1861, Archivo General de Indias (hereafter, AGI): Cuba 1018 (Libro), p. 3; "Secretaria del Gobierno," *Gaceta de Santo Domingo*, no. 50, January 4, 1862, 1.

59. "De Oficio," *Gaceta de Santo Domingo*, no. 51, January 11, 1862, 1.

60. Expte. 119 de la Junta Superior de Medecina, Cirujía y Farmacia, February 18, 1863–64, AGN-RD: Anexión 29, Expte. 37; *Gaceta de Santo Domingo*, no. 56, February 6, 1862, 1.

61. Min de Guerra to Joaquín Manuel del Alba, Madrid, October 7, 1861, AHN: Ultramar 3527, Expte. 57.

62. AHN: Ultramar 3529, Exptes. 13, 14, 15, June-October 1861, Pensions: e.g., AHN: Ultramar 1122, Exptes. 37–38.

63. Mariano Álvarez to Cap. Gen. de Cuba, July 20, 1861, AGI: Cuba 2266, Pieza 1, n.p.

64. Secretaria de Estado to Min. de Guerra y Ultramar, April 4, 1862, AHN: Ultramar 3540, Expte. 16.

65. Minuta de Min. de Guerra y Ultramar, October 5, 1861, AHN: Ultramar 3540, 5; Minuta de Min. de Guerra y Ultramar, October 29, 1861, AHN: Ultramar 3540, doc. 10; Felipe Rivero to Min. de Ultramar February 4, 1863. AHN: Ultramar 3540, Expte. 8; Cap. Gen. de SD to Min de Guerra y Ultramar, December 21, 1862, AHN: Ultramar 3531, Expte. 28.

66. Gob. Superior Civil to Min. de Guerra, SD, January 30, 1862, AGN-RD: Anexión 11 (DE/1800), Expte. 34; AHN: Ultramar 79, Expte. 23, n.p.; Manuel del J. Galván (Expte. del Gob. Sup. Civil), SD, August 19, 1862, AGN-RD: Anexión 11 (DE/1800), Expte. 37; Noel Henriques to Min. de Ultramar, September 29, 1861, AHN: Ultramar 3540, Expte. 4.

67. Manuel de Jésus Galván to Gob. Superior Civil, December 14, 1861, AGN-RD: Anexión 1 (DE/1378), Expte. 31.

68. Pedro Valverde to Gob. Superior Civil, October 13, 1862, AGN-RD: Anexión 26 (DE/000152), Expte. 15. A wealthy Venezuelan immigrant initiated the Dominican

Republic's rum industry in 1852 (Edwin Rafael Espinal Hernández, "Los apellidos del ron: Bérmudez," *Hoy* [Sección Sabatina: Cápsulas Genealógicas], August 29, 2009, http://www.idg.org.do/capsulas/agosto2009/agosto200929.htm, accessed September 18, 2009). For further discussion of rum, see José Chez Checo, *El ron en la historia dominicana* Vol. 2, *Desde los antecedentes hasta finales del siglo XIX* (Santo Domingo: Ediciones Centenario de Brugal, 1988).

69. E.g., Pedro Santana to Sr. Intendente Gral. de Ejercito y Hacienda, SD, August 23, 1861, AHN: Ultramar 6160, Expte. 26; Ministerio de Guerra y Ultramar to Comisario Regio de SD, October 7, 1861, AHN: Ultramar 2785, Expte. 16.

70. Real Decreto de 12 Octubre de 1862, Anexión 26 (DE/000152), Expte. 13.

71. Expediente . . . del Cédula de privilegio a Don Juan A. Cohen, September–October 1861, AGN-RD: Anexión 1 (DE/1378), Expte. 16; Expte. del Gobierno Superior Civil, May 13, 1862, AGN-RD: Anexión 10, Expte. 41. Various government inquests about cotton continued (e.g., Gob. de SD to Min. de Ultramar, May 1862–September 1863, AHN: Ultramar 3542, Expte. 1, docs. 1–8).

72. Jose Rocas to Comisario Regio, April 15, 1861, AGN-RD: Anexión 24 (000150), Expte. 13.

73. Real Orden de 27 de Septiembre de 1863, 22 de Febrero de 1864, in AGN-RD: Anexión 26, Expte. 23.

74. Don Francisco de Olazarra to Cáp. General de SD, January 11, 1862, AGN-RD: Anexión Leg. 11 (DE/1800), Expte. 40.

75. From Felipe Rivero to Min de la Guerra y Ultramar, SD, June 19, 1862, AHN: Ultramar 3525, Expte. 15.

76. Don Francisco de Olazarra to Cáp. General de SD, January 11, 1862, AGN-RD: Anexión Leg. 11 (DE/1800), Expte. 40.

77. [R. Caymare] to Ministro de Ultramar, January 30, 1862, AGN-RD: Anexión 4 (DE/1383), Expte. 20, doc. 1. The proposal, like many others of its kind, demonstrated a total unwillingness to acknowledge the other state of the island, referring instead to the "island of Santo Domingo," "bringing prosperity to the island," and so forth.

78. Eusebio Soler to Gob. Superior Civil, SD, July 4, 1864, AGN-RD: Anexión 16, Expte. 1, doc. 3.

79. Felipe Rivero to Min de la Guerra y Ultramar, SD, June 19, 1862, AHN: Ultramar 3525, Expte. 15.

80. Cuba had a "Junta de Población Blanca" since 1817, although the numbers were somewhat small in the 1850s and 1860s. Dirección de Armamentos del Ministerio de Marina to Min. de Guerra y Ultramar, San Ildefonso, September 19, 1861, AHN: Ultramar 3526, Expte. 4; Serrano to Min. de Guerra, Habana, October 7, 1861, AHN: Ultramar 3625, Expte. 6.

81. Manuel de Cruzat to Felipe Rivero (passed on to the Queen), SD, August 15, 1862, ANC: Audiencia de la Habana, Leg. 245, Expte. 2.

82. Min. de Guerra y Ultramar to Santana, Madrid, August 1, 1861, AHN: Ultramar 5485, Expte. 11.

83. William Cazneau and Joseph Fabens to Ministro de Ultramar, January 2, 1863, AGN-RD: Anexión 4 (DE/1383), Expte. 20, doc. 2. See also AHN: Ultramar 3531, Expte. 42, doc. 2 (a copy); Martínez-Fernández 1994, 217.

84. E.g., Luís Ramírez to Min. de Guerra, Madrid, July 6, 1861, AHN: Ultramar 3527, Expte. 3.

85. From Felipe Rivero to Min de la Guerra y Ultramar, SD, June 19, 1862, AHN: Ultramar 3525, Expte. 15.

86. Pedro Valverde to Gob. Sup. Civil, August 28, 1863, AGN-RD: Anexión 23 (000149), Expte. 11.

87. "Bando de Policia y Gobernación," in *Colección de leyes*, 150.

88. Pedro Valverde to Gob. Sup. Civil, August 28, 1863, AGN-RD: Anexión 23 (000149), Expte. 11.

89. Gob Sup. Civil to Pedro Valverde, September 5, 1863, AGN-RD: Anexión 23 (000149), Expte. 11.

90. Pedro Santana, Bando de 29 de Agosto de 1861, AGI: Cuba 948, "Bandos," doc. s/n. The low-level local administrators called *alcaldes pedáneos* were responsible for supplying the information to their superiors. The edict borrowed directly from such strict legislation as Puerto Rico's 1849 "Bando de Policía y Buen Gobierno," which restricted travel, nighttime activities, and other security measures (Martínez-Fernández 1994, 66).

91. "Bando de Policia y Gobernación," in *Colección de leyes*, 149; Lizardo, *Cultura africana en Santo Domingo* (Santo Domingo: Editora Taller, 1979), 69.

92. "Bando de Policia y Gobernación," 161.

93. "Bando de Policia y Gobernación," in *Colección de leyes*, 150.

94. Expte. "Relativo a las examenes que deben de sufrir las mugeres . . . ," June 24, 1864, AGN-RD: Anexión 29, 2.

95. "Bando de Policia y Gobernación," in *Colección de leyes*, 147.

96. Benito Cuadron to Gob. Político de SD, April 22, 1863, and José Leyba to Gob. Político de SD, June 26, 1863, AGN-RD: Anexión 28, 6. Each was armed with a pistol, a light, and a whistle. Authorities instructed them to listen for insults against authority (*Colección de leyes*, 163–65).

97. Santana to Min. de Guerra y Ultramar, June 15, 1862, AGI: Cuba 1018, p. 108.

98. Eduardo Alonso y Colmenares to Cap. Gen., SD, January 10, 1862, AGN-RD: Anexión 1 (DE/1378), Expte. 12.

99. A soldier from the Crown Regiment, serving a ten-year sentence in Santiago de los Caballeros and without any family to send food, was among the prisoners so poor that Santana feared he would die of hunger, despite his begging for money during street cleaning (Santana to Superintendente Gral. de Ejército y Real Hacienda, December 10, 1861, AHN: Ultramar 2785, Expte. 24, Doc. 3).

100. Comisaria Regia de SD Joaquin M de Alba, to Min. de la Guerra y Ultramar, July 12, 1862, AHN: Ultramar 2785, Expte. 4.

101. Santana to Min. de Guerra, April 30, 1862, AHN: Ultramar 3531, Expte. 33; Real Orden de 19 de Agosto 1862, AGI: Cuba 974A.

102. Joaquín Manuel del Alba to Min. de Guerra, March 10, 1862, AHN: Ultramar 2784, Expte. 42; "Expte promovido por el Regent de la RA relativo a la mala alimentación que se da a los presos de la Real Carcel de esta Capital," Fall 1864, AGN-RD: Anexión 27, Expte. 9.

103. Consul Hood to Cap. Gen. Felipe Rivero, October 7, 1862, AGN-RD: Anexión 4 (DE/1383), Expte. 26.

104. Serrano to Min. de Guerra, July 25, 1861, AGN-RD: Colección Herrera, Leg. 21, Expte. 169, p. 20; Min. de Guerra to Cap. Gen. de Santo Domingo, AHN: Ultramar 3527, Expte. 15.

105. Expediente formado para la plaza de Ministro de Justicia de Santo Domingo, August 1861–February 26, 1863, ANC: AP Leg. 53, Expte. 15.

106. Min. de Guerra to Santana, March 6, 1862, AHN: Ultramar 3626, Expte. 11, doc. 13.

107. Expte. de Ministro de Guerra, October 17, 1861, AHN: Ultramar 3626, Expte. 11, doc. 11.

108. Santana to Min. de Guerra y Ultramar, February 5, 1862, AGI: Cuba 1018, p. 36.

109. Santana to Min. de Guerra y Ultramar, February 5, 1862, AGI: Cuba 1018, p. 35.

110. Sumaria Instruida en averiguación de la fuga del confinado José Poce Camboy, October 1862, AGI: Cuba 1012B; José Hungria to Cap. General, September 5, 1862, AGN-RD: Anexión 28, Expte. 9.

111. Pedro Valverde to Gob. Sup. Civil, January 8, 1863, AGN-RD: Anexión 26, 33; Pedro Valverde to Gob. Sup. Civil., January 28, 1864, AGN-RD: Anexión 29, 16.

112. Cap. Gen de Puerto Rico to Min. de Guerra, PR, November 13, 1863, AHN: Ultramar 3626, Expte. 11, doc. 16.

113. Although this statement was reported secondhand by the British consul—who might, perhaps, have had reason to stir up abolitionist anxieties—it was reportedly said by none other than Manuel Cruzat, the famously racist and difficult former ambassador to Haiti who had almost brought the country to the brink of diplomatic disaster there in the 1850s (Hauch 1947, 251).

114. Regente de la audiencia, Don Eduardo Alonso y Colmenares to Min. de Guerra y Ultramar, sin fecha (spring 1862), AHN: Ultramar 3525, Expte. 13, doc. 4.

115. *El Telegrafo Constitucional*, no. 2, April 12, 1821.

116. Real Orden de 24 de Junio de 1861, Reservado, AHN: Ultramar 5485, Expte. 6.

117. Pedro Santana to Min. de Guerra, February 18, 1862, SHM: Ultramar 5639, Expte. "Esclavitud/Esclavos 1849–1862," doc. s/n.

118. Lower-ranking officers often brought their families, even when embarking from as far away as Madrid. Min. de Guerra to Min. de Ultramar, January 30, 1862, AGN-RD: Anexión 8, 23.

119. Regente de la audiencia, Don Eduardo Alonso y Colmenares to Min. de Guerra y Ultramar, sin fecha (spring 1862), AHN: Ultramar 3525, Expte. 13, doc. 4.

120. Regente de la audiencia, Don Eduardo Alonso y Colmenares to Min. de Guerra y Ultramar, sin fecha (spring 1862), AHN: Ultramar 3525, Expte. 13, doc. 3.

121. Pedro Santana to Min. de Guerra, February 18, 1862, Servicio Histórico Militar (hereafter, SHM): Ultramar 5639, Expte. "Esclavitud/Esclavos 1849–1862," doc. s/n.

122. The Valverdes were a prominent family in Santo Domingo. Valverde had continued in the position since the republic; he is referred to in other Spanish documents as a "persona de buenas circunstancias" and was on the list of prominent men to be rewarded with *gracias* and *cruces* after the annexation (Serrano to Min. de Guerra y Ultramar, Habana, September 1, 1861, AHN: Ultramar Leg. 3526, Expte. 3, Doc. 2; Serrano to Min. de Guerra y Ultramar, 10/7/1861 AHN: Ultramar Leg. 3526, Expte. 10, doc. 5).

123. Gob. Sup. Civil to Pedro Valverde, SD, February 19, 1862, AGN-RD: Anexión 11 (DE/1800), Expte. 27, doc. 1.

124. Gob. Superior Civil de Puerto Rico to Cap. General de SD, November 27, 1862, AGN-RD: Anexión 27, 25.

125. From Felipe Rivero to Min de la Guerra y Ultramar, SD, June 19, 1862, AHN: Ultramar 3525, Expte. 15.

Works Cited

Alexander, Leslie. 2010. "'The Black Republic': The Influence of the Haitian Revolution on Northern Black Political Consciousness." In *African Americans and the Haitian Revolution*, edited by Maurice Jackson and Jacqueline Bacon, 57–80. New York: Routledge.

Álvarez López, Luís. 1986. *Dominación colonial y guerra popular 1861–1865*. Santo Domingo: Universidad Autónoma de Santo Domingo.

Asaka, Ikuko. 2012. "'Our Brethren in the West Indies': Self Emancipated People in Canada and the Antebellum Politics of Diaspora and Empire." *Journal of African American History* 97, no. 3 (Summer): 219–39.

Barry, Sara. 1992. "Hegemony on a Shoestring: Indirect Rule and Access to Agricultural Lands." *Africa* 62, no. 3: 327–55.

Beckert, Sven. 2015. *Empire of Cotton: A Global History*. New York: Knopf.

Bosch, Juan. (1982) 1998. *La Guerra de la Restauración*. 9th ed. Santo Domingo: Editoria Corripio.

Breen, Henry Hegart. 1844. *St. Lucia: Historical, Statistical, and Descriptive*. London: Longman, Brown, Green, and Longmans.

Brown, Laurence. 2005. "Experiments in Indenture: Barbados and the Segmentation of Migrant Labor in the Caribbean, 1863–1865." *New West Indian Guide* 79, nos. 1–2: 31–54.

Calhoun, Ricky-Dale. 2012. "Seeds of Destruction: The Globalization of Cotton as a Result of the American Civil War." PhD diss., Kansas State University.

Dalby, Jonathan R. 2015. "'Such a Mass of Disgusting and Revolting Cases': Moral Panic and the 'Discovery' of Sexual Deviance in Post-Emancipation Jamaica, 1835–1855." *Slavery and Abolition* 36, no. 1: 136–59.

de la Gándara y Navarro, José. 1884. *Anexión y guerra de Santo Domingo*. Madrid: Impresora de "el correo militar."

Dhormoys, Paul. 1859. *Une visite chez Soulouque: Souvenirs d'un voyage dans l'Île d'Haïti*. Paris: Librairie Nouvelle.

Dixon, Chris. 2000. *African Americans and Haiti: Emigration and Black Nationalism in the Nineteenth Century*. Westport, CT: Greenwood Press.

Febres-Cordero Carrillo, Francisco. 2008. "La anexión y la Guerra de Restauración dominicana desde las filas españolas (1861–65)." PhD diss., University of Puerto Rico.

Fontecha Pedraza, Antonio, and Eduardo González Calleja. 2005. *Una cuestión de honor: La polémica sobre la anexión de Santo Domingo vista desde España (1861–1865)*. Santo Domingo: Fundación García Arévalo.

Fryar, Christienna. 2013. "The Moral Politics of Cholera in Postemancipation Jamaica." *Slavery and Abolition* 34, no. 4: 598–618.

Geffrard, Fabre Nicholas. 1859. "Haïtiens!" *Le Moniteur Haïtien*, no. 11 (February 19).

Geffrard, Fabre Nicholas. 1860. "Arrêté." *Le Moniteur Haïtien*, no. 13 (March 3).

Geffrard, Fabre Nicholas. 1861. "Circulaire aux généraux commandant les arrondissements de la République." *Le Moniteur Haïtien*, no. 12 (February 23).

Geffrard, Fabre Nicholas. 1865. "Adresse au peuple et à l'armée." *Le Moniteur Haïtien*, no. 25 (May 20).

Hauch, Charles Christian. 1947. "Attitudes of Foreign Governments towards the Spanish Reoccupation of the Dominican Republic." *Hispanic American Historical Review* 27, no. 2: 247–68.

Hopkins, A. G. (1973) 2014. *An Economic History of West Africa*. New York: Routledge.

Inikori, Joseph. 2009. "English versus Indian Cotton Textiles: The Impact of Imports on Cotton Textile Production in West Africa." In *How India Clothed the World: The World of South Asian Textiles, 1500–1850*, edited by Giorgio Riello and Turthankar Roy, 85–114. Leiden: Brill.

Joseph, F. Jn. 1860. "Rapport." *Le Moniteur Haïtien*, no. 37 (July 18): 1–4.

Jung, Moon-Ho. 2006. *Coolies and Cane: Race, Labor, and Sugar in the Age of Emancipation.* Baltimore: Johns Hopkins University Press.

Kale, Madhavi. 1998. *Fragments of Empire: Capital, Slavery, and Indian Indentured Labor in the British Caribbean.* Philadelphia: University of Pennsylvania Press.

Kerr-Ritchie, Jeffrey R. 2013. *Freedom's Seekers: Essays on Comparative Emancipation.* Baton Rouge: Louisiana State University Press.

Landolfi, Ciriaco. 1981. *Evolución Cultural Dominicana, 1844–1899.* Santo Domingo: Editora de la UASD.

Levy, Claude. 1980. *Emancipation, Sugar, and Federalism: Barbados and the West Indies, 1833–1876.* Gainesville: University Press of Florida.

Lightfoot, Natasha. 2015. *Troubling Freedom: Antigua and the Aftermath of British Emancipation.* Durham, NC: Duke University Press.

Logan, Rayford W. 1941. *The Diplomatic Relations of the United States with Haiti, 1776–1891.* Chapel Hill: University of North Carolina Press.

López, Cathy. 2013. *Chinese Cubans: A Transnational History.* Chapel Hill: University of North Carolina Press.

Lora Hugi, Quisqueya. 2012. *Transición de la esclavitud al trabajo libre en Santo Domingo: El caso de Higüey (1822–1827).* Santo Domingo: Academia Dominicana de Historia.

Marsh, Kate. 2012. "'Rights of the Individual,' Indentured Labour and Indian Workers: The French Antilles and the Rhetoric of Slavery Post 1848." *Slavery and Abolition* 33, no. 2: 221–31.

Martínez-Fernández, Luís. 1994. *Torn between Empires: Economy, Society, and Patterns of Political Thought in the Hispanic Caribbean, 1840–1878.* Athens: University of Georgia Press.

May, Robert E. 1979. "Lobbyists for Commercial Empire: Jane Cazneau, William Cazneau, and U.S. Caribbean Policy, 1846–1878." *Pacific Historical Review* 48, no. 3: 383–412.

Monfleury, A. 1862. "Fabrication du Sucre." *L'Opinion Nationale,* no. 6 (February 8): 1.

Nicholls, David. 1974. *Economic Dependence and Political Autonomy: The Haitian Experience.* Montreal: McGill University Centre for Developing Area Studies.

Northrup, David. 2000. "Indentured Indians in the French Antilles: Les immigrants indiens engagés aux Antilles Françaises." *Revue Française d'Histoire d'Outre-Mer* 87, nos. 326–27: 245–71.

Pani, Erika. 2002. "Dreaming of a Mexican Empire: The Political Projects of the 'Imperialistas.'" *Hispanic American Historical Review* 82, no. 1: 1–31.

Paton, Diana. 2004. *No Bond but the Law: Punishment, Race, and Gender in Jamaican State Formation, 1780–1870.* Durham, NC: Duke University Press.

Ramsey, Kate. 2011. *The Spirits and the Law: Vodou and Power in Haiti.* Chicago: University of Chicago Press.

Ratcliffe, Barrie M. 1982. "Cotton Imperialism: Manchester Merchants and Cotton Cultivation in West Africa in the Mid-Nineteenth Century." *African Economic History* 11: 87–113.

Renault, François. 1976. *Libération d'esclaves et nouvelle servitude: Les rachats de captifs africains pour le compte des colonies françaises après l'abolition de l'esclavage*. Abidjan: Les Nouvelles Éditions Africaines.

Rodney, Walter. 1981. *A History of the Guyanese Working People, 1881–1905*. Baltimore: Johns Hopkins University Press.

Rodríguez Demorizi, Emilio. 1955. *Antecedentes de la anexión a España*. Ciudad Trujillo [Santo Domingo]: Editora Montalvo.

Schmidt-Nowara, Christopher. 1999. *Empire and Anti-slavery: Spain, Cuba, and Puerto Rico, 1833–1874*. Pittsburgh: University of Pittsburgh Press.

Schmidt-Nowara, Christopher. 2006. *The Conquest of History: Spanish Colonialism and National Histories in the Nineteenth Century*. Pittsburgh: University of Pittsburgh Press.

Schuler, Monica. 1980. *"Alas, Alas Kongo": A Social History of Indentured African Immigration into Jamaica, 1841–1865*. Baltimore: Johns Hopkins University Press.

St. John, Spenser. 1884. *Hayti: Or, the Black Republic*. Pittsburgh: Ballantyne Press.

Thompson, Alvin. 1997. *The Haunting Past: Politics, Economics and Race in the Caribbean*. Armonk, NY: M. E. Sharpe.

Watts, Isaac. 1871. The *Cotton Supply Association: Its Origin and Progress*. Manchester: Tubbs and Brook.

The Fight against *Patronato*

Labra, Cepeda, and the Second Abolition

Luis Miguel García Mora

In 1999 Christopher Schmidt-Nowara published *Empire and Antislavery*.[1] The book was based on extensive and diligent research conducted for his doctoral thesis. This influential book allowed us to discover an important historian and placed him in the area of knowledge that has since been shaped by his work. *Empire and Antislavery* is located within the tradition of his mentor, Rebecca Scott, who during the 1980s made important contributions to the study of abolition in Cuba, culminating in the publication of *Slave Emancipation in Cuba: The Transition to Free Labor, 1860–1899* (1985). Schmidt-Nowara was within this immediate tradition, but his study went much further and had other implications. Scott was interested above all else in how and to what degree slaves had been protagonists in their own liberty, given their integration in postcolonial society. It was, to a certain extent, a history of Cuba, of Cuban slaves, where Spain appeared only as a backdrop, while in the work of Schmidt-Nowara, the empire, Spain, occupies the stage. His book was not a history of Cuba. It was instead a history of nineteenth-century Spain where two colonial spaces, Cuba and Puerto Rico, become meaningful through their relationship with the mainland. This was a very successful perspective. On many occasions the history of Cuba and Puerto Rico in the nineteenth century has been studied without placing enough emphasis on their relationship with Spain. It seems as though everything starts and ends in the islands. It is not so; it may start there, but complete understanding lies within the relationship of dependence they had with a territory that was over seven thousand kilometers away on the other side of the Atlantic.

Second Empire, Second Slavery, and Second Abolition

In his study, Schmidt-Nowara was preoccupied with how an ideology and a movement such as antislavery developed within a determinate period, between 1833 and 1874, at a moment during which the liberal order was being constructed in Spain, a form of liberalism that was being conceived at two different paces within one single state on two sides of the Atlantic. Antislavery or abolitionism is not a colonial ideology. Abolition is a commitment of conscience; there are many reasons for one to become opposed to slave labor. Thus, it is not necessarily a colonial ideology. Nevertheless, abolitionism put into practice deeply influences the colonial world where slaves work. Cuban and Puerto Rican reformism, on the other hand, were indeed colonial ideologies: they were conceived as ways to explain and transform the relationship between these territories and Spain and the role that creoles should play within that relationship. Slavery and the control of the abolitionist process was a basic problem for reformism, albeit not the only one. Schmidt-Nowara's great contribution was understanding how those who fought to transform the colonial world in the Caribbean found other reformists in the mainland, who could share abolitionist ideas as a further objective in the construction of a modern capitalist order, in opposition to the oligarchies, and were able to separate the Church from the state and public education. This project, implemented by those who fought for free trade and any reform they deemed fit, such as the education of women and workers, was sustained by the urban middle classes and caused the necessary transformation of the public sphere, particularly after 1854, to such an extent that ideas about modifying the colonial order and the abolition of slavery became plausible. Thus, free trade and abolition appear as two sides of a single coin. Those in the Asociación para la Reforma de los Aranceles (Association for the Reform of Tariffs) were also in the Sociedad Abolicionista (Spanish Abolitionist Society) and were those who emerged from democratic and republican ranks to fight for a new colonial order. They were always opposed to those who defended a protectionist market and sought to perpetuate slavery while maintaining a colonial status quo that benefitted them. The former were the men of the *Sexenio Democrático*, and their opponents were those who made the *Restauración* possible.

By developing his argument in this way, Schmidt-Nowara placed his research within the tradition that had been established by Alberto Gil Novales many years prior, who pointed out the close relationship between abolitionism and free trade while explaining the figure of Rafael María de Labra (Gil Novales 1968, 154–81).

There was a certain continuity between metropolitan reformism and that of the Antilles. When figures such as Saco, Del Monte, Angulo y Heredia, Vizacarrondo, and Acosta arrived in the capital they found the right environment to carry out the reform programs they advocated with other figures such as Joaquim Maria Sanromá, Laureano Figuerola, Francesc Pi i Maragall, Gabriel Rodríguez, and Labra and in the associations and publications that they created. From the pages of *La América* and the *Revista Hispanoamericana* it was much easier to create a new colonial order that reality insisted on rejecting.

Little by little Schmidt-Nowara was hinting at the success or failure of abolitionism and from that point he established an alternative to the traditional economic explanation of the end of slavery. It was no longer only the profitability of the institution, nor, as Scott emphasizes, the slaves' own strategies. Instead, what also influenced change was the political and institutional framework, more concretely the Revolution of 1868, headlined by a group of metropolitan reformists who deeply believed in abolition. Here, Schmidt-Nowara's analysis approached that of other historians (Blackburn 1988): the emancipation of slaves occurred within the context of a political revolution that affected the entire empire. It was something that happened relatively easily in Puerto Rico while proving slower and more complicated in the case of Cuba, which later culminated in the abolitionist process.

Empire and Antislavery is also intertwined within another historiographical tradition: the second slavery. It was Dale Tomich who, in an enlightening article published in 1988, established that while the capitalist order (which was obviously against the continuation of slavery as it was conceived during the seventeenth and eighteenth centuries) was being consolidated, the globalization of the economy and the new international distribution of labor enabled the development of a new type of slavery in the Atlantic world. This second slavery was fueled by the demand for products such as cotton, coffee, and sugar, and it undoubtedly influenced political organization and eventual abolition in the spaces of which it was a part (Tomich 1988, 103–17). Tomich's contribution denotes the true complexity behind the continuation of slavery and abolition by incorporating many other factors into economic profitability. In the case of nineteenth-century Spain, this second slavery corresponds to a "second empire," or, in other words, to the transition from empire to nation, where this new creation, the nation, must integrate and incorporate the remains of the old empire (Fradera 2015). It is within this juncture, marked by the second slavery and the construction of the liberal state, that Schmidt-Nowara weaves his analysis of the origin, strategies, and results, both in the colonies and in the mainland, of Hispanic abolitionism, institutionalized in 1865 as the Spanish Abolitionist Society.

Although his study ends in 1874, he concludes by predicting what was to come, Restoration and abolition in Cuba within a completely different paradigm than what occurred in Puerto Rico in 1873, where the process was immediate and indemnified. Instead, in Cuba, what was established by law in 1880 was a form of abolition substituted by an eight-year period of *patronato* during which former slaves, now *patrocinados*, would compensate their former masters for losses with their own work. Abolition was a fact, it had a date, but slavery remained, regardless of how the new law protected and safeguarded former slaves under patronato. From an antislavery perspective this amounted to a new challenge, since the goal of all abolitionist movements was achieved with the passage of the law that came into effect in 1880. Nonetheless, it was clear that slavery persisted. Consequently, the fight would have to endure but with a different strategy. In this context, we can speak of a second abolition, referencing Tomich's concept of second slavery.

Declaring immediate abolition and submitting newly freed slaves to a master for a determinate amount of time was not a novelty. This form of gradualism or second abolition had been practiced by the British in Jamaica (1833–38) under the name of "apprenticeship" and by the Danes in their West Indian territories who also named it patronato. In both cases, definitive abolition was achieved prior to the period established by the laws due to the opposition by part of the abolitionists and by the pressure that former slaves generated against their new situation. Prime Minister Segismundo Moret's Free Womb Law (Ley de vientres libres) also established a period of patronato, and when the abolition law of 1880 was being discussed, conservative Cuban representatives—some of whom criticized the government's project and others who endorsed it—referred to the British experience. Autonomists, who were withdrawn from Parliament at the moment of the debate, defended immediate abolition and displayed their knowledge of European abolitionism by explaining to anyone who was willing to listen how patronage was destined to failure.[2]

Until 1880 many supported the abolitionist policy on their own initiative. Once the law was passed, support diminished. As Rafael María de Labra acknowledged to Francisco Cepeda in a series of interviews conducted in 1889 and published a year later, the campaign against abolitionism was driven by elements that were in great measure peninsular (Cepeda 1890, 141). Nevertheless, the last part of the campaign, the part that fought against patronage, was carried out thanks to the Cuban autonomist drive. The Spanish Abolitionist Society was similarly faltering in those years. It was unable to either restart or establish an adequate periodical, *El Abolicionista*, as its means of expression. It was mainly Antillean income that paid for the campaign. The fight for the abolition of patronato was an endeavor undertaken by Cuban autonomism that made of it one of its principal claims, financing the campaign and counseling the slaves in the attainment of their rights. Abolition remained, in this manner, strictly tied to a colonial ideology that sought the transformation of overseas Spanish territories during the nineteenth century.

As an example of what I propose I will concentrate on two figures and two publications. The first is Rafael María de Labra, a specialist politician, tireless champion first for abolition (after 1864), and for autonomy thereafter. Labra is the quintessential colonial reformist. Despite having been born in Cuba and being acquainted with slavery as a child, he never set foot on the island again. In exchange for being the standard-bearer for abolition and autonomy, Cuba granted him the possibility of having continuous parliamentary representation, something that would have been quite difficult during the Restoration for a politician with republican and democratic ideas (García Mora 2006). Opposite to Labra, Francisco Cepeda was a mainlander whose time in Cuba, where he arrived as a civil servant, made him embrace the cause of colonial autonomy and from it the abolition of slavery. Labra represented a pact-based tendency within autonomism, a politician who believed that the campaign would be long, and thus negotiation between parties was necessary in order to slowly obtain partial reforms. He was a prestigious lawyer; his firm was one of the main firms in Madrid. He had encyclopedic knowledge of colonial history and politics. He was an academic man who never attended the university, but who was well considered among scholars of the colonial world. In contrast, Cepeda never held a position in the institutions or in Cuban autonomism; he was, in the parlance of that time, an agent for autonomy who also had to accept abolition. He represented an exalted autonomism, stemming from the press, first in Cuba, with the *Revista Económica*, and later in Madrid, with the *Revista de las Antillas*, and finally in 1886 in Puerto Rico with the *Revista de Puerto Rico* where he was fully integrated into political life and was a founding member of the board of the Autonomist Party of Puerto Rico. Cepeda's work consisted in arousing party supporters, which also benefited him economically: his magazine was targeted at the segment of Cuban creoles that wanted colonial reform to move faster than what autonomist management in Havana and parliamentary representatives in Madrid could allow. Cepeda was the rallier, while Labra was the one who managed to get reforms approved in Court.

Labra is a well-known figure and all who have approached the subject of abolition have also had to approach him, since he was the president and main backer of the Spanish Abolitionist Society. Cepeda is less well known. He was a second tier abolitionist. In March 1882 the lives of Labra and Cepeda were intertwined. At that moment, having been banished by the general governor of Cuba, Luis Prendergast, Cepeda arrived in Madrid and, with the funds provided by autonomists, he founded a weekly, the *Revista de las Antillas*, with the objective of generating debate on the colonial problem in the mainland press. At the same time, that same month, Labra was able to start a newspaper in Madrid, *La Tribuna*, the keystone of Antillean autonomism and, consequently, defender of the abolition of the patronato. The lives of their directors, Labra and Cepeda, are certainly not parallel, but to some extent the publications are. Both were established in May 1882; both were mediums for Cuban autonomism and were funded by it. *La Tribuna* disappeared first due to disagreements between Labra and its Cuban stakeholders. The crisis of 1884, which saw sugar prices plummet, entailed the end of the *Revista de las Antillas*. But both managed, in this brief period of time, to conduct a campaign in which the fight for abolition and colonial autonomy were interwoven in their pages (Cepeda 1890, 191–94; Labra 1897, 191–96).

The Abolition of Slavery: An Open Debate

We have over one hundred years' worth of studies on slavery in Cuba. From the initial studies by Fernando Ortiz (1916) and Hubert Aimes (1907) to the many others that have followed, they have allowed us to understand and evaluate slave legislation, how many Africans arrived in Cuba, and how many remained in its territory during different periods. We also have important contributions on plantations, less on city life; we know about the rebellions; about marronage and stockades. There are works on the lives of women slaves; in later years, legal sources have allowed us to establish concrete series on slave prices and how, to some extent, slaves were able to rely on these prices in order to attain their freedom. In these one hundred years there has been a shift that has led from the study of slavery as an institution to an interest in the slave as a person and key actor of this period. It is a pity Ortiz, who, when writing his work, could have chosen to speak to former slaves, decided instead to focus his efforts on re-creating their lives in the sugar mills from secondhand sources despite being an anthropologist and a disciple of Bronisław Malinowski (Ortiz 1916, 180–83).

There is, however, a subject within the historiography of slavery that still generates a certain amount of controversy and that is the subject of abolition. The explanation that has been most widely supported is that of Cepero Bonilla (1976) and Moreno Fraginals (1978), which argues that production by slaves ended when it ceased to be profitable for the sugar mills, the economic sector in which slave labor was in highest demand. It was a hermetic explanation: the moment the sugar mills completed their process of technicification, slaves ceased to be profitable. Plantation owners had to wager: either invest in more slaves or invest in technology. A cause-effect relationship between both factors was posited, something we now question. We believe that these are processes that coincide in time, but there is not necessarily a causal relationship between them. The sugar industry in Cuba during the nineteenth century had to resolve two issues: the decline in prices and the concentration of exports into one single market. The cause of these problems was the influx of beet sugar; the solution: the modernization of production that was accomplished though boosting the most abundant and cheapest production factor, land, versus capital and labor, which were far scarcer (García Mora and Santamaría 2002, 169).

Cepero-Moreno's explanation, which defended abolition as a historic necessity, began to be put into question when Rebecca Scott (1989, 28) and Laird Bergad (1989; 1990, 228) established that the most modern sugar mills were those that employed a greater number of slaves. Industry statistics demonstrate that slave labor continued to prove efficient.

Sugar plantation censuses for 1860 and 1877 have allowed us to establish an alternative interpretation to that of Cepero-Moreno. Slaves continued to be the fundamental and most profitable workforce within the industry, much more so than wage laborers. From the evolution of sugar we also know that slaves were not solely and directly replaced by wage laborers. *Colonatos* (tenant farmers) also played their part. The industrial segment centralized production in a few sugar mills that were completely mechanized, while sugar cane supply was partly in the hands of *colonos*, which allowed for savings in labor, expansion of the crop (farmers who also harvested other crops would now be dedicated to sugar cane), and a greater yield of raw materials, thus helping to reduce costs and compete with beet sugar. The meaning of this industrial transformation is explained by the relative endowment of resources: land and capital was used to cheapen labor. Nevertheless, labor remained crucial and censuses prove sugar producers' preference for slave labor. However, in the mid-nineteenth century, due to noneconomic circumstances, slavery was an institution in the process of extinction (García Mora and Santamaría 2002, 184).

The aforementioned concepts move us toward completing the economic explanation of abolition with another explanation. They provide grounds for incorporating new perspectives and actors in order to obtain a more adequate explanation. Throughout the nineteenth century, abolitionism and anticolonialism walked hand in hand. The continuation of slavery was what linked Cuba and Spain, a political dependence that was confronted by its economic structure, which demanded fewer tariffs and more free trade. While beet sugar was not in the market, tariffs were not a great issue. But when markets were lost to competition, Spain's guarantee of slavery, which required the upkeep of tariffs, weighed ever more heavily. Plantation owners were *slaves to their slaves*, which was precisely what prevented them from demanding a new colonial order with more fervor. Anticolonial and abolitionist discourse was driven from exile. It was advocated from abroad and its incidence was limited in the island. The revolution of 1868 developed within this context, at the state level, and in Cuba, the Ten Years' War ended with an agreement that recognized the freedom of the *mambise* slaves (guerrilla independence soldiers) and opened the floodgates for the rest. In February 1880, abolition was passed as a law (Ortiz 1916, 510–14).

The abolition approved in 1880 was neither immediate nor simultaneous; it was a gradual law that entailed converting the slave into the patrocinado during a period of eight years. A patrocinado was a slave who knew he was going to be free in a determinate amount of time and who also was granted a series of rights, among others, a small wage. Day to day life, however, was that of a slave. Abolition had been passed as a law but slavery continued and thus the need for abolitionist activity to continue.

There are few studies on the patronato. It is in great measure due to Rebecca Scott's work that we know the strategies of masters and slaves (Scott 1989, 165–241). Abolitionism until 1874 is well known through the work of Schmidt-Nowara, who surmises how abolition during the Restoration must have been. Nevertheless, knowledge is still scarce on how patronato committees worked and on how abolitionists, aside from having a political sense, also had a practical one, giving the patronato political backing in order to achieve freedom. We also do not know much about the press campaigns in the mainland to mobilize and generate awareness among the public with the objective of obtaining a law in Parliament. In May 1882 Rafael María de Labra founded *La Tribuna* and Francisco Cepeda the *Revista de las Antillas*. Two generations of abolitionism in this last stage had to support themselves with a colonial ideology, autonomism, in order to gain financial and political support.

Rafael María de Labra and Francisco Cepeda

When both Labra and Gabriel Rodríguez drew up the history of Spanish abolitionism they defined three periods (Rodríguez 1886–87; Labra 1903). The first are the precursors, from the Cortes de Cádiz until 1865 with the foundation of the Spanish Abolitionist Society. From 1865 to 1870 they distinguish the propaganda phase, and, from 1870 to 1886, the legal solution phase. We locate the second abolition within this third phase, between 1880 and 1886, defined by the fight against the patronato and characterized by its close relationship with autonomism as a colonial ideology that advocated the transformation of the framework of the relationship with the mainland through definitive abolition. With the maintenance of slavery (under whatever name it was given) and without having a model for a postabolitionist society, for which European immigration was preferred, an autonomous Cuba where creoles and whites could decide on tariffs and on what was more convenient for economic development in the island could not be achieved. This meant bringing to the island the form of abolitionism that had been previously endorsed by Cuban exiles, and had been the analogue to anticolonialism, at a moment during which colonial politics were shifting away from stale pro-Spanish thought as an ideology that justified everything and entitled anyone who advocated it. This was also the time when autonomist lawyers began to arbitrate practical solutions against the patronato. Within this context we can situate Labra and Cepeda, and the periodicals they funded: a campaign that developed in the mainland and complemented actions taken in Cuba, occasionally with unnecessary limitations.

As mentioned above, the lives of these men were not parallel and were separate from one another until Cepeda arrived in Madrid in 1882.[3] Yet certain parallelisms remain. They are part of the same generation. Labra was born in 1840, and Cepeda was born five years later. Both had ties to the region of Asturias in Spain, although Labra was born in Havana, where his father, a soldier who had endured exile and prison for his liberal ideas, had been deployed. In contrast, Cepeda arrived in Cuba when he was seventeen years of age as a typical immigrant who, with the help of his fellow countryman, Mariano Cancio Villamil,[4] a politician and economist, found opportunities he was lacking in his immediate environment within the colonial administration. Labra, who had already returned to Spain, studied law, philosophy, and humanities, spoke several languages, played the piano, drew, and was a talented fencer and horseback rider.

While Labra successfully established his law firm and flourished within the democratic and reformist circles in the mainland, Cepeda advanced within the colonial administration. With the revolution of 1868 Labra fully entered the political scene, specializing on overseas matters, which he always considered related to and part of the general reform of the state. He defended the social and political integration of the Antilles within the Spanish ensemble. In order to accomplish this, relationships within production had to be equalized on both sides of the Atlantic. In other words, abolition of slavery was required in order to level civil rights and correlatively autonomy, which he understood as the most adequate model for the relationship between the colony and mainland (Labra 1901, 3–10; García Mora 2006, 126–27). While Labra strove to become a member of Parliament in order to put all these ideas into practice, Cepeda, who entered the Volunteer Corps, an armed militia, during the Ten Years' War, would go on to criticize Labra during the Cortes del Sexenio (parliamentary sessions from 1868 until 1873). Cepeda's progression within the colonial administration led him to become mail administrator in Corralillo and to make his debut in the world of journalism when he founded the *Hoja Económica del Puerto de Sagua la Grande* in 1870 (Catálogo 1965, 210).[5]

It seemed as though Cepeda stood for everything Labra detested. Nevertheless, with the triumph of Restoration and the end of the war in Cuba their lives came closer. If Labra, undoubtedly a man of '68 who had voted for the republic, wanted to continue in politics he had to, without renouncing his ideals, tone down his discourse and manage to have Cubans and Puerto Ricans consider him as their spokesperson in Madrid, a spokesperson with enough contacts and with the necessary political background to grant them the sort of colonial reform Antilleans desired. In exchange, Labra would obtain parliamentary representation allowing him to promote his political agenda, which was not solely related to overseas matters. Meanwhile, in 1876, Cepeda abandoned Sagua and his publication and had moved to Havana, where he worked for the colonial administration under Joaquín Jovellar and Arsenio Martínez Campos who tried to implement a policy of attraction in order to end the war. Within the general government he moved through several positions on the Debt Board. He managed to become chief of personnel in the central section for statistics and taxes, and culminated his career as a civil servant holding the position of printing press censor, a beautiful paradox for someone who years later would be banished for a *thought crime*.[6] In May 1877 he founded the *Revista Económica*, a publication similar to the one he had led in Sagua. It was a magazine on applied economics and avoided politics, which remained the case until the signing of the Peace of Zanjón when the magazine became the unofficial arm of the most radical and advanced autonomism, closer to the grassroots, more belligerent and less committed to maintaining the colonial order. We are unsure if this choice was driven by conviction or convenience.

If within politics Labra appeared to be a more moderate actor than Cepeda due to his role as a member of Parliament and the responsibility this position entailed, in terms of abolition he agreed completely with the propositions the latter made through the *Revista Económica*. While the heads of the autonomist party eventually accepted abolition with the patronato, Labra, from Madrid, and the most advanced autonomist leaders such as Enrique José Varona and José Antonio Cortina, fought for immediate abolition (García Mora 2016a). As Ramón Blanco (the governor general of Cuba when the debate on abolition was approaching) stipulated, autonomism was debated in the space between the desire for radical abolition and the consequences this would entail for the world of sugar. Blanco had no doubts: limitations and transaction formulas would impose themselves and in fact this is what happened.[6] Cepeda's reaction was to deny the legitimacy of the leaders, whom he accused of betraying the entire autonomist party. It was through this grievance that the *Revista Económica* laid the foundations for the campaign against the patronato, which was in turn accepted by the entire party due to pressures from the party's militants. The patronato was a form of covert slavery in which the former slave compensated his master for his loss through work. Any advantages the patronato might have, such as knowing when one would be free, a series of rights, and the possibility of exercising them to obtain one's freedom, were disregarded. At the same time, the disadvantages of the patronato—everything that would put it on the same level as slavery or worsen the lives of patrocinados—were highlighted, while any and all infringements of the new law would be reported. This was the basic strategy against the patronato. It was at this point that Labra and Cepeda were finally united, one as a politician and the other as an agent mobilizing public opinion. When they finally met in Madrid in May 1882, both were under the protection of autonomism, which granted political representation to one and readers to the other, while providing the two with funding for the campaign.

Francisco Cepeda's incarceration and his banishment from Cuba was the most important political event after the Peace of Zanjón (García Mora 2016b). Events transpired quickly between late December 1881 and early February 1882. In late December 1881 Cuban autonomist representative Bernardo Portuondo disembarked in Cuba. He was on an official trip as an engineer sent to conduct a series of works for the construction of what was known as the *ferrocarril central de Cuba* (the Cuban central railroad) and also traveled as a representative of a Spanish company based in Paris that had an ambitious project for the colonization of the Bay of Nipe. Beyond this, Portuondo took advantage of his trip through the entire island in order to give lectures defending autonomy in an attempt to reorganize the party in the provinces of Puerto Principe and Santiago de Cuba. Authorities were not pleased with Portuondo's tour of the island, but were unable to do much due to his status as a representative. Nevertheless, in Santiago de Cuba, the local governor dictated a ban on pronouncing "*Viva!*" in reference to autonomy, a shout that was constantly heard throughout Portuondo's rallies.

Restraint on behalf of the authorities remained, regardless of their inherent desire for a different approach. The *españolista* press, in particular *La Voz de Cuba*, did not follow this restraint. Not surprisingly, rebuttal came from the *Revista Económica*. The debate became even more fervent as *La Voz* called for Asturian expatriates in Havana to rally against Cepeda, an aggression that was halted by authorities who asked him for moderation in the debate. Nevertheless, Cepeda's response was the article "Los Cipayos en Campaña," a violent attack on the Volunteer Corps of which he was still supposedly a member (Estevez y Romero 1899, 117–21). Reaction by the authorities entailed the detention and deportation of Cepeda under the pretext that his life was endangered and the need to avoid further turmoil. In reality this measure infringed on all civil liberties, from the Constitution on down, and was one the governor general was not warranted to promulgate. The autonomists' reaction was prompt. They called on the militants to evaluate the possibility of the party's disappearance, something that would mean leaving a great part of Cuba's political mass without representation at a moment when those who favored independence challenged colonial power once again (Partido Liberal de Cuba 1882).

For abolitionists, the detention and deportation of Cepeda was also related to the pressures from large plantation owners who had grown increasingly unhappy with the tough campaign the *Revista Economica* carried out against the patronato law and against the rulings that applied it. At the moment he was detained, plantation owners were resisting the elimination of the shackle and clamp, and Cepeda's name may have come up when discussing this matter in meetings with the authorities. The governor himself noted that the decision to deport Cepeda was taken according to a committee of authorities, without specifying who composed it. (We are unsure if it was the same committee that established the decree of attributions of the general government in June 1878.) Perhaps it was the same committee as the one he was dealing with about the elimination of the shackle and clamp, visits to the factories, and verifying how the patronato was being carried out. For the autonomist movement it was clear, and Labra reported the close relationship between Cepeda's deportation and his radical abolitionism to the press in Madrid. Even José Martí was aware of this relationship.[8]

La Tribuna, La Revista de las Antillas, and the Second Abolition

When *La Tribuna* and the *Revista de las Antillas* were first published in May 1882, they did so in a more liberal atmosphere. From February 1881 there had been a liberal government in Madrid, which was supposedly in favor of colonial reform and abolition of the patronato. In fact it had enacted the Constitution and applied the Press Law and the Gatherings Law. In May, the court of Havana had declared autonomist propaganda legal, but the trip made by representative Portuondo had highlighted that in the colonial world it was more important to maintain public order than respect for laws. Cepeda's deportation and the decree by which the local governor of Cuba prohibited the chanting of "Viva la autonomía" (long live autonomy) stemmed from this situation. This in turn produced a radicalization of the autonomist program that was based on the defense of democracy, the abolition of slavery, and colonial autonomy. Finally, the press and many political circles in Madrid had only gotten ahold of the versions offered by the more recalcitrant pro-Spanish sectors. Aside from a few republican newspapers, the rest seemed to give credit to what was said in *La Voz de Cuba* (García Mora 2016b).

From 1879 autonomist representatives called for their own vehicle of expression that would also speak for the party in Madrid. It was imperative that the colonial problem be kept alive within public opinion while exerting a form of political pedagogy that would promote autonomist solutions as a panacea for all ailments. Beginning in 1880 the editorial board of *La Tribuna* was constituted and endowed with statutes that shielded Labra's authority. This is what perhaps held the autonomist leadership back from providing sufficient funding for realizing the idea. The political situation created after Portuondo's trip to Cuba and the unexpected presence of Cepeda in Madrid made the release of *La Tribuna* and the *Revista de las Antillas* possible. Labra would have his national newspaper, tailored to his interests, in which colonial issues were subordinated to the "alignment of the diverse elements of Spanish democracy."[9] Cepeda was able to release a ten-issue publication dedicated exclusively to overseas issues and autonomist solutions, where suppression of the patronato was a priority. It was the only propaganda campaign that boasted the abolition of slavery as one of its pillars. Autonomists paid for this enterprise and also contributed the readers. Nevertheless, *La Tribuna* catered to Labra's every whim, occasionally with Labra making decisions without even consulting with his fellow autonomist representatives in Parliament, while at the *Revista de las Antillas*, Cepeda was closely dependent on the directives he received from Havana because of financing, readers, and the nature of the publication. There overseas subjects were given priority over all else, without necessarily having to finance the democratic and republican campaigns in the mainland with Cuban money. The *Revista de las Antillas* could be a publication open to the influence of other autonomist representatives, something these representatives had demanded from the management in Havana.[10]

We have figures referring to distribution costs for *La Tribuna*, and an approximation for the distribution of the *Revista de las Antillas*. *La Tribuna* could never have been justified on its sales. Statistics found in the *impuesto del timbre* (tax stamp) allow us to ascertain that the publication was running at a loss of approximately 3,353 *pesetas* in the improbable case of selling the entire print run. Pricing overseas made the publication more competitive, but the cost of transport decreased its profit margins. The profitability of *La Tribuna* was not a business in itself; its profitability was political, and costs were diluted by reusing the same press to print other publications related to the same campaign. We have been able to document that the Aurelio Alaria printing press, aside from producing the *Revista de las Antillas*, also produced a number of publications authored by members of the editorial board. Labra himself produced eleven publications with them between 1880 and 1883 (García Mora 2005, 308).

In terms of distribution, the economic burden entailed by *La Tribuna* was compensated for by its widespread circulation. Undoubtedly it was never a dominant reference within the press at the time, as were *La Correspondencia, El Imparcial, El Globo*, and *El Liberal*, but in a list of about sixty papers that were published monthly by *La Gaceta de Madrid*, drawn from statistics provided by the *timbre* or stamp taxes, the autonomist paper was between number fourteen and fifteen. The few times the *Revista de las Antillas* managed to enter the list, it was always at the bottom. This situation varies if we consider mainland newspapers being distributed in the Antilles, where *La Tribuna* was always the most widely circulated paper between June 1882 and February 1884, and the second most widely circulated between March and June 1884 when statistics are no longer available. On the other hand, the *Revista de las Antillas* figured in the statistics from June 1882 until June 1883, and always held a top-ten position within a list of thirty to forty publications.[11] In this way *La Tribuna* managed to have some effect on public opinion in the mainland. The *Revista de las Antillas*, on the other hand, did not. Autonomism, in order to make itself heard, had to keep on purchasing space in other publications. Nevertheless, in the Antilles, both these papers were widely circulated and could convey the impression that the overseas problem and its solutions were one of the preoccupations of mainland public opinion to autonomist voters. More than simply trying to obtain more followers, it was the newspaper the autonomist wanted to read to reaffirm his ideas, situating the debate where readers wanted it instead of where it really was.

Once initial doubts and fears were surpassed, the board in Havana, representatives in Madrid, and their publications shared a radical abolitionism that opposed the patronato, which they considered a form of covert slavery; a type of abolitionism that was insatiable in denouncing the treacherous noncompliance of authorities; one that was necessary when slavery was on its way out; the last push in the second to last American territory in which it existed. Manual Moreno Fraginals argues that the abolitionist campaign was conducted at the only time it could have been, when the institution of slavery was collapsing and losing its salience, a period in which the law proved itself "an [essential] weapon towards its definitive suppression" (Moreno Fraginals 2003, 480). Autonomists were dedicated to finding the contradictions and breaches of the latest abolitionist law while safeguarding the Spanish Abolitionist Society both within and beyond Parliament.

Articles dedicated to abolition in *La Tribuna* and in the *Revista de las Antillas* constituted a perfect web in which the proslavery "flies" were trapped. On the one hand, there were articles denouncing the government, if conservative for implementing the law, and if liberal for not repealing it as they had promised when not in power. Other articles were propaganda for the activities of the Abolitionist Society in the street and for autonomist representatives in the courts: ultimately two sides of the same coin. On other occasions, abolitionist articles focused on how the law was implemented in practice, the strategies of slave owners to circumvent the law, and the violations slaves were subject to. It constituted a very effective form of pedagogy. Finally, and aside from abolition but closely related to it, the issue of postabolitionist societal construction was treated alongside the recommendation of what type of immigrant Cuba needed, though always from the orthodox position of the autonomist message. Let us study a few examples.

Within autonomist discourse, self-government was always presented as the solution to all of the problems with the colonial model. It was a blank page. It had never been implemented and nothing could be said against it as such. On the other hand, no one doubted that the policies applied by the different nineteenth-century governments were the cause of the turmoil that led to the loss of the continent and the war in Cuba, policies that, according to autonomist thought, had no other fundamental value than the continuation of slavery. If slavery did not disappear completely, nothing could be done to preserve the empire. This was a straightforward discourse without nuances and was very effective when targeting the weakest points of pro-Spanish thought—in other words, targeting the loss of territory. The Peace of Zanjón had seen the dawn of a new colonial order based on political representation in which, supposedly, old practices had disappeared. In fact, the first important law that was approved was abolition, a law autonomists did not completely oppose when it was passed even though it was not the law they wanted. Once this initial moment had subsided, any deviation from the norm, any position alien to immediate and definitive abolition was publicly denounced and equated with the old colonial order, the order that had ended in armed conflict and exhausted the island. Both publications presented the idea that pro-Spanish ideology and slavery were one and the same: in the corruptness of slavery lay the advantage of the pure Spaniards, the ones who could register a free black man in a slave census as easily as they could bribe authorities to have them look the other way. An article entitled "La vieja política colonial" (The old colonial policy) from the first issues of *La Tribuna* accurately described the situation:

> The Spanish flour producer who has the monopoly of the Antilles for his wheat and for the *foreigner*'s wheat that enters Santander and is sent overseas with a new stamp; the slave owner, who cannot find any other flags in the

world except for those of Brazil and Spain in order to guarantee the exploitation of the black man by the white man, which necessarily implies a general policy of repression and distrust; the ambitious classes generally known as *clases presupuestivoras*, those classes from which administrative cadres have traditionally been recruited, and who now find themselves deprived of the ability to exploit the peninsula [that is, the Spanish metropolis] because the choice of personnel for administrative positions [there] is increasingly being left to the opposition and to *concursos*, or public competitions, but who still have before them the juicy salaries and more or less legitimate subsidies of the large overseas bureaucracy, where there are neither statutory promotions nor conditions for admission. . . . all of them, it is clear, must register any minor variation of the political, economic, and social lives of our Antilles as a formidable attack, with an even greater motive, when their interests, by their own nature, are not long-lasting and their energy and efforts must be in inverse reason to their viability. ("La vieja política colonial," *La Tribuna*, May 5, 1882)

Maintenance of the patronato constituted the seed of public corruption and placed the island on the path toward a new insurrection. In this sense, we can recall the words of Fernando de León y Castillo when he was still a member of the opposition in the Parliament: "The immediate abolition of slavery is a terrible weapon that if not brandished by us against the insurgent, the insurgent will brandish against us." Further on he continued: "It is an axiom for all who deal with these matters, liberty granted on a long term produces impatience in the slave. A precursor to rebellions." Putting his argument into the mouths of those who occupied power at the time, recapitulating what they had promised and had later gone on to breach, was a perfect strategy and legitimated his discourse, more so when the attack was directed against mainland politicians, liberals, heirs of the Sexenio, who were meant to have reformed the state and, in consequence, the colonial model, something that was nothing more than a sterile exercise if a decisive attitude against the patronato was not taken.[12]

Aside from liberal and conservative governments, the fight was also directed at other powers such as the Catholic Church. Unlike other European abolitionist scenarios where Protestantism was an important advocate for the movement, Catholicism had never been characterized by its opposition to slavery (Drescher 2009, 252–54). Clericalism was situated in the same semantic field as slavery. They were two obstacles to the modernization of politics: "because, finally, to reject all of that, here and there, liberals have spilt generous rivers of blood and have sacrificed lives and fortunes. [Their] memory is slandered by those who persevere in the objective of maintaining, in the interests of a meager, but rowdy minority, the clamp and shackle, clerical privilege, and discretionary powers of soldiers above civil authority" ("La autonomía colonial," *La Tribuna*, February 8, 1883). Moreno Fraginals has written eloquent pages on how sugar plantation owners adapted religion to the sugar mill and how they made its practice an effective mechanism for social control: property had to be protected and the first lesson taught to the slave was that suicide was a sin (Moreno Fraginals 1963, 11–28; 1978, 2:10). This collusion on the part of the church was denounced mainly because it supported the regulations of May 1880 in which corporal punishment, which had been eliminated by the Moret Law, was reintroduced, an attitude that autonomists and abolitionists considered far from being part of the behavior of a good Christian.[13]

Nevertheless, the main criticisms were directed toward the colonial authorities who were supposed to be ensuring compliance with the law, but who instead avoided visiting the sugar mills in order to verify such compliance and who time after time postponed one of the basic requirements of the patronato: the registration through personal identification cards of all patrocinados. It is clear that, in order to procure this registration, the patrocinados should have been registered in the census of 1867, something that was also criticized as hollow. The law, something perfect in the mainland, was breached when it crossed the Atlantic and interests came into play that did not abide by what the law ordered. The gradual nature of the process, the patronato itself, caused unlawfulness. There are even objections to governments that were closer to abolitionist ideology. When in February 1883 the ministry of Gaspar Nuñez de Arce made one of his longtime aspirations a reality—the freeing of all the slaves who were not enrolled in the census of 1867—it was noted that the decree did not clearly establish how or when the freeing of forty thousand slaves was to be carried out. Moreover, a year later, there was no hesitation in pointing out that

> the decree of February 9, 1883, that granted the emancipation of 40,000 blacks, which according to authorized calculations is the number of blacks who have not been registered as slaves by their masters, has reached a mere 1,000 to 1,500 blacks. The rest have been illegally included in the slave registry or are found on the plantations under fake names, replacing dead or freed blacks. ("*La abolición del patronato*," *Revista de las Antillas*, May 28, 1884)

This function of surveillance in the interest of legislative compliance was a fundamental characteristic of the second abolition since it was a period during which a general framework existed for regulating the processes and measures that were to ensure its completion. With denunciation as the starting point, a practical form of abolitionism could be developed that would allow the transformation of the slave into a free man. Legislation, however, was no more than a temporary fix. The ultimate objective was another, immediate, and simultaneous abolition: "The decree for the freedom of the 40,000 *patrocinados* has been put forth with many doubts, and it is believed in Cuba that it will only be successful when the *patronato* ends."[14]

Aside from denouncing the dangers posed by the maintenance of the patronato to the future of the colonial model, which was the cause of the possible venalities incurred by the authorities and something always difficult to demonstrate, the autonomist narrative had to muster concrete facts. The reintroduction of physical punishment in the regulations of May 1880 as part of the implementation of abolition law of February of that same year was always one of the most compelling arguments used by the campaign (Labra 1881; Ortiz 1916, 514–31). It signified brutality at the gates of liberty. If theoretically slavery had been abolished and patrocinados were getting ready for free life, why then did physical punishment return, something that was characteristic of an institution that was said to have disappeared (Sociedad Abolicionista 1882)? This was one of the paradoxes of the patronato. It was an institution that was capable of sending slaves to school while simultaneously allowing a master, at his own discretion, to impose "corporal punishment that the law applied to bandits and incendiaries which in Cuba was used as work stimuli for the poor blacks" for a minor offense.[15] The campaign against the shackle and the clamp was tenacious. Even when it was eliminated it served as a means of casting doubts: At what point could the end of corporal punishment be verified? And, on the other hand, once these punishments were eliminated, the slave owner could still benefit because he had the capability of withholding the wages of the patrocinado by just claiming his work was not done satisfactorily. Abolitionists did not hesitate to assert that under the patronato there would be few former slaves who would be paid their full wages. Every argument had its rebuttal.[16]

The bitter accusations directed at the government and authorities by Labra's and Cepeda's publications turned into sweet honey when narrating the activities against the patronato conducted by autonomists and abolitionists, two sides of the same coin. Everything had its own logic: the first reform, then abolition of slavery, followed by the modification of tariffs, and, as a consequence, colonial autonomy. For this reason the epic nature of commentary was heightened, dwelling upon how abolitionists in Cuba suffered repression by the authorities but did not cease in their effort to aid the patrocinado population. *La Tribuna* and *La Revista* did not forget to review every rally, banquet, or meeting held by the members of the Spanish Abolitionist Society and the action against the patronato that representatives and senators conducted in the courts. Those who had been at a Spanish Abolitionist Society rally the day before were the same people who presented petitions by Spanish cities against patronage in Parliament. Moreover, both publications gathered and amplified the references other newspapers made to the subject of abolition. This task was more oriented toward Cuban readers rather than to readers in the mainland. In a similar way, they would take advantage of any triumph accomplished by Cuban abolitionists, such as the one of José Antonio Cortina rehabilitating the poet Placido, in order to quickly share the news with his readers in Madrid. In the same way that they would reflect how an audience in a theater in Madrid was surprised by seeing slavery represented on stage: "It is excellent abolitionist propaganda . . . contributing towards the formation of a critical mass of thought that must fall on slavery and crush it." The campaign was unique; it was not a Cuban issue. It was an issue that affected the entire Spanish state.[17]

Regardless, the strategy they were able to take most advantage of was denouncing slave owners and the injustices suffered by slaves directly. It was practical pedagogy. The most forceful argument was about the slaves that should not have been slaves according to the different laws. The majority of the slave population had been born into slavery or had been brought in as slaves. But the slave trade had been forbidden since 1820 and after the Moret Law of 1870 all slaves older than sixty should have been freed. Therefore, there should have been few Cuban slaves. During the drafting of their documentation abolitionists also encountered irregularities. When a slave died, the master would give his identity to another; an emancipated slave would become the deceased slave and was automatically registered in the census: "In this way, or leaving them for dead, pretending they had absconded, or moving them to another plantation or to a different jurisdiction and selling them as slaves, all have suffered the horrible fate of slavery" ("Cien mil españoles esclavos," *Revista de las Antillas* [Madrid], February 8, 1884). On other occasions, once having obtained and deposited all the money for emancipation, the slave was sold before obtaining his freedom; or on others, and against what was established by the law, mothers were separated from their children, wives from their husbands, and slaves were transported from the city to the plantation. Denunciations against patronato committees, in which plantation owners acted as judge and jury, were another of the arguments abolitionists used frequently. They would adamantly point out how allegations were not processed because they had not been written up on official paper, or how slave owners would only accept gold as payment. These were all different subterfuges used to prevent slaves from obtaining the rights that the law theoretically granted them.[18]

Together with abstract denunciations, concrete examples were used. Abuse perpetrated against slaves with names and surnames, who on occasion suffered the clamp and shackle, on others were separated from their children, and on others were simply abused: "a black child of approximately ten years of age, who was dragged by a trotting horse from his town to the plantation," a child who should be free if the law was applied properly.[18] Cases such as those of Francisca Rodriguez, who sued her patron for not paying her salary; or Matilde García, who requested her liberty because she was not accounted for on any of the slave censuses could be found in the pages of *La Tribuna* and the *Revista de las Antillas*. The latter sounded the alarm and called for a joint strategy: "As these matters must be simply resolved, without the need of formalities other than certification of the census, we call on our esteemed colleagues at *La Tribuna* and *El Abolicionista* not to desist in requesting the prompt dispatch of the petition being alluded to, so that it is not misplaced as many others have been."[20] Or the case of a married couple under the patronato trapped by the workings of the law:

> The *pardo* Antonio Zamora, *patrocinado* of *don* Francisco Causa y Roque has declared to *La Discusión,* from Havana, that he is united in legitimate and canonical marriage with the *pardo* woman Emilia Francisca, *patrocinada* of *doña* María Regla de Casas: while this lady was alive there was no obstacle to him visiting his wife and children, but today *don* José Pereira y Gómez, widower of that lady, and current patron of Emilia will not allow him to enter the house, with the intention of forcing him to free his wife, or else take charge of a daughter of seven months that seems to bother him. ("Antonio Zamora, pardo y víctima," *Revista de las Antillas*, August 8, 1882)

In the case of Francisca Entenza we find a concrete example of corruption within the legal superstructure that regulated the patronato, but was not enforced by mainland governments, who were completely inactive in abolitionist activities and in attempts to aid slaves even though they called themselves liberals. Since 1874 Francisca Entenza had worked on her own and supplied her masters with between twenty-five and thirty-four pesos a month. Some of the payments were even accompanied by a receipt. She was married to a free black man called Domingo Entenza, with whom she had two daughters. Because of a complaint Domingo made against his former masters, who were the same as Francisca's, his wife and daughters were taken to the Recurso plantation, disregarding the claims made by the delegation of the Spanish Abolitionist Society to the board of the patronato. The *Revista de las Antillas* remarked:

> The amount of wages paid by Francisca to her masters since 1874, and the seven grown children she has also given these masters, who now work for them, are reason enough for that poor woman to be granted her freedom. . . . She has been stripped of her home, shredding articles 60 and 61 of the regulation passed on May 8, 1880, which categorically prevent patrocinados, who had partaken in labor not relating to the fields for at least four months, to be taken to the fields against his or her own will.

The autonomist paper considered that what had been done with Francisca's daughters, who at the time were enrolled in school, was kidnap, even more so if Domingo paid for the ransom, in this case, purchasing the freedom of his wife and daughters. Their conclusion was clear: under Prime Minister Práxedes Mateo Sagasta the Cánovas law had been more harshly enforced, a law he had initially rejected in an emphatic manner ("Los abolicionistas de Sagasta," *Revista de las Antillas*, September 8, 1882).

When presenting the case of Facundo Socarrás, the *Revista de las Antillas* pointed out that they were doing it "so that knowledge of these things could reach the peninsula, and so that Mr. León y Castilla, who is a famous abolitionist, would be able to read them." Facundo Socarrás had been recognized as a free man by a local committee for freed slaves in May 1879 because his master had been unable to procure his registration. However, the central committee for freed slaves decided otherwise and returned him to his master. Subsequently, in May 1880, and in great measure because of the defense by Miguel Villanueva y Gómez, a representative of the Unión Constitucional, he was declared a free man once again, something that was reported in the *Gaceta de la Habana*. Nevertheless, the slave still remained in servitude. This decision was commented upon by the *Revista*: "If he has been declared a free man, know that he has a right to claim every wage he might have won since the moment he was first declared free" ("Ah, delicioso patronato," *Revista de las Antillas*, July 18, 1882).

Commentary by the autonomist lawyer, who assisted the former slave, was also present in the complaint and finally allowed for his case to succeed when everything seemed to be against him. The fact that he filed the suit in a Cuban court, and if necessary would have carried the case up to the Supreme Court in Madrid, was something unheard of in prior periods of the abolitionist campaign (Labra 1884–86b, 269–87; Martínez Girón 2002).

Apart from petitions to governments and authorities, praise for contributors to the campaign, and concrete denunciations, abolitionists, and in this specific case, perhaps more autonomists than abolitionists, were able to denounce the type of immigration upon which they did not want to construct postabolition society. The defense of free labor ultimately constituted the best form of abolitionist propaganda. In this regard, figures were drawn up at abolitionist's whim. Arguing that the decrease in the numbers of slaves had not affected production hid the fact that the majority of emancipated slaves were on the margin of the plantation and that they had not been freed until the end.[21]

There was no argument against any particular immigrant. Instead, the argument was made against how they had arrived in Cuba. In the same way that trafficking was rejected, now contracting was put in doubt, where the contractor benefitted and the immigrants lost regardless of whether they were white, black, or Chinese. Autonomist contempt for slavers translated equally to those who contracted whites (*blanqueros*) or Chinese (*chineros*). Autonomists demanded individual and free immigration, in families, preferably white, and directed at establishing them in rural areas. This was the ideal that was to sustain the future autonomist Cuba, the country of creoles. It was a societal model that was already present in the discourse of renowned reformists such as the Count of Pozos Dulces. It was a type of manpower that could be achieved now that abolition was looming over the horizon. The *Revista de las Antillas* posited this idea: "Cuba needs hands, but white and intelligent hands that will honor the country that grants them hospitality. The scandalous speculation of slavers must cease, since it has been dire for Cuba, and consequently for all of Spain. If white immigration is protected, industry and agriculture will be bolstered" ("Inmigración asiática," *Revista de las Antillas*, April 8, 1883).

The new immigrant had to be white and the freed slave had to conform to white cultural patterns. *La Tribuna* referred to a correspondent in Havana: "An individual initiative has constituted a corporation in Santa Clara with the objective of bringing in white immigrants for agricultural tasks. It is composed of men of all parties. If we continue on this path the country will progress." *La Tribuna* further complained about how the Havana Immigration Committee, constituted to promote white immigration, had agreed to "bring Chinese immigrants at the nation's expense, requesting the provision of a large portion of the budget. Are the Chinese white?" Finally, and in an ironic fashion, it extracted a political reading of the issue: "Autonomist spokesmen have argued that only white immigration in family units must be favored, mainly peninsular immigration, while fundamentalists argue for the Chinese. Who will be more favorable to the conservation of integrity, Spaniards from the peninsula or the Chinese? This is our separatism" ("Desde la Habana," *La Tribuna*, May 26, 1883).

However, the example that summarizes opposition to the unwanted concept of immigration to Cuba is the campaign conducted against the project for colonizing the Bay of Nipe, in the eastern part of the island (Moisand 2015). This business had it all: great capitalists who had become politicians in order to gain profit within the colonial framework (Leon Crespo de Serna, from the Unión Constitucional); politicians from both sides of the spectrum, including autonomists such as Bernardo Portuondo and José Güell y Renté, and others such as Francisco Serrano and Nicolás Salmeron, former presidents, who all offered their reputation in exchange for a seat on the board of directors.[22]

The Bay of Nipe was a territory that had been awaiting development since the late eighteenth century. The project involved the union of very large properties, the construction of four *centrales* (sugar processing plants), and the necessary parcels for settlers to grow crops and supply the factories. In theory the plan was more than viable. The company, based in Paris, supplied the land that was to be rented out, financed the settlers, and would construct the factories and other necessary buildings. In practice, when not enough settlers were attracted, clearing of the land had to be performed by the military, from which another business opportunity arose: feeding and maintaining the soldiers. In reality, the great business opportunity lay in the fact that the lots were less extensive than what had been initially stated, and there was a need to provide the region with a railroad line, as well as to bring settlers into Cuba and to get paid for the budgeted grants. The other part of the business was the issuing of stock, since everything sounded great, but in practice it was all smoke and mirrors. It was a business plan conducted under the shadow of colonial domination.

Nipe is the example of what was not wanted. Criticism by the *Revista* managed to quash the project when autonomist and democratic representatives who were part of the board were compromised: "The system of colonization and the unconscionable and incredible conditions that have been stipulated . . . could have only been rejected" ("Reformas en lo de Nipe," *Revista de las Antillas*, September 28, 1883). For both the *Revista de las Antillas* and *La Tribuna*, as well as for autonomists, abolition was only the first step toward constructing a free and racially homogeneous society only to the degree that was possible in a territory that had resorted to slavery since the sixteenth century.

The End of the Campaign

Who benefited from the campaign of warnings, insinuations, and specific reports on the patronato? Did they have an influence on its demise? This is something difficult to ascertain. After the end of the American Civil War, British pressure to abolish slavery, and now American pressure, intensified. The 1868 La Gloriosa Revolución in Spain on the one hand, and the Ten Years' War on the other, only accelerated the process even further. In the provinces of Santiago de Cuba and Puerto Príncipe, which had been the main setting for the conflict, slavery had all but disappeared. After the Peace of Zanjón, which recognized the freedom of slaves enlisted in the *mambises*, abolition could not be delayed. Nevertheless, as we have mentioned previously, slave labor continued to be preferred by great plantation owners, who resisted until the very end putting it aside and missing out on an opportunity to obtain profits. Abolition under the patronato was a solution that aimed at appeasing everyone. Faced with the impossibility of compensating the masters, slaves were forced to work for a further eight years in order to be freed. This measure might have convinced timid abolitionists, but not radicals, who rapidly restarted the campaign against it.

Abolition was more a consequence of international pressures, the democratic revolution in Spain, and the war in Cuba, and less a consequence of the obsolescence of slave labor. This being said, abolition had an expiration date. The strategies of the slaves, of the abolitionists in Cuba and in the mainland, and the development of abolitionist law all contributed to ending the institution more rapidly. In contrast to what had occurred with systems of gradual abolition, such as those implemented in Jamaica and in the Danish Antilles (Drescher 2009,

248, 264, and 280), in Cuba neither the extreme pressure nor a revolt by part of the slaves ended the institution. It was, instead, the development of the law to which plantation owners had been opposed (Scott 1983; Piqueras 2011, 230). It was within this environment that the autonomist/abolitionist campaign played its part. Following the British model by a considerable number of years, rallies in the street, petitions to Parliament, in sum, the mobilization of public opinion, once these became possible in the peninsula and in Cuba, helps to shed light on the contradictions the maintenance of slavery entailed. We are unsure to what point the campaign was effective, or if, aside from it, the patronato would have disappeared. We believe that it would have. But what we do know for certain is that autonomism understood this process as something that was necessary and put its resources toward this goal.

Among those who undoubtedly benefited from the campaign were Labra and Cepeda. For Labra this was the opportunity to manage a national newspaper that granted him influence and that allowed him to grow as a politician. For Cepeda it was something as simple as the opportunity to keep earning a living. There was a market of Cuban readers who believed a weekly radical autonomist paper was necessary in Madrid. The same readers who up to 1882 had been purchasing the *Revista Económica* were those who until 1884 bought the *Revista de las Antillas*. The colonial world opened myriad opportunities for sharp writers such as Cepeda who knew how to sell what the creole autonomist wanted to read. The controversy about Nipe is a good example. The journalist who wrote the series for the *Revista de las Antillas* denounced the project ("Los fantoches de Nipe" and "La sentencia de Nipe," *Revista de las Antillas,* January 18 and March 28, 1884, respectively). He ultimately received a criminal conviction for it and was banished from Madrid for three years and seven months. Germán González Peñas, was also the same person who in 1880, two years prior, had begun selling the publication in Havana (González Peñas 1880).

Labra's independent criteria caused Cuban autonomism to withdraw its financing of *La Tribuna*. On July 20, 1883, the last issue of the national edition was published, while the offshore edition lasted until December 28. The *Revista* managed to survive for exactly one more year, until December 1884. Labra and Cepeda understood how to be efficient agents for abolition and autonomy. Nevertheless, the lack of practical results, the even more ominous perspective for autonomists after conservatives returned to power in 1883, and the economic crisis affecting Cuba during that year contributed toward the decision by the management in Havana to give up their own publications and to renew buying space in other venues, which was perhaps a more economically sound and effective strategy.

Labra continued his campaign in favor of abolition and autonomy, in Parliament and outside of it; Cepeda left for Puerto Rico, where in 1887, following the model of the *Revista Económica* and the *Revista de las Antillas*, he founded the *Revista de Puerto Rico*, a publication that survived until 1894, when Cepeda, who had fought to lead *boricua* autonomism, abandoned the island (Gargallo García 2014). Labra and Cepeda encountered each other once again in 1889 when Cepeda conducted a series of interviews with Labra that were published as a book. In that meeting, when recalling the campaign by *La Tribuna* and the *Revista de las Antillas*, Labra did not hesitate to assert that the first publication had died from not realizing that the publication was more a political instrument than an editorial business, and, as such, it could not survive solely from the support of readers. He was adamant: "It could not be a business, it had to be a sacrifice" (Cepeda 1890, 193). The same could be said of the *Revista de las Antillas*. The problem was that Cuban autonomism only bore the sacrifice for twenty months in the case of Labra and thirty-two in the case of Cepeda.

In 1886 the abolition of the patronato was achieved. Labra then dedicated himself to colonial autonomy and social reform. He was also a lawyer who on multiple occasions defended former slaves against the racial abuse that substituted for slavery (Labra 1894). For his part, Cepeda, who had so emphatically criticized immigrant contracting, did not hesitate to put himself in charge of a contract sending immigrants to Brazil, through which he made a small fortune ("Francisco Cepeda," *El Liberal*, July 26, 1911). The colonial world generated rich business opportunities, but in the criticism of these lie other opportunities. Undoubtedly both Labra and Cepeda acted in good conscience, but without the support of island autonomists, Labra would have not been able to enjoy parliamentary longevity and Cepeda would not have been able to prosper in the press. Labra always had his firm, through which he had many clients and dealings with Cuba: "I lost my parliamentary position, my firm, and my peace in 1898" (Labra 1916, 27). But when Cepeda ran out of money, he accepted as just and necessary something he had refuted in the pages of his publications only a moment before.

Notes

Research conducted under the framework of the MINECO, HAR2012-32510 project. The Spanish version of this text appeared in Consuelo Naranjo Orovio (ed), *Sociedades esclavistas y racializadas en el Mundo Atlántico*, Doce Calles, 2017. This chapter was translated by Manuel Borja Burbano.

1. In terms of the assessment he made in *Empire and Antislavery* I retake much of what was written in the analysis I made in the *Revista de Indias* (García Mora 2001, 216–218).

2. On abolition in general, Drescher (2009, 333–348). On British learning experience, see Labra (1884–86a, 139–64), and Danish patronage, Labra (1873, 11–14), Ahumada y Centurión (1870, 119–31) and Hall (1994, 208–27). Moret Law in Ortiz (1916, 495–98). The debate on abolition in the *Diario de Sesiones del Congreso de Diputados* (Madrid), January 14, 15, 16, and 17, 1880.

3. Bibliography on Labra is extensive. Among others see Domingo Acebrón (2006), Serrano de Haro (1996), Hernández Sandoica (1994), Bayrón Toro (2005), and Laguna Ochoa (1991). In order to find information on Cepeda one must review his own works published in 1907 and 1910, biographical repertoires of Puerto Rico (Cifre de Loubriel 1989, 434–25; Enciclopedia 1976, 14:72–73, and Reynal 1988, 61–62) and Asturias (Suárez 1936, 2:416–18) as well as the obituaries published by the press. See *El Liberal* (Madrid), July 26, 1911, and *El País* (Madrid), August 11, 1911. Likewise it is worth consulting the letter that Cepeda himself wrote to *La Época* (Madrid) March 15, 1882, that sheds light on his first years in Cuba, and also the biography published by Antonio Cortón in *Correo de Ultramar* on March 18, 1895. Recently, Gargallo García (2014, 72–79).

4. "Francisco Cepeda," *El País*, August 11, 1911.

5. *La Época*, March 15, 1882.

6. On his role as a printing press censor: González del Valle (1918, 168–71 and 177).

7. Archivo Histórico Nacional, Ultramar, Gobierno, Leg. 4794, Caja 2º. "Carta de Ramón Blanco al ministro de ultramar, Salvador Albacete," La Habana, 15-5-1879.

8. Labra's articles are "Torpes manejos" and "The Insurrection in Cuba," both in *El Liberal* (Madrid), February 22 and March 27, 1882, respectively. The knowledge of Martí is in Archivo Histórico Nacional, Ultramar, Gobierno, Leg. 4801, exp. 256 caja 2ª "Copy of a Letter Addressed from Havana to José Martí," Havana, February 27, 1882.

9. "Nuestros propósitos," *La Tribuna*, May 2, 1882.

10. Archivo Nacional de Cuba, Donativos y Remisiones, Caja 124, no. 128: "Carta de José Ramón Betancourt a Vidal Morales," Madrid, March 8, 1882.

11. Revenue by tax stamp (*derecho de timbre*) is data published by the monthly *Gaceta de Madrid* under the epigraph: "Nota de la recaudación obtenida por derecho del timbre de periódicos para la península, Antillas y Filipinas, con expresión del número de ejemplares de cada uno de los periódicos cuya tirada está intervenida por Hacienda." On the other hand, Pascual Martínez (1994, 1:141 and 146) from another source, the *Padron de matrícula de contribución industrial*, states that *La Tribuna* paid fifty-five pesetas for this concept in 1882 and 1883, which placed it between the thirty-third and thirty-fifth position of tax-paying newspapers.

12. See "Concluyamos" and "Más hechos y menos palabras," *La Tribuna*, June 20, 1882 and June 27, 1883, respectively. "Cuba y partido de Sagasta en 1880" and "El señor Balaguer y Cuba," *Revista de las Antillas*, June 5 and 8, 1882, respectively.

13. "Abolición del cepo y el grillete," *Revista de las Antillas*, December 8, 1883. On the relationship between the world of the factory and the Catholic Church, aside from the article by Moreno Fraginals cited previously, see Klein (1967, 87–126), and on the relation with abolitionism, see Bergad (2007, 273–75).

14. "Sin embozo," *La Tribuna*, June 5, 1883. See also "Cuarenta mil esclavos en Cuba," *La Tribuna*, February 10, 17, and 20, 1883. On the difficulties of knowing the exact number of slaves during this period, see Piqueras (2011).

15. "Si cepo, ¿para qué escuela?" and "El cepo y el grillete," *Revista de las Antillas*, November 28, 1882 and August 28, 1883, respectively.

16. "Abolición del cepo y el grillete," *Revista de las Antillas* (Madrid), no. 2, 76 December 8, 1883. On the elimination of the clamp and shackle, see Suárez Inclán (1884, 33–43).

17. See from *La Tribuna*: "El movimiento abolicionista en Cuba" (May 8, 1882); "Hombre al Agua" (May 14, 1882); "Correo de Cuba" (June 2, 1882); "Interpelaciones sobre la política del Gobierno en Ultramar" (February 24, 1883); and "Sorpresa" (June 10, 1883). From the *Revista de las Antillas*: "La cuestión negra en el Senado" (February 26, 1883); "El cepo y el grillete en el Senado" (March 18, 1883); "Abolición del patronato" (December 28, 1883 and May 28, 1884); and "Meeting abolicionista" (December 18, 1883). The claim of Plácido is in "Otro triunfo de Cortina," *Revista de las Antillas* (Madrid), no. 1, July 15 and 28, 1882. The theatrical representation of slavery and its influence throughout public opinion is in "Las mil y una noches," *Revista de las Antillas* (Madrid), no. 1, July 13 and 18, 1882.

18. See *La Tribuna*: "El Sancta Santorum" (July 30, 1882); "Sinceridad Liberal" (August 18, 1882); "El patronato por dentro" (October 10, 1882); and "Las dulzuras del patronato" (October 15, 1882). From the *Revista de las Antillas*: "Cipayos al natural" (June 8, 1882); "Pobres esclavos" (July 6, 1883) and "Cepo y grillete" (August 28, 1883).

19. "Las atrocidades en Cuba," *La Tribuna*, December 22, 1882, facts that had already been recorded in *Revista de las Antillas* in the article "¡Que viva el patronato!" (August 18, 1882).

20. See "La negra Francisca Rodríguez," *La Tribuna*, December 10, 1882, and "La criolla Matilde," *Revista de las Antillas*, July 8, 1882.

21. "El trabajo libre" and "Abolición del patronato," *Revista de las Antillas*, July 18, 1882 and January 18, 1884.

22. See "Desde la Habana," *La Tribuna*, March 9, 1883, and the following articles in the *Revista de las Antillas*: "La tramoya de Nipe" (May 18, 1883); "El embrollo de Nipe–El monstruo de Nipe" (May 28, 1883); "El güiro de Nipe" (June 8, 1883); "El enredo de Nipe–Nipe no es Cuba" (June 18, 1883); "Brisas de Nipe" (July 8, 1883); "El maltrana de Nipe" (July 18, 1883); "Reformas en lo de Nipe" (September 28, 1883); "Los miserables

de Nipe" (October 28, 1883); "El dinero de Nipe" (November 8, 1883); and "La cortina de Nipe–Bahía de Nipe" (December 8, 1883).

Works Cited

Ahumada y Centurión, José. 1870. *La abolición de la esclavitud en países de colonización europea*. Madrid: Imprenta de F. López Vizcaíno.

Aimes, Hubert H. S. 1907. *A History of Slavery in Cuba 1511 to 1868*. New York: G. P. Putnam's Sons.

Bayrón Toro, Fernando. 2005. *Labra: Biografía, bibliografía e ideas sobre abolición de la esclavitud, autonomismo y el Tratado de París de 1898*. Mayagüez: Editorial Isla.

Bergad, Laird W. 1989. "The Economic Viability of Sugar Production Based on Slave Labor in Cuba, 1859–1878." *Latin American Research Review* 24, no. 1: 95–113.

Bergad, Laird W. 1990. *Cuban Rural Society in the Nineteenth Century: The Social and Economic History of Monoculture in Matanzas*. Princeton: Princeton University Press.

Bergad, Laird W. 2007. *The Comparative Histories of Slavery in Brazil, Cuba, and the United States*. Cambridge: Cambridge University Press.

Blackburn, Robin. 1988. *The Overthrow of Colonial Slavery, 1776–1848*. London: Verso.

Catálogo de publicaciones periódicas cubanas de los siglos XVIII y XIX. 1965. La Habana: Biblioteca Nacional José Martí.

Cepeda, Francisco. 1890. *Conferencias de Abulí celebradas con el jefe de la minoría autonomista parlamentaria, D. Rafael M. de Labra sobre política antillana, sus relaciones con la política peninsular y procedimientos que deben seguirse*. Ponce: Tipografía de la Revista de Puerto Rico.

Cepeda y Taborcias, Francisco. 1907. *Armonías familiares. Primera y segunda parte. Anales de Navia: libro IV*. Madrid: Centro Gráfico Artístico.

Cepeda y Taborcias, Francisco. 1910a. *Notas de papeles viejos: Afectuosidades de versos y prosas y adición de Rivero Andante*. Madrid: Centro Gráfico Artístico.

Cepeda y Taborcias, Francisco. 1910b. *Papeles viejos, primera parte. Anales de Navia: Libro V*. Madrid: Centro Gráfico Artístico.

Cepeda y Taborcias, Francisco. 1910c. *Rivero andante: Apéndice de Papeles viejos*. Madrid: Centro Gráfico Artístico.

Cepero Bonilla, Raúl. 1976. *Azúcar y abolición*. Barcelona: Grijalbo.

Cifre de Loubriel, Estela. 1989. "Cepeda Taborcias, Francisco." In *La formación del pueblo puertorriqueño: Contribución de los gallegos, asturianos y santanderinos*, 424–25. Río Piedras: Editorial de la Universidad de Puerto Rico.

Dirección General de Hacienda de la Isla de Cuba. 1877. *Noticia de los ingenios o fincas azucareras que en estado de producción existen actualmente en toda la isla, según los datos que arrojan los padrones aprobados para la contribución del 30% con expresión del partido en que se encuentran situados y jurisdicción municipal a que este pertenece.* La Habana: Imprenta del Gobierno y Capitanía general por S. M.

Domingo Acebrón, María Dolores. 2006. *Rafael María de Labra: Cuba, Puerto Rico, las Filipinas, Europa y Marruecos, en la España del Sexenio Democrático y la Restauración, 1871–1918*. Madrid: Consejo Superior de Investigaciones Científicas.

Drescher, Seymour. 2009. *Abolition: A History of Slavery and Antislavery*. Cambridge: Cambridge University Press.

Enciclopedia. 1976. "Cepeda Taborcias, Francisco." In *La gran enciclopedia de Puerto Rico*, 14:72–73. Madrid: R.

Estévez y Romero, Luis. 1899. *Desde el Zanjón hasta Baire: Datos para la historia política de Cuba*. La Habana: La Propaganda Literaria.

Fradera, Josep Maria. 2015. *La nación imperial (1750–198): Derechos, representación y ciudadanía en los imperios de Gran Bretaña, Francia, España y Estados Unidos*. Barcelona: Edhasa,

García Mora, Luis Miguel. 2001. "Empire and Antislavery." *Revista de Indias* 61, no. 221: 216–18.

García Mora, Luis Miguel. 2005. "Los intereses solapados: La Tribuna de Madrid y la autonomía colonial." *Ibero-Americana Pragensia. Supplementum* 15: 299–314.

García Mora, Luis Miguel. 2006. "Rafael María de Labra (1840–1918): La abolición de la esclavitud y la autonomía colonial." In *Figuras de la Gloriosa: Aproximación biográfica al Sexenio Democrático*, edited by Rafael Serrano García, 125–37. Valladolid: Universidad de Valladolid.

García Mora, Luis Miguel. 2016a. "The Paths of Freedom: Autonomism and Abolitionism in Cuba, 1878–1886." In *The Politics of the Second Slavery*, edited by Dale Tomich, 113–44. Albany: State University of New York Press.

García Mora, Luis Miguel. 2016b. "Órdenes contrapuestos: El viaje del diputado Bernardo Portuondo a Cuba en 1882." In *Orden político y gobierno de esclavos*, edited by José Antonio Piqueras, 99–124. Castellón: Universidad Jaume I.

García Mora, Luis Miguel, and Antonio Santamaría. 2002. "Centrales por ingenios y colonos por esclavos. Mano de obra y cambio tecnológico en la industria azucarera cubana, 1860–1877. Un estudio cuantitativo." In *Azúcar y esclavitud en el Caribe: El final del trabajo forzado*, edited by J. A. Piqueras, 165–85. Madrid: Fondo de Cultura Económica.

Gargallo García, Oliva. 2014. *La prensa autonomista en Puerto Rico: El caso de El Buscapié y la Revista de Puerto Rico, 1877–1898*. Morelia: Universidad Michoacana de San Nicolás Hidalgo.

Gil Novales, Alberto. 1968. "Abolicionismo y librecambio (Labra y la política colonial española en la segunda mitad del siglo XIX)." *Revista de Occidente* 59: 154–81.

González del Valle, Francisco. 1918. "El clero y la revolución cubana." *Cuba Contemporánea* 18, no. 2: 140–205.

González Peñas, Germán. 1880. *Proyecto de inmigración González Peñas, propuesto a los Sres. Estéfani y Crespo, de Matanzas, para la población y explotación de los terrenos que poseen en la gran bahía de Nipe, parte oriental de la isla de Cuba: Desarrollado en la teoría, fundada en el trabajo libre, y como consecuencia, plan de ingenios centrales*. La Habana: Imprenta del Gobierno y Capitanía General por S. M.

Hall, Neville A. T. 1994. *Slave Society in the Danish West Indies: St. Thomas, St. John and St. Croix*. Kingston, Jamaica: University of the West Indies Press.

Hernández Sandoica, Elena. 1994. "Rafael María de Labra y Cadrana: Una biografía política." *Revista de Indias* 54, no. 200: 107–36.

Klein, Herbert. 1967. *Slavery in the Americas: A Comparative Study of Virginia and Cuba*. London: Oxford University Press.

Labra, Rafael María de. 1873. *La abolición de la esclavitud en el orden económico*. Madrid: Imprenta de J. Noguera.

Labra, Rafael María de. 1881. *Un reto del esclavismo: El reglamento esclavista de 8 de mayo de 1880*. Madrid: Sociedad Abolicionista.

Labra, Rafael María de. 1884–86a. "La abolición de la esclavitud en las colonias inglesas." In *Discursos políticos, académicos y forenses de D. Rafael M. de Labra*, 2:139–64. Madrid: Imprenta de Aurelio J. Alaria.

Labra, Rafael María de. 1884–86b. "El negro Faustino." In *Discursos políticos, académicos y forenses de D. Rafael M. de Labra*, 2:269–87. Madrid: Imprenta de Aurelio J. Alaria.

Labra, Rafael María de. 1894. *La raza de color de Cuba*. Madrid: Tipografía de Fortanet.

Labra, Rafael María de. 1897. *La república y las libertades de Ultramar*. Madrid: Tipografía de Alfredo Alonso.

Labra, Rafael María de. 1901. *La crisis colonial de España, 1868 a 1898: Estudios de política palpitante y discursos parlamentarios*. Madrid: Tipografía de Alfredo Alonso.

Labra, Rafael María de. 1903. "La educación política en España." *Nuestro Tiempo* 7, no. 31: 17–33.

Labra, Rafael María de. 1916. *Política hispano-americana: Españoles y cubanos después de la separación de 1900: Interview con D. Rafael M. de Labra*. Madrid: Imprenta de Jaime Ratés Martín.

Laguna Ochoa, Fernando. 1991. *Las ideas hispanoamericanistas de Rafael María de Labra: Ultramar y sus problemas durante el siglo XIX*. Madrid: Universidad Complutense.

Martínez Girón, Jesús. 2002. *Los pleitos de derecho privado sobre esclavitud ultramarina en la jurisprudencia del Tribunal Supremo (1857–1891)*. Madrid: Civitas.

Moisand, Jeanne. 2015. "Migrant-e-s entre deux empires: Journaliers agricoles espagnols à Cuba et en Algérie dans les années 1880–1890." *Revue d'histoire du XIXe siècle* 51: 89–106.

Moreno Fraginals, Manuel. 1963. "Iglesia e Ingenio." *Revista de la Biblioteca Nacional José Martí* 5, nos. 1–4: 11–28.

Moreno Fraginals, Manuel. 1978. *El ingenio: Complejo económico social cubano del azúcar.* 3 vols. La Habana: Ciencias Sociales.

Moreno Fraginals, Manuel. 2003. "La abolición de la esclavitud." In *La construcción de las naciones latinoamericanas, 1820–1870*, edited by Josefina Zoraida Vázquez, 465–81. Madrid: UNESCO / Ediciones Trotta.

Ortiz, Fernando. 1916. *Los negros esclavos: Estudio sociológico y de derecho público.* La Habana: Revista Bimestre Cubana.

Partido Liberal de Cuba. 1882. *La junta magna del Partido Liberal de Cuba celebrada el día 1º de abril de 1882.* La Habana: Imprenta de El Triunfo.

Pascual Martínez, Pedro. 1994. *Escritores y editores en la Restauración canovista.* 2 vols. Madrid: Ediciones de la Torre.

Piqueras, José Antonio. 2011. "Censos *lato sensu*: La abolición de la esclavitud y el número de esclavos en Cuba." *Revista de Indias* 71, no. 251: 193–230.

Rebello, Carlos. 1860. *Estados relativos a la producción azucarera de la isla de Cuba.* La Habana: Intendencia del Ejército y Hacienda.

Reynal, Vicente. 1988. "Cepeda Taborcias, Francisco." In *Diccionario de hombres y mujeres ilustres de Puerto Rico y de hechos históricos*, 61–62. Río Piedras: Edil.

Rodríguez, Gabriel. 1886–87. "La idea y el movimiento antiesclavistas en España durante el siglo XIX: 35ª conferencia." In *La España del siglo XIX: Colección de conferencias históricas celebradas durante el curso de 1885–86 [y curso de 1886–87]*, 3:321–55. Madrid: Librería de Don Antonio San Martín.

Schmidt-Nowara, Christopher. 1999. *Empire and Antislavery.* Pittsburgh: University of Pittsburgh Press.

Scott, Rebecca J. 1983. "Gradual Abolition and the Dynamics of Slave Emancipation in Cuba, 1868–86." *Hispanic American Historical Review* 63: 449–77.

Scott, Rebecca J. 1989. *La emancipación de los esclavos en Cuba: La transición al trabajo libre, 1860–1899.* Mexico City: Fondo de Cultura Económica. [Translation of English original: *Slave Emancipation in Cuba: The Transition to Free Labor, 1860–1899.* Princeton: Princeton University Press, 1985].

Serrano de Haro, Antonio. 1996. "Tres notas sobre Rafael María de Labra." In *La nación soñada: Cuba, Puerto Rico y Filipinas ante el 98*, edited by Consuelo Naranjo, Miguel Ángel Puig-Samper, and Luis Miguel García Mora, 49–64. Aranjuez: Ediciones Doce Calles.

Sociedad Abolicionista. 1882. *El cepo y el grillete (la esclavitud en Cuba).* Madrid: Sociedad Abolicionista Española.

Suárez, Costantino. 1936. "Cepeda y Taborcias, Francisco." In *Escritores y artistas asturianos*, 2:416–18. Madrid: N.p.

Suárez Inclán, Estanislao. 1884. *El Gobierno del Ministerio presidido por el Sr. Posada Herrera con respecto a la administración de las provincias de Ultramar.* Madrid: Fortanet.

Tomich, Dale. 1988. "The 'Second Slavery': Bonded Labor and the Transformation of the Nineteenth-Century World Economy." In *Rethinking the Nineteenth Century: Movements and Contradictions*, edited by Francisco O. Ramirez, 103–17. Westport, CT: Greenwood Press.

Atlantization and the First Failed Slavery

Panama from the Sixteenth to the Seventeenth Century

Javier Laviña

From Columbus's intended first voyage to India the objective of the Spanish Crown and its admirals was to arrive in Asia, the land of spices.[1] Following the "discovery" of the Caribbean islands efforts to find the passage to the Pacific Ocean grew. Upon reaching the continent known as "Castilla del Oro," Panama became a key site for settlement and colonization, and thus the expansion of slavery, due to its geostrategic location.

Upon arriving in Panama, however, the terrain proved inhospitable and the first settlement of Santa María la Antigua del Darién had to be abandoned. Following this no large cities were founded on the Atlantic coast of Central America until the establishment of Nombre de Dios, which became a key strategic port in the colonization of the Pacific. Despite the strategic importance of Nombre de Dios the city never became very populous and it primarily served as a port of entry from Europe and as a key route through which silver and precious metals were sent to Europe. As peninsular shipping routes opened up, the city filled with traders from the Americas and became an important nodal point for voyages to the isthmus as much as to the south of the continent.

The territories adjacent to the continental Caribbean coast presented huge economic potential. Despite this, the alluvial deposits of gold and the crops that could be offered to European markets eager for spices and precious metals were not enough to spur on population growth in the territory. Furthermore, attempts at colonization were hampered and unsuccessful due in part to opposition from the indigenous populations and the climate, which according to Europeans was unhealthy and not conducive to consolidating settlements.

Regardless of the excuses presented when abandoning these settlements on the Atlantic coast, during the sixteenth and seventeenth centuries the occupation of Central America's Caribbean coastline was limited and had little success.

The First Slavery in Panama and the Atlantic

The concept of the "first slavery" is inherently linked to that of Atlantization. We cannot talk about slaves and slavery in the Americas without considering the opening and connecting of the New World to other Atlantic shores, as much in Africa as in Europe. The concept, which emerged in the 1970s, was an attempt to explain and classify the revolutions that took place on the European and American continents in a way that transcended national accounts and expanded the study of bourgeois revolutions by linking them to ideological processes that had taken place since the beginning of the eighteenth century. These revolutionary processes were, in part, a fruit of these changes. Nevertheless, the concept grew during the Cold War as it attempted to make sense of the new politics that implicated postwar Europe in the conflict with the Soviet Union. The countries of the Atlantic world, in this regard, came to a common understanding in order to jointly address the Soviet influence in the West.

Nevertheless, today the concept of Atlantization has more to do with an attempt to contextualize and understand the historical phenomena that were created in a particular time than it does with political responses to the Cold War order. The concept of Atlantization, as has been argued by many authors (Armitage 2004; Bailyn 1996, 2005; Bailyn and Denault 2009; Canny and Padgen 1987; Falaola and Roberts 2008; Gilroy 1993; Greene and Morgan 2009; Laviña and Zeuske 2008; Putman 2006; Solow 1991; Strobel 2015; Suranyi 2015; Tomich and Zeuske 2008), brings together the continents of America, Africa, and Europe as their histories become interconnected. As the following quote illustrates, the concept of Atlantization develops the idea of a circum-Atlantic history. Following the European colonial expansions, the social, cultural, and economic worlds of Africa, America, and Europe became intertwined:

Circum-Atlantic history is the history of the Atlantic as a particular zone of exchange and interchange, circulation and transmission. It is therefore the history of the ocean as an arena distinct from any of the particular narrower oceanic zones that comprise it. It certainly encompasses the shores of the Atlantic but does so only insofar as those shores form part of a larger oceanic history rather than a set of specific national or regional histories abutting onto the Atlantic. It is the history of the people who crossed the Atlantic, who lived on its shores and who participated in the communities it made possible, of their commerce and their ideas, as well as the diseases they carried, the flora they transplanted and the fauna they transported. (Armitage 2004, 13)

As we can see the concept of Atlantization has shaped how authors view the oceanic history of the Atlantic, and from there the conceptual union of the three continents emerged. This perspective does not attempt to treat the history of the Atlantic as a Braudelian geographic concept, but regards it as fundamentally an asymmetric space of communication between the three continents.

At the heart of this asymmetric space Europe established itself as the economic, technological, and military strength on the three shores of the Atlantic. South America was identified as a land of milk and honey where a new world could be started, while Africa would be the source of the labor that the colonizers required for the extraction of wealth. In this context, Panama was the nexus of the union between the Pacific and the Atlantic, where slavery and the commercialization of slavery was a common link connecting imperial powers and interoceanic trade.

African slavery in the Americas brought about a quantitative increase in the scale of the Mediterranean slavery that had developed since the Middle Ages. While Iberian monarchies had mostly been driven by the demand to increase their control over African coasts alongside mercantile interests in commodities such as spices and sugar, African slavery in the Americas brought about a quantitative increase in the slave trade as the sub-Saharan African coast was integrated into the construction of the new Atlantic world (Hidalgo Pèrez 2016). In this new space, relations of power and interdependence were established, creating new economic realities as the regions contributed to the growth of the hegemonic centers. This process transformed the Atlantic into a space of transnational communication that crossed empires, national borders, and oceans, creating a new space that would transform the cultures and the histories of the three continents (Thornton 2012; Blackburn 1997; Zeuske 2006; Heywood and Thornton 2011; Wheat 2016).

This connection does not assume that the history of the Atlantic is the same for all the empires that developed their trade on the ocean, but that the Atlantic was the nexus of union and confrontation of the Atlantic empires. Alongside this global narrative, local and regional histories developed, as shown by the work of Alencastro (2000), notwithstanding the fact that it was the globalizing Atlantic perspective that served as the basis of the shrinking of distances between different worlds (Wheat 2016).

Colonial slavery formed and ordered the Atlantic world as it connected all the shores of the ocean and created a new form of capitalism built on the movement of bodies from one side of the ocean to the other. It is in the scope of this development that the "first slavery," which precedes and complements the "second slavery,' a concept developed by Tomich and Zeuske (2008) and other work by Laviña and Zeuske (2014), is located.

The new international conjuncture that emerged from the Portuguese and Castilian expansion toward the coasts of Africa forged a new system of slavery, heir to the Iberian model of the Middle Ages but with an intensity that had not been experienced until then. The New World was transformed into a bottomless pit where the enslaved would be absorbed by work. Despite this the enslaved not only managed to survive but they developed alternatives to the established order that were successful in many regions where they were transferred. Through resistance the enslaved managed to establish social and economic alternatives that served as a refuge for other fleeing slaves.

In some cases the refuge found in *palenques* or *rochelas*,[2] relatively isolated from the society, called into question the capacity of colonial forces to effectively control the enslaved and slavery. *Palenques* were found across the region and differed in size, composition, and origin. In areas where the indigenous population remained organized they collaborated with freed slaves against the Crown in order to help consolidate territory (Tardieu 2006), as was the case in the province of Esmeraldas. In other places, such as in Cuba or Santo Domingo, where the indigenous population was subjugated or had been wiped out, runaway slaves resorted to their own strategies of survival and territorial occupation.

Social Structures in the Audiencia of Panamá

From the moment Vasco Nuñez de Balboa crossed the Isthmus of Panama the Crown of Spain began to develop plans to unite the Atlantic and Pacific Oceans. To do this, they had to turn to forced indigenous labor in order to clear passage, construct infrastructure, and obtain food. The Spanish who migrated to the New World saw a land of milk and honey and hoped the Crown would grant them dominion over the natives in order to enrich themselves and the empire. They hoped that good fortune would reward them upon arrival in a land covered in gold and in no case did the conquistadors go to the Americas in search of work on the land or in the mines.

The exhaustion of the workforce, as well as the pressure from the mercantile centers, led to the importation of slave labor, replacing the spent or indomitable indigenous labor force. These circumstances by themselves created a slave system, or rather a slave society. In the case of Panama, the majority of slaves were owned by the Crown and were employed in public works. There were also private landowners with estates and ranches who used the indigenous workforce to manage the lands and territories. In some cases, these lands proved less profitable than imagined, as many sites were difficult to access and often remained in territories controlled by militant natives. These circumstances ensured that the slavery system in Panama would not have the same success as had been seen in the Antilles.

The development of slavery in Panama followed a trajectory that differed from the traditional exploitation of labor for agricultural use and the development of a plantation economy. In the case of the Audiencia de Panamá[3] a flexible and variable model was created that moved private slave owners in agriculture to largely dedicate themselves to the extraction of minerals and precious metals. At the same time the Crown's slaves would construct roads and fortifications.

Researchers who have worked on slavery in Panama, especially during the first two centuries, present a clear idea of the slave reality under these conditions. Primarily they affirm that the "first slavery" in the Isthmus of Panama was of two distinct varieties: activities relating to mining[4] and to service slavery. There were also a considerable number of slaves working in agriculture, though it is hard to estimate exact numbers. For example, in 1607 the city of Panama had a total of 3,696 slaves, of which 1,421 were employed in houses, ranches, mills, and sawmills, although we do not know how many of them were engaged directly with agricultural work (Castillero Calvo 2004). In other words, many slaves may have been organized under the same roof and controlled by the same foreman.[5]

Mining and public works also contributed significant numbers, with slaves in public works the property of the Crown. According to Tardieu (2006), in 1575 there were 8,629 slaves, including 2,100 in the cities of Panama and Nombre de Dios. The joining of the Atlantic and the Pacific Oceans through the union of these two cities across the isthmus depended on the slave labor of nine hundred slaves working as mule drivers and rowers. At this time the number of Spaniards was extremely low, with only some eight hundred settlers, while the enslaved made up 70 percent of the population of the Audiencia (Mena García 1984; Ward 1993).

In the early years in Panama colonial society responded to the migratory reality that saw settlers largely outnumbered by slaves. Although the settlers maintained power, this was limited to the cities, ranches, and through the sporadic lines of communication between agricultural plantations. As the indigenous population was decimated by disease, war, and work, their population began to rapidly decline (Castillero Calvo 2004), up to the point that natives enslaved from elsewhere, such as the West Indies, were sent to Panama (Reséndez 2016; Ahlert 2015).

The continued growth of the slave population (Wheat 2011) through the sixteenth century, especially after their arrival in the Pacific, led to the resistance and the flight of runaway slaves who became the scourge of landowners in the Audiencia. Since the early years in Panama the Maroons[6] were very active in the area, and particularly the zone surrounding the Camino Real.[7] These were slaves who escaped the working conditions imposed by their owners, who in their scant numbers were unable to control the growing slave population.

But the Maroons were not the only problem that the settlers and colonial authorities of the Real Audiencia had to confront. Attacks from European pirates and corsairs were another cause for concern, with the Maroons collaborating with the pirates to help them navigate and attack the cities of Panama and Nombre de Dios.

Runaway Slaves and the Failure of the "First Slavery"

Marronage[8] directly affected slave owners and was possibly the most destabilizing element of the slave system. The Maroons not only represented an alternative to the organization of labor but also to the political and economic arrangements underpinning the occupation of the territory. Furthermore, the communities of Maroons led to the creation of new Afro-American ethnicities through the cultural mixing between the African cultures transported to the Americas and the indigenous and European cultures.

The description and political classification of the Maroons by those who fought them was always influenced by their cultural traditions. This does not mean that the Maroons would not form kingdoms, but it is clear that they tended toward confederations or communities that came together when under attack from settlers and the colonial authorities. The occupation of a territory by groups of Maroons guaranteed the communities' security, and once these communities had grown sufficiently they would form the basis for new communities in the area. This allowed some coordination between leaders, as was the case between the Bayano Maroons, which split into two groups—one that remained in Bayano and was led by Domingo Congo and Antón Mandinga, and another new community that began on the outskirts of Portobelo and was led by Luis de Mozambique.

As far as the organization of the Maroons was concerned, we must take into account that the information we have is always from external sources, which interpreted the slaves' realities in terms of their political socialization. Thus, it is no surprise that in the sixteenth century one could find examples of monarchies or governments in any Maroon stronghold. That being said, we must take into account that monarchies were not a foreign means of political or social organization in sub-Saharan Africa. Indeed, some communities, such as that led by Benkos Bioho in Cartagena, attempted to reproduce forms of organization that were similar to those in Africa.

This monarchical reorganization reached its peak with the proclamation of the Kingdom of Haiti following the expulsion of the French from the colony with the assistance of auxiliary troops close to the king of Spain. In the communities of Maroons, at least those that we know to have survived, leaders acted only as mediators as decisions were taken in community assemblies. Nevertheless, in periods of war or confrontation with colonists or slave owners, command structures changed as the Maroons engaged in military actions of attack and defense. In doing so titles like captain, general, governor, and king were attributed at different historical moments to Maroons by their pursuers, giving rise to the diversity of positions and multiple interpretations regarding the social organization of communities of Maroons.

Regardless of the social organization of the slaves they were enormously active in their attempts to make the colonial system fail. The Maroons offered refuge to any dissident of the system and maintained collaborative ties with the indigenous population, which allowed them to remain in their territory. Integrating fleeing slaves into these communities helped the movement grow but it also presented more challenges in terms of the subsistence of the group. In this regard the Maroons needed the colonists in order to obtain food and supplies that they could not make themselves.

In Panama, the free indigenous populations and the Maroons worked with European corsairs in attacking the cities and residencies of the Audiencia, causing enormous amounts of damage to the owners and the estates. This was one of the causes of the failure of slavery in Panama.

The Maroons represented a significant percentage of the population in relation to the inhabitants of the Audiencia de Panamá in the sixteenth century (Jaén Suárez, 1998), It was estimated that the population of Maroons for the last third of the sixteenth century ranged between twenty-five hundred and three thousand.

This posed a serious problem in light of the difficulties in controlling the slave population, and it prompted the authorities to begin negotiations with fleeing slaves while attacking communities of Maroons that refused to surrender. As early as 1534, Pascual de Andagoya organized an expedition in Nombre de Dios to reduce the numbers of Maroons with "licence to kill blacks who had fled or refused to surrender without compensation for their Masters" (Mena García 1984, 52). However, the lack of efficiency in restraining the Maroons, along with the support they offered to English corsairs, continued to harm interoceanic trade in the region.

In Panama the phenomena of marronage was so significant that, of a total of fifty-six hundred slaves, some twenty-five hundred were Maroons (Castillero Calvo 2008, 78–104).

Table 1. Evolution of the Population of Panama City, 1575–1607

	1575	1607
Whites	800	1,267
Indians (natives)	0	27
Free Colored People	300	718
Slaves	2,809	3,696
Total	3,909	5,708

Source: Castillero Calvo 2008, 82.

As an enormous numerical inequality developed in colonial society between Europeans and slaves, the authorities were left with little room to maneuver, forcing them to negotiate with Maroons in order to avoid greater risks.

Trade between Panama and Nombre de Dios was regularly attacked as Maroons, allied with the natives who had helped free them, disrupted the circulation of goods on the transatlantic trading routes:

> In Nombre de Dios on the 24th of August, 1551, the residents denounced a very dangerous situation for them. . . . they estimated that en route to Panama the number of Maroons exceeded six hundred individuals who robbed, and even killed, travelers and mule drivers. They dared to enter Nombre de Dios with the same intent, or to take black men and women to enlarge their ranks. . . . In spite of killing many of them they did not manage to end the insurgency. (Tardieu 2009, 67)

A few years later the situation had barely changed, and colonial authorities had to ask for outside help to fight the Bayano Maroons. A further reason why the authorities were forced to ask for assistance was the economic impossibility of winning the war, largely due to the characteristics of the terrain (Saco 1937, 208–9).

Furthermore, the alliances created between Maroons and corsairs in the areas around Nombre de Dios and Portobelo created serious problems for the Crown:

> The King, Dr. Loarte, President of our Real Audiencia that resides in Panama, of the Province of Tierra Firme . . . from the many deaths and robberies that the black Maroons commit every day . . . that war will be waged against the black Maroons and the corsairs, until they are punished and undone . . . and the corsairs who in this have understood and will understand that to be punished with so much rigor, so that the others will not dare similar things. (CODOIN 1864–84)

However, this alliance between Maroons and corsairs, recorded in 1568, was not the last that Panama would experience. When Francis Drake attacked Nombre de Dios in 1572, he was supported by Maroons. They saw the English as allies in their quest to undermine Spanish control of the area and assure freedom in the highlands. For the authorities this problem continued throughout the sixteenth century and for part of the seventeenth century. After the sacking of Nombre de

Dios the English sunk various vessels along the coast. A few sailors from Drake's expedition disembarked near Nombre de Dios and walked toward the interior of the Audiencia. This group of attackers were guided by Maroons who not only facilitated their entrance but gave them lodgings in their town.

Arriving at Venta del Chagres, the settlement was attacked.[9] According to a report, one of the consequences of this attack was verification of the threat posed by corsairs and Maroons in the area. While the Crown continued the policy of punishment of Maroons, it is possible that the panic caused by the attack on Venta del Chagres may have provoked them to reconsider their position and offer pardon to the Maroons who laid down their weapons (Encinas 1946, 4:394). These types of pacts were common between both the Spanish and English Crown and slaves in all colonial territories. In these situations, where the colonial authorities could not win militarily against the slaves they opted for a truce and in all cases the results were similar: land was transferred to newly freed slaves while their freedom was recognized in exchange for surrender. On the other hand, all remaining fugitive slaves would return to work or face punishment, and the pacified Maroons had to collaborate in the prosecution of Maroons who resisted.

Despite the apparent willingness of the colonial authority to forgive the Maroons, this was not the reply that they had expected. Marronage represented a social and political alternative and means of resistance to the colonial powers, as much as it represented a freedom that most would not consider renouncing (Laviña and Ruiz-Peinado Alonso 2006). Before the Consejo de Indias issued orders to resolve the situation peacefully in the area it had already been proposed that any rebel who voluntarily surrendered would not be punished (Tardieu 2009, 57–58). The amnesty had its intended effect and some gangs of rebels negotiated peace with the authorities. Despite this neither Emperor Carlos V nor his successor Felipe II managed to end the problem of Marronage.

In spite of the metropolitan authorities' optimism, those tasked with administering daily life in the colonies saw the Crown's measures as detrimental to the accumulation of wealth, as the freed slaves were a great loss to their owners, particularly those working in mines established far away from the urban centers who remained at the mercy of attack by Maroons (Tardieu 2009, 58).

Moreover, the presence of Maroons in and around the Camino Real continued to present an obvious danger to communication and trade. In these contexts the colonial authorities did not hesitate to wage war against uprisings that stopped the circulation of precious metals, which were fundamental to the economic march of the empire (Mena García 1984, 400–401).

When this occurred the Maroons sought shelter in the nearby hills, which made their persecution very difficult. The difficulties of the terrain compounded the impossibility of victory over the rebels, leading colonial authorities, with the approval of the Crown, to negotiate a lasting peace. During the most difficult period of confrontation between 1575 and 1580 there were between twenty-five hundred and three thousand Maroons, representing about a third of the total slave population of Panama (Tardieu 2009, 174; Jaén Suárez 1998, 361).

As a result, in conflicts between slaves, their owners, and the authorities the exercise of violence was not always the key element in solving conflicts. Despite the number of Maroons this did not imply that the authorities abandoned violence in their repression. Even so, faced with the impossibility of ending marronage through violence and war, the authorities were forced to cede to the wishes of the runaway slaves. In return for the recognition of their freedom the Maroons would have to work with the colonial authorities to put a stop to the continued attacks on colonial lands by those who did not surrender.

Some groups near to the main roads thought it more convenient to accept the conditions of freedom offered by the Crown and collaborate, as subjects, with the colonial authorities. Nevertheless, other Maroons decided not to accept the amnesty and conditions of peace offered by the Crown and continued to disrupt the flow of commerce and trade between the two oceans.

The Maroons of Portobelo agreed to sign a peace with the Crown in recognition of their freedom:

> Those of Portobelo have continued to be reduced peacefully so that the treaty has made them [created] a settlement a league and a half from Nombre de Dios. They have populated the town and called it Santiago del Principe, where they have a priest who indoctrinates them and administers justice. . . . it appears that Captain Antonio de Salcedo is still there with twenty soldiers. (Jopling 1994, 375–78)

The primary objective behind the foundation of Santiago de Príncipe by the Maroons led by Luis Mozambique was to guarantee peace in the area and allow commerce and trade to move fluidly between Panama and Nombre de Dios. Despite the losses caused to owners who had to recognize the freedom of their ex-slaves the benefits of peace were without doubt greater.

The negotiations brought about peace between the colonial authorities and the Maroons. The Maroons recognized the authority of, and pledged allegiance to, the Crown, which in return founded a town that would maintain a garrison of a captain and soldiers to guarantee the peace. Luis de Mozambique was made governor of the new town, which would help maintain peace by contributing money toward the capture of other Maroons (Jopling 1994, 375–78). Furthermore, the town would replicate the order of the empire and was founded around a central plaza and a church dedicated to the Virgin of Candelaria.

The Crown recognized the authority of Luis de Mozambique within the community and the Maroons were granted land for tillage. From that moment they were considered settlers. Meanwhile, the colony contributed to the maintenance of garrisons of captains and guards, alongside the upkeep of the clergy, while the petty crimes committed by Maroons would be pardoned. Other objectives of the Maroons included the promise of land by the Crown to establish another settlement. In principle this town was to be established in a swampy area named Chilibre, but this was exchanged for better land that allowed the subsistence of the group in the hills of the Piedra next to Nombre de Dios.

These new free subjects served as an example to other Maroons and mediated in conflicts with other groups who still operated in the area. In 1580 there is an account from Cepeda (no first name reported) telling of how the pacified slaves now served as auxiliaries in the suppression of other Maroons in the areas around Portobelo:

> Another group of negroes are those who lived in Puerto Velo near Nombre de Dios. . . . after having granted them general pardon for their crimes and freedom to their people, children and women, and having brought them to the place where they had settled . . . they live contently and in peace, they made their own elections of mayors from the commanders of the squadrons they had before being subdued. The friendship that is kept (with pacified black slaves) confuses the stubborn rebels who have seen some of those subdued Puerto Velo blacks serve against them with good zeal, knowing the benefits they receive in allowing themselves the good friendship and protection that is done to them, and I understand that this serves as an obstacle to these perverse people. (De la Guardia 1976, 91)

Thus, the expectations of the Crown and the colonial authorities were fulfilled by the collaboration with the subdued Maroons. Nevertheless, the conflict between the authorities and the Maroons continued throughout the sixteenth century.[10]

The Bayano Maroons, who were seen as the most unruly and mistrusted, continued opposition to the Crown until 1581 when Antón Mandinga and other leaders were captured by the colonial authorities. A new settlement called Santa Cruz la Real was founded in January 1582, and following the surrender of the Bayano Maroons on April 5, 1582 they were regrouped across Panama based on their ethnic origins. In surrendering, the Maroons committed themselves to dressing and attending mass, while the Crown would provide subsidies to buy food and animals.

In 1583 there was a report from Antonio de Salcedo in which he recounts the merits that accompanied the management of peace on his part:

> I have relieved of service to your majesty the black Maroons that were scattered around Portobelo, where there have been notable robberies and deaths, that they committed before they were subdued . . . and I have kept them in great stillness and peace without distrust that I can see no reason, or unease, on their part because of the great contentment and tranquillity that they have caused.[11]

But this did not mean the end of marronage or remove the danger of rebellion, as highlighted in September 1586 in a letter from the Audiencia de Panamá to the Consejo de Indias expressing fears rooted in the old revolts in the streets. As new slaves were brought into the colonies the fear returned that slaves armed with knives and other weapons might rise up once again against the authorities. Furthermore, the Bayano Maroons never entirely gave up pillaging and trafficking goods along the Camino Real. At the same time, the excessive mistreatment and punishment against the new slaves by their masters continued. Thus, in the early seventeenth century, the number of Maroons in the hills still represented some 35 percent of all slaves in the Audiencia of Panamá. The cycle was repeated and a new psychosis about the indecency and ferocity of the Maroons contrasted with the clever—more strategic—approach of the subdued Maroons who exerted a form of resistance "without renouncing their freedom" (Tardieu 2009, 242).

Along with problem of the Maroons the colonial authorities had to face conflicts with the indigenous people who resisted conquest, especially the Cuna who remained in the Darién region and facilitated the safe passage of the English attackers, along with other Maroons, from Atrato to Panama. The Cuna had also contributed to the sacking of Panama by an Anglo-French battalion, which surprised the inhabitants of the two commercial cities of the isthmus.[12]

The Darién region became one of the weak spots of the Spanish Empire: the impossibility of controlling the terrain and pacifying an indigenous population made trade and commerce between Cartagena and Nombre de Dios difficult. Furthermore, this situation continued for almost the whole colonial period (Rediker 2004), as the area served as a point of entry for pirates and corsairs who hindered Spanish trade.

The Maroons of Panama actively contributed to the failure of the slave system during the "first slavery." Flight and confrontation with colonists, and the frequent attacks on traders along the Camino Real created a permanent state of insecurity. In the case of Panama, the attacks of slaves not only saw them interrupt trade, but they actively collaborated with European pirates and corsairs to facilitate marches on Panama or Chagres. The sackings and attacks at the hands of pirates alongside unruly Maroons was a decisive factor in changing the policies of the Crown. The signing of treaties transferring land and recognizing the freedom of the slaves allowed them to maintain more effective control of trade in the area. Nevertheless, the problems of marronage remained alive with the arrival of more slaves from Africa.

Notes

1. Translation by Aidan Gabriel McGovern.

2. *Palenques and rochelas* were the names given to refuges established by fleeing slaves. These were usually found in the forest, making it difficult for the Crown to pursue, while also becoming sites from which the Cimarrons (escaped slaves) could attack.

3. La Real Audiencia de Panamá was the governing body and court of the empire of Spain in Panama. This was the third government established by the empire in the Americas following the Real Audiencia de Santo Domingo and the Real Audiencia de México.

4. While not considered a mining activity "proper," the extraction of pearls is here considered as an extractive mining activity.

5. This was the case of the sugar mills in Puerto Rico where forty to fifty slaves would regularly be involved in the production of sugar.

6. Maroons was the name given to the enslaved Africans in the Panama who had escaped the Spanish Crown and their private owners and formed independent settlements.

7. The Camino Real was the main road constructed by the Crown to move goods across the Isthmus of Panama, and it ran from Nombre de Dios to Panama City. It connected the trade of the Atlantic and Pacific Oceans.
8. Marronage is the name given to the act of escaping from slave owners.
9. A.G.I. Panamá, 237, L12 f12v–13; Kesley 2000, 46–50.
10. A.G.I. Panamá, 13, R 20,123.26 de febrero de 1581.
11. A.G.I. Panamá, 42.
12. A.G.I. Panamá, 95.

Works Cited

Sources

Archivo General de Indias, Panamá 237, L12.
A.G.I. Panamá 13, R 20, 123.
A.G.I. Panamá 42.
A.G.I. Panamá 95.

Published Sources

CODOIN. 1864–84. *Real Cédula autorizando la guerra contra los cimarrones de Tierra Firme. San Lorenzo 23 de mayo de 1568.* Vol. 17. Madrid: M. Bernaldo Quirós.
Encinas, D. de. 1946. *Cedulario Indiano.* Recopilado por Edición y estudio preliminar de Alfonso García Gallo. Libro IV. Madrid: Ediciones de Cultura Hispánica.

Bibliography

Ahlert, R. 2015. *La pestilencia más horrible . . . Die Geschichte der indigenen und schwarzen Skleverei in Nicaragua.* Berlin: LIT Verlag.
Alencastro, L. F. de. 2000. *O trato dos Viventes.* Sao Paulo: Companhia das Letras.
Altez, R., and M. Chust, ed. 2015. *Las revoluciones en el largo siglo XIX latinoamericano.* Madrid: Iberoamericana Vervuert.
Armitage, D. 2004. "Tres conceptos de historia atlántica." *Revista de Occidente*, no. 281: 7–28.
Bailyn, B. 1996. "The Idea of Atlantic History." *Itinerario*, no. 20: 19–44.
Bailyn, B. 2005. *Atlantic History: Concept and Contours.* Cambridge: Harvard University Press.

Bailyn, B., and P. L. Denault, ed. 2009. *Soundings in Atlantic History: Latent Structures and Intellectual Currents, 1500–1830*. Cambridge: Harvard University Press.

Blackburn, R. 1997. *The Making of New World Slavery: From the Baroque to the Modern, 1492–1800*. London: Verso.

Canny, N., and A. Padgen. 1987. *Colonial Identity in the Atlantic World, 1500–1800*. Princeton: Princeton University Press.

Castillero Calvo, A. 2004. *Historia General de Panamá*. Vol. 1. Panamá: Comité Nacional del Centenario de la República de Panamá.

Castillero Calvo, A. 2008. "Afromestizaje y movilidad social en el Panamá colonial." In *Africanos y afromestizos en la sociedad colonial de Centroamérica*, vol. 1, edited by Rina Cáceres, 78–104. San José: Oficina regional de la UNESCO para Centroamérica y Panamá.

Chust, M. 2015. "Sobre revoluciones en América Latina . . . Si las hubo." In *Las revoluciones en el largo siglo XIX latinoamericano*, edited by R. Altez and M. Chust. Madrid: Iberoamericana Vervuert.

De la Guardia, R. 1976. *Los negros del Istmo de Panamá*. Panamá: Instituto Nacional de Cultura.

Encinas, Diego de. 1946. *Cedulario Indiano*. Recopilado por Edición y estudio preliminar de A. García Gallo. Madrid: Libro IV Ediciones de Cultura Hispánica.

Falaola, T., and K. D. Roberts. 2008. *The Atlantic World: 1450–2000*. Bloomington: Indiana University Press.

Gilroy, Paul 1993. *The Black Atlantic: Modernity and Double Consciousness*. London: Verso.

Godechot, J. 1969. *Las revoluciones (1770–1799)*. Barcelona: Ed. Labor.

Greene, J. P., and P. D. Morgan. 2009. *Atlantic History: A Critical Appraisal*. New York: Oxford University Press.

Heywood, L. M., and J. K. Thornton. 2011. *Central Africans, Atlantic Creoles, and the Foundation of the Americas, 1585–1660*. Cambridge: Cambridge University Press.

Hidalgo Pèrez, M. 2016. "Cimarrones atlánticos: Historia atlántica como perspectiva historiográfica para el estudio del cimarronaje en Panamá." Comunicación presentada en el VII congreso AJHIS, Salamanca (ejemplar mecanografiado).

Jaén Suárez, O. 1998. *La población del Istmo de Panamá: Estudio de geohistoria*. Madrid: Agencia Española de Cooperación Internacional.

Jopling, C. F. 1994. *Indios y negros en Panamá en los siglos XVI y XVII: Selecciones de los documentos del Archivo de Indias*. Guatemala City: Centro de Investigaciones Regionales de Mesoamérica.

Kesley, H. 2000. *Sir Francis Drake: The Queen's Pirate*. New Haven: Yale University Press.

Kossok, M. 1981. *Vergleichende Geschichte der neuzeitlichen Revolutionen*. Berlin: Akademie-Verlag.

Kossok, M. 1989. *In tyrannos: Revolutionen der Weltgeschichte von den Hussiten bis zur Pariser Commune*. Leipzig: Edition Leipzig.

Laviña, J., and J. L. Ruiz-Peinado Alonso. 2006. *Resistencias esclavas en las Américas.* Madrid: Ed. Doce Calles.

Laviña, J., and M. Zeuske. 2008. "Failures of Atlantization: First Slaveries in Venezuela and Nueva Granada." *Review Fernand Braudel Center* 31, no. 3: 297–342.

Laviña, J., and M. Zeuske. 2014. *The Second Slavery: Mass Slaveries and Modernity in the Americas and in the Atlantic Basin.* Berlin: LIT Verlag.

Mena García, M. C. 1984. *La sociedad de Panamá en el siglo XVI.* Sevilla: Diputación de Sevilla.

Molina Castillo, M. J. 2011. *Panamá una sociedad esclavista en el periodo colonial, 1501–1821.* Chiriquí: Impresos modernos.

Portillo Valdés, J. M. 2006. *Crisis Atlántica.* Madrid: Marcial Pons, Col. Ambos Mundos.

Putman, M. Lara. 2006. "To Study the Fragment/Whole: Microhistory and the Atlantic World." *Journal of Social History* 39, no. 3: 615–30.

Rediker, M. 2004. *Villains of All Nations: Atlantic Pirates in the Golden Age.* London: Verso.

Reséndez, A. 2016. *The Other Slavery: The Uncovered Story of Indian Enslavement in America.* Boston: Houghton Mifflin Harcourt.

Roura, L., and M. Chust, ed. 2010. *La ilusión heroica, colonialismo, revolución e independencia en la obra de Manfred Kossok.* Castelló de la Plana: Universitat Jaume I.

Saco, J. A. 1937. *Historia de la esclavitud desde los tiempos más remotos hasta nuestros días.* Vol. 4. La Habana: Ed Alfa.

Solow, B. L., ed. 1991. *Slavery and the Rise of the Atlantic System.* New York: Cambridge University Press.

Strobel, C. 2015. *The Global Atlantic, 1400–1900.* New York: Routledge.

Suranyi, A. 2015: *The Atlantic Connection: A History of the Atlantic World, 1450–1900.* New York: Routledge.

Tardieu, J-P. 2006. *El negro en la Audiencia de Quito: Siglos XVI–XVIII.* Quito: Ed Abya Ayala, Ifea, Coodi.

Tardieu, J-P. 2008. "Perlas y piel de azabache: El negro en las pesquerías de las Indias Occidentales." *Anuario de Estudios Americanos* 65, no. 2: 91–124.

Tardieu, J-P. 2009. *Cimarrones de Panamá: La forja de una identidad afroamericana en el siglo XVI.* Madrid: Iberoamericana Vervuert.

Thornton, J. K. 2012. *A Cultural History of the Atlantic World, 1250–1820.* New York: Cambridge University Press.

Tomich, D., and M. Zeuske. 2008. "The Second Slavery: Mass Slavery, World Economy, and Comparative Microhistories." *Review: A Journal of the Fernand Braudel Center* 3: 91–100.

Ward, C. 1993: *Imperial Panama: Commerce and Conflict in Isthmian America, 1550–1800.* Albuquerque: University of New Mexico Press.

Wheat, D. 2011. "The First Great Waves: African Provenance Zones for the Transatlantic Slave Trade to Cartagena de Indias, 1570–1640." *Journal of African History* 52: 1–23.

Wheat, D. 2016. *Atlantic Africa and the Spanish Caribbean, 1570–1640*. Chapel Hill: University of North Carolina Press.

Zeuske, M. 2006. *Sklaven unsd Sklaverei in den Welten des Atlantiks*. Berlin: LIT Verlag.

Slavery in the Paraíba Valley and the Formation of the World Coffee Market in the Nineteenth Century

Rafael Marquese and Dale Tomich

The new formations of the second slavery were the vehicles for the mass production of key commodities of the material culture of modernity. Not only cotton and sugar but also coffee became important items of everyday consumption that were densely woven into the patterns of urban industrial life through the expansion of slave production into new commodity frontiers during the first half of the nineteenth century. Coffee consumption had been limited to luxury consumption among elite circles before Brazilian production transformed the world coffee market. Contrary to conventional views of slave production the Brazilian coffee frontier may be seen as a zone of innovation as Brazilian planters pioneered new ways of organizing nature and slave labor on an unprecedented scale in order to reinvent coffee as an item of mass production and mass consumption.

In 1828, the value of Brazilian coffee exports surpassed that of sugar, and Brazil emerged as the world's leading coffee producer.[1] Almost all of Brazilian production came from a single region. The valley of the Paraíba do Sul River, or simply the Paraíba Valley, encompassing lands in the provinces of São Paulo, Rio de Janeiro, and Minas Gerais, underwent a complete transformation in the course of two generations. Relatively unoccupied in 1800, the Valley acquired all of the characteristics of a slave plantation region over the next fifty years. Something similar had happened in other moments and spaces in the history of Brazil, for example the Zona da Mata in Pernambuco and the Bahian Recôncavo in the passage from the sixteenth to the seventeenth centuries, or in Maranhão and in

Campo dos Goitacases in the final decades of the eighteenth century. However, the scale of activity in the Paraíba Valley was unprecedented and its impact, not only on the economy but also on shaping the Brazilian national state, was decisive. It was already written during the nineteenth century that if coffee cultivation had put down roots in another region of the national territory and not in such close proximity to the Court, the history of the empire could well have been different. This is the origin of the saying "Brazil is the Valley," which has had a long career both in common-sense understanding and in historiography. It could equally well be said that the Valley was coffee. Beyond Brazil's complete domination of the world coffee market throughout the nineteenth century, the unheard of volume of its production was central for the transformation of the nature of the market itself, which passed from restrictions linked to luxury consumption to a qualitatively distinct scale of mass consumption (Topik 2003, 21–49).

Interpretations of Brazilian Coffee Culture

The interpretation of the Brazilian coffee industry has been the subject of historiographical discussion since the 1940s. Treating coffee cultivation as a sort of Brazilian "manifest destiny," historians have tended to relate it to the crisis of the mining industry and the resumption of agro-export activities at the turn of the nineteenth century. In this interpretation, coffee, fully suited to the natural conditions of Brazil's Center-South (virgin soil, climate, altitude, proximity to seaports), began to be produced on a large scale at the moment that world demand increased, mobilizing idle resources—capital and slaves—derived from the mining crisis (cf. Simonsen 1940; Prado 1985, 159–67; Stein 1990; Furtado 1974, 110–16; Valverde 1985; Costa 1982; Canabrava 2005). With variations, all these studies fall within what Stuart Schwartz calls the "dependency paradigm" of analysis of the Brazilian past. This interpretive model emphasizes Brazil's slave, agro-export character, oriented toward the generation of wealth in the centers of the capitalist world-economy (Schwartz 2003).

Beginning in the 1970s, efforts to revise this model in combination with empirical verification that the slave labor force employed on the first coffee plantations was not from the old mining zones led some historians to shift their focus away from the dependency paradigm to local social dynamics. The work of João Fragoso is a good example of this perspective (Fragoso 1992; Fragoso and Florentino 2001).

Taking his point of departure from the fact that the definitive expansion of slave coffee production coincided with a fall in world coffee prices (1822–30), Fragoso focuses his analysis on the forms of production and circulation articulated around the Rio de Janeiro market. Forming a "mosaic of non-capitalist forms of production," these activities permitted the accumulation of capital by the big merchants resident in Rio de Janeiro who monopolized the transatlantic slave trade and operated in the internal market. This capital was reinvested on a large scale in slave production in the frontier zones despite its lower return in relation to commercial activities. The entire movement was driven by an "archaic" ideal that conformed to a seigneurial-slaveholder ethos in which the possession of land and men was the decisive mark of social distinction. In Fragoso's words, "in the given system, investment in production obeys a logic that reproduces fixed differences between social groups on the basis of prestige" (Fragoso 1992, 297). Brazilian slave coffee cultivation was uniquely and exclusively the result of local actions and considerations. The response to the world market is excluded from consideration.

The empirical and theoretical inconsistencies of the Fragoso model have been duly criticized by historians (Gorender 1990, 81–83; Schwartz 1996; Mariutti, Nogueról, and Denieli Neto 2001). In all of these criticisms, scholars insist on the impossibility of understanding the formation of the Brazilian coffee frontier without having recourse to broader world processes, examining their interconnections with local conditions. Thus, in this chapter we examine the role of the Paraíba Valley in the formation of the world coffee market over the course of the nineteenth century. On the one hand, our analysis of the global framework presumes that various productive spaces form in relation to one another. Consequently, our unit of analysis is not the colonies or agro-exporting countries taken in isolation, but rather the broader arena of the world-economy. This is even more urgent in the case of tropical commodities. As we shall demonstrate, the movements of coffee and sugar maintained a close relation to one another during the course of the eighteenth and nineteenth centuries. On the other hand, our analysis of the local framework will take into account not only the regional composition of land, labor, and capital but also the political relations between planters, enslaved workers, and the national state. The formation of coffee plantation agriculture in Brazil depended upon political actions that were synchronized at the national level in order to create the institutional conditions necessary to set activity in motion and to regulate the world coffee market. These actions took place within the field of the politics of slavery. The period of the formation of the great coffee *fazendas* of the Paraíba Valley coincided with the period of the illegality of the transatlantic slave trade (1835–50) and the acquisition of slave gangs that, according to the terms of the imperial law of November 7, 1831, were formally free. Without an internal structure that gave political and juridical security to masters who possessed illegally enslaved Africans, Brazil certainly would not have supplied endless sacks of coffee to the ports and warehouses of the Northern Hemisphere.

World Coffee Production in the Age of Revolution, 1790–1830

Even though coffee was one of the most valuable agricultural products to enter world trade since the sixteenth century, European colonial powers were slow to produce it. Until the end of the seventeenth century the countries of Southwest Asia monopolized this sphere of activity. The Dutch were the first Europeans to produce the crop. During the 1690s the East India Company (VOC) introduced its cultivation to Java. The French soon followed in Réunion. During the 1720s, the coffee bush was adapted to the colonies of the New World (Surinam, Martinique, Guadeloupe), and the Dutch and the French introduced substantial quantities of coffee into metropolitan markets for the first time. Nonetheless, until the mid-1700s the volume of coffee did not increase over previous levels. The Dutch imported about three thousand metric tons annually, an amount similar to what the French obtained from Martinique in 1750 (May 1972).

The jump in production occurred after the Seven Years' War, in large measure as a result of the explosion of coffee cultivation in Saint-Domingue. Exports from this colony jumped from about thirty-one hundred metric tons in 1755 to nearly thirty-two thousand metric tons in 1790. In the latter year, the total production of French colonies of the Caribbean and the Indian Ocean (Saint-Domingue, Martinique, Guadeloupe, Cayenne, and Réunion) reached about forty-eight thousand metric tons, about 70 percent of the world total, which was estimated at sixty-four thousand metric tons. On the eve of the Revolution, Saint-Domingue by itself was responsible for almost half of the world production of coffee, as well as nearly one-third of world sugar production (Trouillot 1982, 337). Nonetheless, the coffee market was relatively restricted, limited to luxury consumption of urban strata in continental Europe and the Levant.

The growth of coffee cultivation in Saint-Domingue was at the heart of the events that led to the Revolution. For technical and environmental reasons, coffee was grown on lands that were not suitable for sugar cultivation. The geomorphology of the hills or *mornes* in the interior of the colony impeded the formation of large rural holdings there. Nonetheless, with initial investment requirements much lower than those required for sugar, coffee cultivation offered a path to the accumulation of wealth and social mobility for small- and medium-sized slave owners, especially the growing number of mulattos and free blacks with little capital (Trouillot 1982; Girault 1981, 51). During the 1780s, the economic success of coffee cultivation heightened conflicts between these racially subaltern but prosperous groups and the white population of the colony, that is to say, the large sugar planters and the poor whites (*petit blancs*). This highly explosive configuration of social forces unraveled with the outbreak of revolutionary events in the metropolis. In 1789 the National Assembly in Paris aroused the autonomist anxieties of the Caribbean planter classes. As early as the second half of 1789, the planters of the various French West Indian colonies, especially those of Saint-Domingue, formed colonial assemblies to press their claims for greater economic and political freedom. However, the white slave owners were not the only ones to organize themselves in order to benefit from the new political situation. The free men of color, many of whom were prosperous coffee planters, also mobilized to expand their political rights. These black and mulatto slaveholders demanded, above all, the right to participate in the elections for the National Assembly in France. The conflict of the blacks and mulattos against whites sharpened during 1790 and rapidly gave way to open conflict. Until the middle of 1791 these struggles did not threaten the economy of Saint-Domingue. But in August 1791 the massive slave revolt destroyed the tenuous equilibrium between whites and mulattos (cf. Dubois 2004).

What is important for our purposes is that beyond having ended slavery on the battlefield and transformed the condition of slaveholding throughout the Americas, the Haitian Revolution completely altered the configuration of the world coffee and sugar supply. In the years of the conflict and in the decades immediately after, the volume on the market of these two products fell to less than half of what it had been in 1790. In contrast to sugar, coffee continued to be cultivated in independent Haiti, but now as a peasant crop. Only at the end of the nineteenth century did it reach prerevolutionary levels, of about thirty thousand tons annually. In conjunction with rising consumer demand, the dramatic withdrawal of Saint-Domingue from the market had an immediate impact on the other zones of world coffee production.

Initially the zones that most benefited from the vacuum created by Saint-Domingue were those that had produced coffee before 1790, above all the British West Indies. Throughout the eighteenth century coffee production grew slowly in the British Caribbean, in response to the tariff policy adopted by the metropolis. Around 1730, the British government established a heavy tax on coffee imports in order to protect East India Company tea imports. With the reduction of these tariffs in the 1780s, colonial coffee production increased to the point that Jamaica produced about a thousand metric tons in 1790. Jamaican planters responded immediately to the slave uprising in Saint-Domingue and the radicalization of the revolutionary process. Production jumped by six thousand tons in the last years of the eighteenth century and reached a historic high of 13,500 tons in 1808 (Smith 1998, 73).

The lands employed for coffee cultivation in Jamaica differed from those used for sugar cultivation, for reasons that were similar to those that obtained in Saint-Domingue. Even though there was not competition between sugar and coffee over land, the same could not be said for labor. The competition for labor was aggravated after the abolition of the transatlantic slave trade to the British colonies. It is perhaps not surprising that the high point of Jamaican coffee production was in 1808, the year after the passage of the abolition bill. Beyond environmental depletion and limited metropolitan consumption, Jamaican coffee planters needed to confront the strong local demand for slave labor on the part of the sugar planters who struggled to maintain their economic viability in the decades following abolition of the slave trade. Despite almost two centuries of uninterrupted exploitation of the soil and an inadequate agro-manufacturing plant compared with the innovations introduced by their international competitors, the Jamaican sugar planters proved to be more efficient than the coffee planters of the island (Ward 1988). The problem of competition between sugar plantations and coffee plantations for increasingly scarce slave manpower, always to the disadvantage of coffee, was confirmed in Demerara, the former Dutch colony acquired by the English during the Napoleonic Wars.

If Jamaican planters responded satisfactorily to the vacuum left by Saint-Domingue in the decades from 1790 to 1800, the same cannot be said of the Dutch East India Company in the Indian Ocean, something all the more notable in view of the role that Java was to play in the world coffee market after 1830. After 1725, during the first years of systematic activity, the VOC collaborated with indigenous authorities in Priangan and Ciberon, in the west of the island, in order to supply coffee at fixed prices. The local authorities compelled their subjects to cultivate coffee on a small scale and retained all or part of the product obtained from the peasants in the form of taxation. This method was applied to other parts of the island in the final decades of the eighteenth century and was maintained after the dissolution of the VOC and the beginning of direct colonial control by the Dutch government in 1800. The organization of this production process inhibited rapid response to the increase in world demand since it necessarily entailed negotiation with local authorities. Further, the peasants cultivated coffee on a small scale, outside of the system of world prices, as the amount paid per unit was arbitrarily established by the VOC. Dutch efforts to increase production in the wake of Saint-Domingue resulted in a serious rebellion in Ciberon in 1805. During the rebellion, the peasants uprooted the coffee bushes that they cultivated and burned the warehouses where previous harvests were stored. Afterward the entire system of colonial exploitation had to be reconstructed, which yielded results only three decades later (Elson 1994, 24–25; Clarence-Smith 1994, 241–43).

The world coffee market underwent considerable fluctuations between 1790 and 1830, not only as a result of the Haitian Revolution but also because of the military conflicts among the Atlantic powers. Amsterdam experienced a period of sustained high prices during the course of the conflict in Saint-Domingue (1791–1804). The Continental Blockade and the intensification of the conflict between Britain and France from 1808 to 1812 created a disjuncture between the high prices in Amsterdam and low prices in the ports of the producing regions (González Fernández 1989, 157). Global coffee prices were exceptionally high with the return of peace in 1815, and remained so until 1822. In the following decade prices fell continuously until they reached the level that they had had twenty years before. Thus, the years from 1812 to 1830 can be seen as a period of market adjustment. The first phase from 1812 to 1822 was a period of high prices with an artificial contraction at the end of the Napoleonic Wars. Prices fell during the second phase from 1822 to 1830, leading to the equalization of supply and demand and the expulsion of inefficient producers from the market.

Thus, it was no accident that the period from 1822 to 1833 marked the clear differentiation of the world coffee market between old and new producing regions. This process of differentiation was set in motion three decades earlier. The Haitian Revolution marked a disjuncture in the history of the Atlantic, at once initiating the simultaneous decline of colonial slavery in the French and British Caribbean and the formation of new historical structures of nineteenth-century slavery—whose centers were the vast areas of virgin land in Cuba, Brazil, and the United States (Tomich 2004). These new spaces were outside of traditional imperial relations and were not subject to the restrictions of built environment that were present in the British and French Caribbean. Of these new spaces, the US South—the keystone of the new structure of nineteenth-century slavery—is beyond the limits of this study. It never produced coffee for the world market and the sugar produced in the Lower Mississippi Valley was not prominent in the world market. In contrast, Cuba and Brazil were strong rivals in the international sugar and coffee trades from the 1790s onward.

The roots of this cycle of coffee and sugar production in Cuba is to be found in the Bourbon Reforms. Cuba possessed ample natural resources for the establishment of a plantation economy, but remained underexploited until the end of the eighteenth century. Between the 1760s and the 1780s, a policy of gradual commercial liberalization promoted by the ministers of Charles III and decisive action by local oligarchies led to the development of a dense network of sugar mills in the western part of the island around the port of Havana. At the end of the eighteenth century Cuban sugar production was the equivalent of the total production of Portuguese America (Moreno Fraginals 1978, 3:59–60; Alden 1999 313–14). Among the first measures taken by the new monarch, Charles IV, in 1789 was a decree permitting free trade in slaves for two years, a measure that Cuban planters had long sought and which was reiterated on several occasions in subsequent years. Up until 1807 English and North American merchants were the primary suppliers of Africans to Cuba. Although the Spanish-Cuban slave traders would not be capable of dominating the transatlantic slave trade for several decades, it became perhaps the most important engine of the Cuban slave economy (Murray 1980; Johnson 1999).

With the collapse of Saint-Domingue, Cuban planters were well prepared to take advantage of the new conditions of the world market. The rapid growth of the Cuban slave plantation economy was dazzling after 1791. New sugar plantations were founded, and old ones significantly increased their levels of production. For the first time, slave coffee plantations were established in both the east and the west of the island. This sudden shift in production depended upon the reorganization of Cuban commerce, which occurred as a response to the conjuncture of the revolutionary wars. From 1796 to 1802, Cuba's trade with the Iberian Peninsula was interrupted. After a brief period of normalization, trade between Cuba and Spain was again interrupted between 1804 and 1812. During these critical years the United States became the principal trading partner of the Spanish colony. Cuban sugar and coffee were purchased by North American merchants who reexported what was not consumed in their country to continental European markets. (The United States was neutral in the Atlantic conflicts of the period.) With the return of peace and the end of the war between the United States and Britain between 1813 and 1816, the British merchant marine controlled Cuban exports. With the erosion of its position as the reexporter of Cuban products, Spain authorized free trade in its colonies in 1818, opening Cuban commerce to the merchants of all nations. From the promulgation of this decree onward, Spanish control over the Cuban economy was only fiscal. The metropolis facilitated the export of Cuban products to the world market with low tariffs, but protected the importation of Spanish goods to the colony with high taxes (Fradera 2005, 327–420).

The links between the Haitian Revolution and Cuban coffee production were much closer than mere market incentives. The generalized conflict that broke out in the French colony after 1791 sent many slave owners into exile, among them a number of coffee planters, who often brought their slaves with them. The majority of them went to the mountainous region of eastern Cuba because of its geographical proximity and favorable environmental conditions. These new immigrants played a decisive role in transferring technology and knowledge of coffee cultivation to Cuba. This knowledge was quickly transferred to planters who were building coffee plantations on the Havana–Matanzas axis in the west of the island. Until 1807 Cuban coffee production was insignificant, not going above the one thousand ton level. But the large-scale planting that began in 1804 brought production to forty-six hundred tons in 1810. In the following decade, it oscillated significantly, reaching about ten thousand metric tons annually in the high years of 1815 and 1821 (Pérez de la Riva 1944; Marrero 1984, 11:108).

In 1821, Cuban coffee production was equivalent to that of Jamaica, and both were superior to Java. However, Jamaican production stagnated during the 1820s and both Brazilian and Javanese coffee production increased significantly, the former more than the latter. Even though international coffee prices fell sharply between 1822 and 1830, Cuban production almost tripled during this period, reaching almost 29,500 tons in 1833, a figure close to that of Saint-Domingue in 1790. This was due to the increased area under cultivation and the increased number of slaves employed in coffee production. In 1827 coffee and sugar production in Cuba each employed around fifty thousand slaves (Marrero 1984, 11:114). However, in the west of the island, where the majority of plantations were located, coffee and sugar competed for the same natural resources.

Brazilian coffee production also reached levels equivalent to those of the world's major coffee producers during the 1820s. As in Cuba, coffee cultivation in Portuguese America was irrelevant until the last decade of the eighteenth century. Coffee was introduced into the state of Grão-Pará e Maranhão in the 1720s as part of the same movement that introduced the crop to Martinique and Surinam, but it was simply regarded as an ornamental plant until the end of the century. Although coffee had been part of the Pombal's imperial calculus, which sought to diversify agricultural exports in the 1760s, it did not receive the same attention as other crops such as cotton and rice, which were shipped to Lisbon on a large scale beginning in the 1770s. However, coffee was adapted to the Center-South of Brazil during this period and was cultivated at country houses and on small farms around Rio de Janeiro.

As has been discussed, from the earliest works on the subject, specialists in the history of the Brazilian coffee economy related the establishment of coffee plantations (*fazendas*) to the crisis of the mining economy at the beginning of the nineteenth century. In light of current scholarship, the existence of a link between the two processes can be affirmed, but not in the sense in which it has been conventionally presented. Many of the conditions that were decisive for the emergence of coffee production in Brazil were already present because of the gold economy: a large-scale bilateral slave trade between the ports of Central Africa and Rio de Janeiro controlled by merchants in Rio de Janeiro, the existence of north-south and east-west roads that crossed the Paraíba Valley (the Caminho Novo between Rio de Janeiro and the capitania of Minas Gerais opened in the 1720s, and the Caminho Novo de Piedade, which linked Rio de Janeiro and São Paulo, opened in the 1770s to facilitate communications between the seat of the vice-royalty and the mines o Goiás and Mato Grosso); the availability of a vast area of virgin land in the Serra de Mantiqueira and on the slopes of the Serra do Mar that was the result of the official policy of "forbidden zones"; and, finally, a very efficient transport system based on mule trains that was adapted to the rugged terrain of south-central Brazil.

Nonetheless, this infrastructure was not mobilized by the coffee industry during the 1790s and 1800s. During these years the response of the slaveholders of Portuguese America to the revolution in Saint-Domingue was felt in sugar production. Beyond the recuperation and expansion of sugar production in the Northeast littoral (the Recôncavo Baiano, the Zona da Mata in Pernambuco, and Paraíba), the sugar producers in the Center-South established new mills in Campos dos Goitacases, in the Recôncavo Baiano, the west of São Paulo (Itu, Jundiaí, Campinas), and even along the roads that cut through the Paraíba Valley. In the 1790s the growth of sugar production in Portuguese America followed the same rhythm as Cuban production (Moreno Fraginals 1978, 3:355; Arruda 1980, 360). The conjuncture of the end of the eighteenth century also stimulated the production of provisions and cattle-raising for the internal market, as demonstrated by the diversification of agriculture in the Rio das Mortes district in the south of Minas Gerais and in various parts of the capitania of São Paulo (Bergad 2004, 1–25; Luna and Klein 2005, 28–52).

The flight of the Portuguese royal family to Rio de Janeiro was the turning point for Brazil. In the first place, the rapid increase of population in the new seat of the Portuguese Empire—in addition to the migration stimulated by the new political status of Rio de Janeiro—substantially increased the demand for basic provisions. In order to meet this need, the Crown sought to improve the network of roads that crossed the Center-South of the colony and promoted the construction of roads to directly link the zone producing provisions in the south of Minas Gerais to the new Court. Two of these new roads, the Estrada da Polícia and the Estrada da Comércio, designed to regularize the flow of goods between Minas and Rio, would be absolutely central for the rise of coffee cultivation in the central Paraíba Valley. Their opening generated immense land hunger and two of the most important coffee municipalities in the world, Vassouras and Valença, were soon to be established on their margins (Lenharo 1992, 47–59). Second, the opening of the ports after 1808 permitted a direct connection between the slave owners of Portuguese America and the world market. In conjunction with the demographic growth of the Court, the free trade decree had an immediate impact on the demand for slaves. During the first decade of the nineteenth century an annual average of ten thousand slaves disembarked in Brazil. During the following decade (1811–20), under the new commercial regime, this figure practically doubled. Nearly nineteen thousand Africans were imported as slaves in Rio de Janeiro during this period (Florentino 1995, 74). A portion of these slaves were destined for the growing coffee plantations whose proprietors had at their disposition, in the port of Rio de Janeiro and the length of the littoral down to Santos, a complete commercial system (warehouses, merchant houses, and so forth) that had been built there previously for the exportation of sugar, leather, cotton, and other products (Luna and Klein 2005, 58–59).

Slave owners invested decisively in coffee during the decade of the 1810s in response to the incentives of the world market. Their initiative is documented not only by a series of prices paid directly to producers between 1798 and 1810 but also by the qualitative evidence of Auguste de Saint-Hilaire. While traveling through the Valley of Paraíba from São Paulo to Rio de Janeiro along the Caminho Novo de Piedade in the first months of 1822, the French naturalist noted: "The lands around Taubaté are very suitable for the cultivation of sugar and coffee. Formerly, sugar cane was most frequently cultivated, but after coffee enjoyed a considerable rise in price, planters only wanted to grow coffee." Further along, near Areias, he wrote after interviewing a slaveholder: "According to what he, his son, and others told me, coffee cultivation is entirely new in this region and has already enriched many people" (Luna and Klein 2005, 37; Saint-Hilaire 1974, 78, 100–101).

Saint-Hilaire's evaluation was confirmed by the export data for Brazil. The annual average for the period from 1797 to 1811, which reflects the conditions that obtained before the opening of the ports, was about four hundred metric tons. In the five-year period between 1812 and 1816, Brazilian coffee production rose to an annual average of fifteen hundred metric tons in response to direct access to the world market and rapidly rising prices. In the following five-year period (1817–21) production increased fourfold, climbing to sixty-one hundred tons annually. During the years of independence (1822–23), production doubled, reaching 13,500 tons, the amount that was produced in Cuba that same year. If the total value of coffee exports did not yet surpass that of sugar, its rapid growth since 1812 promised much for the future.

Growth accelerated greatly over the next ten years when production quadrupled from 13,500 tons in 1821 to sixty-seven thousand tons in 1833. This latter figure was the equivalent of total world production in 1790. The ceiling set by prerevolutionary Saint-Domingue, unattainable until then, was definitively a thing of the past. At the beginning of the 1830s, Brazil was world's largest producer, well ahead of the rest of its competitors (Cuba, Java, Jamaica, Haiti). How can the great jump in Brazilian production during the 1820s, a phase of sharply falling prices, be explained? Did producers ignore the price system and organize their strategy in terms of social and symbolic gains, as João Fragoso argues? And is this the reason why production was concentrated almost exclusively in the Paraíba Valley?

In order to respond to the first question it is necessary to take into account two specific characteristics of coffee. First, the coffee tree only begins to produce its full yield after five years. The delay between planting and the sale of the processed beans is at least three years. As a means of getting around this problem planters adopted the practice of planting corn and beans between the rows of coffee trees with the objective of both providing shade for the young coffee plants and furnishing provisions for the slave labor force. Increasing the supply of coffee in response to high prices in any particular year could only make itself felt after a period of three to five years. Second, as Pedro Carvalho de Mello emphasizes, the coffee trees had "a characteristic of a capital good since once they were planted they could produce coffee beans for many years. . . . Therefore, cultivation could not be abandoned without a serious loss of capital. This contrasts to cotton and sugar cane. Even with low prices, planters continued to care for coffee trees that had already been planted in the expectation of a future rise in prices" (Mello 1982, 1:12).

These material characteristics of coffee cultivation in combination with fluctuating exchange rates allowed Brazilian slave owners to supply more coffee to the world market despite the sharp decline in unit prices. The value of coffee sold in New York, the new center of world distribution, fell sharply from 1823 to 1830, going from twenty-one to eight cents per pound (Bacha and Greenhill 1992, 333–34). The fall in dollar prices diminished in intensity between 1827 and 1830 and stabilized at a low level between eight or nine cents. These were exactly the years in which, according to the data collected by Luna and Klein for the lower Paraíba Valley in São Paulo, exchange rates allowed Brazilian planters to gain more in *milreis* (Brazilian currency) per unit of coffee. During these years exchange rates clearly favored exporters. The price series established by Luna and Klein ends in 1830 (Gorender 1990, 82). The series for New York, on the other hand, indicates an increase of almost 30 percent for prices paid in dollars between 1830 and 1835. Brazilian exports correspond to these prices. Production grew sharply from 1826 to 1828, the product of trees that had been planted before 1823, when prices were high. Between 1828 and 1830 (coffee trees planted between 1824 and 1826 with external and internal prices at low levels), production stabilized at around 27,000 metric tons, while from 1831 to 1834 (coffee trees planted between 1827 and 1830, with external prices stationary and internal prices high) production climbed from 32,940 metric tons to 67,770 metric tons. As these figures demonstrate, Brazilian producers responded rapidly to changes in the world market within the parameters allowed by the physical characteristics of coffee cultivation.

Further, the role of the Paraíba Valley as a new zone of coffee production needs to be considered here. We may divide the Paraíba Valley into three subregions. The upper Paraíba, with emerging land occupation up to the zone of Queluz and Rezende at the present division between São Paulo and Rio de Janeiro, was already occupied at the beginning the seventeenth century by Paulistas seeking to enslave

Indians. The lower Paraíba, extending from São Fidélis up to the falls of the Paraíba River, roughly corresponding to Campos de Goitacases, had been occupied since the second half of the seventeenth century, first for cattle-raising and later sugar production. In contrast, the central Paraíba, from Barra Mansa to the region of São Fidélis, was open to coffee cultivation on an unprecedented scale. Occupation was blocked by the official Portuguese policy of "forbidden zones" that was adopted in the 1730s. This ordinance sought to prevent contraband trade in gold by prohibiting construction of new roads and trails in the mountain areas where there were no checkpoints and the forest patrols (*Patrulhas do Mato*) were not active. Clandestine prospectors and small-scale squatters were certainly present on lands to the east and west of the Caminho Novo or Estrada Real before revision of the ordinance in the 1780s, but systematic settlement was effectively blocked (Stein 1985, 10–17; Motta 1999, 34–40). As a result, there was an enormous quantity of virgin land in the central Paraíba Valley at the end of the seventeenth and beginning of the eighteenth centuries. These lands presented no obstacles to settlement and offered excellent conditions for coffee cultivation. They were no more than 150 kilometers distant from the myriad of natural anchorages located along the coast to the south of the port of Rio de Janeiro, and they possessed an adequate transportation infrastructure because of the mining economy.

Vast lands of the central Paraíba Valley offered exceptional conditions for large-scale coffee cultivation. Once the forest was cleared, its rich humus soil, which had been deposited for centuries, was highly productive. Productivity was even higher in the Valley because coffee trees were not planted in the shade. Coffee trees planted this way produced much higher initial yields even if they required constant weeding, had an oscillating yield from harvest to harvest, and produced beans of inferior quality (Dean 1996, 181–82). The available records indicate that the yield of coffee plants in the Paraíba Valley declined over the course of the nineteenth century, but it was extremely high in the early decades. In the document cited above, Saint-Hilaire noted that one thousand trees produced ninety-one arrobas of processed coffee while Father João Joaquim Ferreira de Aguilar, in the first agronomy manual produced in the Paraíba Valley, registered the productivity at one hundred arrobas per one thousand trees in the area around Valença (Saint-Hilaire 1974, 101; Aguiar 1836, 11). In comparison, Carlos August Taunay, basing his observations on the Tijuca region of Rio de Janeiro at the end of the 1820s, reported a yield of twenty arrobas for one thousand trees (Taunay 2001, 130), while the Cuban census of 1829 registered twenty-seven arrobas per one thousand trees planted on the island, a number superior to the 9.8 arrobas per one thousand trees reported by the Cuban agronomist Tranquilino Sandalio de Noa, regarded as the norm for a big plantation in 1829 (Marrero 1984, 11:110–11).

In order to market the growing output of the 1820s it was necessary to overcome the obstacles presented by the mountainous terrain of the Paraíba Valley and the distance to the ports on the coast. The transportation network was the major contribution of the mining economy to coffee cultivation during the nineteenth century. In response to the requirements of the mining industry in the second half of the eighteenth century, a complex system of raising and commercializing mules linked the southern part of Portuguese America to the capitanias of São Paulo, Rio de Janeiro, and Minas Gerais, furnishing the primary means of transport to the entire Center-South of the colony. With the stimulus of the world market, this system was immediately mobilized to transport the coffee production of the Paraíba Valley. Given that the new plantations were no more than a seven-day journey from the ports of the coast (taking as a reference the customary journey of three leagues a day), and given the relatively low cost of acquiring and maintaining mule trains until the mid-nineteenth century, the ratio of the cost of coffee: the cost of freight: the volume of freight: and distance to the ports was viable with the system of mule trains (Klein 1990, 1–25).

The Paraíba Valley Domination of the World Coffee Market, 1830–1880

Brazil's position in the world coffee market after 1830 is clearly demonstrated by the graph of world coffee exports from 1823 to 1888 (figure 9). The harvests from 1831 to 1833 doubled the annual volume of production and put Brazil well ahead of its competitors. The level of production jumped between 1843 and 1847 when output stabilized at about 150,000 metric tons per year, then again in the second half of the 1860s when annual production reached about 225,000 metric tons, and finally at the end of 1870s when it reached the 350,000 metric ton level. With slight variations from one harvest to the next, Brazil, that is to say the Paraíba Valley, dominated world supply in the nineteenth century, at least until the middle of the 1870s when the west of São Paulo and the forest zone (*zona da mata*) of Minas Gerais began producing coffee. Its only competitor was the Dutch colony of Java.

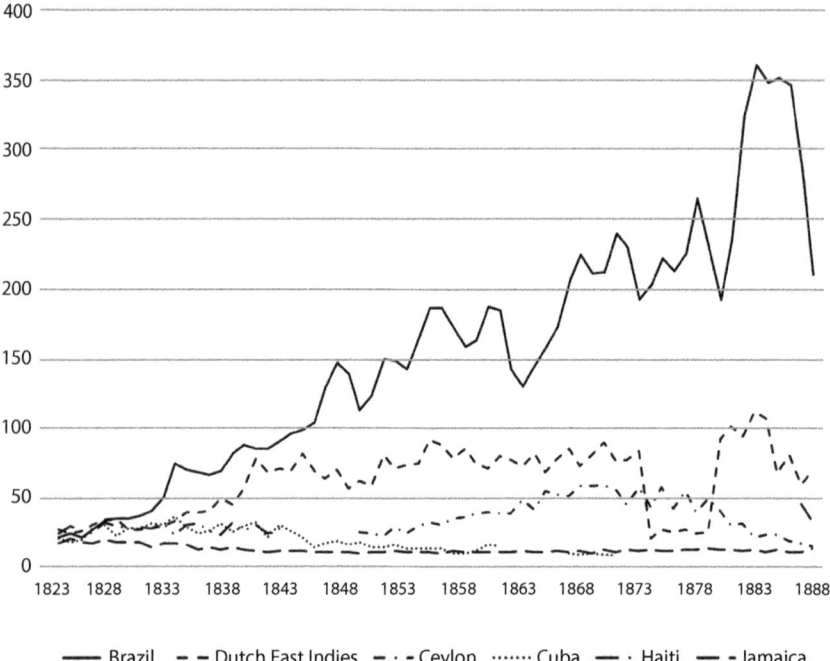

— Brazil   – – Dutch East Indies   – · – Ceylon   ······ Cuba   — · Haiti   — - Jamaica

Source: Mario Samper and Radin Fernando, "Historical Statistics of Coffee Production and Trade from 1700 to 1960," in *The Global Coffee Economy in Africa, Asia, and Latin America 1500–1989*, edited by William Gervase Clarence-Smith and Steven Topik (Cambridge: Cambridge University Press, 2003), 411–62.

Figure 9. Coffee Exports, 1823–1888 (Thousands of Metric Tons).

The scale and character of the world coffee market was profoundly transformed during the nineteenth century. In the 1880s total world production was ten times greater than it had been one hundred years earlier. The appearance of the United States as a consumer was the great change. Its population increased fifteen times and annual per capita consumption rose from only four grams to four kilos during this period. It was an open market, free from import tariffs from 1832, and it did not discriminate with regard to the quality of coffee imported. The other big purchasers of the period, all located in northern Europe and undergoing rapid industrialization and urbanization, where also distinguished by a demographic explosion and increasing rates of per capita consumption. These changes transformed the coffee market from the restricted luxury market of the eighteenth century to the mass industrial market of the nineteenth century whose growth was stimulated by the increased supply and low cost of coffee (Topik 2003, 37–40).

The new conditions of the international market required a constant increase in productivity from tropical producers. For those old producing regions without reserves of land for expansion or which had been affected by the crisis of colonial slavery (as in the case of Saint-Domingue at the end of the eighteenth century or Jamaica and Surinam in the first decade of the nineteenth century) the loss of competitiveness quickly eliminated them from central positions in the market. This was not the case for Brazil and for Spain's Cuban colony whose constitutional monarchies were able to implement policies during the 1810s and 1820s that established secure institutional bases for slavery that were capable of confronting the strong external antislavery pressures promoted by Britain. Nonetheless, in view of Cuba's performance in sugar production, the ample availability of virgin lands, and the continuation of the African slave trade until the 1860s, it exclusion from the world coffee market is noteworthy. Why did this happen? And why did Java, which did not have a slave economy, succeed in maintaining its position alongside Brazil as a major coffee producer?

With regard to the first question, there was a close relation between the coffee boom in Brazil, the crisis of coffee production in Cuba, and Cuba's sugar boom. As we have seen, the coffee plantations in the western region of Cuba had been established in the same zones as the sugar plantations and the two competed with one another for the same resources, especially land and slaves. Until the 1820s it was not unusual that the same slave owners employed their capital simultaneously in both activities (Perez de la Riva 1944, 53). In contrast, the central Paraíba Valley was exclusively a zone of coffee production, distinct from the sugar zones in the lowlands of Rio de Janeiro state and the west of São Paulo state. The difference in the output per coffee tree demonstrates that the land in the west of Cuba was not as well suited to coffee as that in the Paraíba Valley. The coffee tree's character as a capital good created additional difficulties in the west of Cuba, a region that was regularly exposed to hurricanes. If the weather was not a problem for sugar cane, which could recover within a year, it was devastating for coffee plantations, which had to be replanted and required five years to recuperate their full productivity.

Throughout the 1820s Cuban coffee producers were aware of the growing weight of Brazilian competition. Sharply falling world coffee prices that resulted in the ruin of many Cuban coffee plantations were clearly the result of increasing world production. In 1828 the Consulado of Havana reported that perhaps two-thirds of Cuba's coffee plantations had been ruined. The following year a proposal by the Economic Society of Friends of the Country in Havana to abandon coffee production was rejected but there was agreement on the need to reduce costs and increase efficiency in order to compete with Brazil (González Fernández 1989, 164).

When the United States ended duties on coffee at the beginning of the 1830s, Brazilian coffee producers displaced their Cuban rivals in the US market (González Fernández 1989, 164). The inability of Cuban producers to compete with Brazilian coffee planters, together with their exclusion from the US market, sealed their fate. The beginning of the construction of the Cuban railroad network in 1837 increased the relative advantage of sugar planters in international markets and resulted in a massive transfer of land and slaves from coffee to sugar production (Santamaría García and García Alvarez 2004, 129). The devastating hurricane of 1844 was the final nail in the coffin of coffee cultivation in western Cuba. There was, however, another side to the coin. The rapid growth of sugar cultivation in Cuba beginning in the 1830s began to displace Brazilian sugar from its position in the world market. While the transatlantic slave trade was still in operation the Brazilian sugar industry was able to resist Cuban expansion, but after the end of the slave trade it was no longer viable (Moreno Fraginals 1978, 3:356–57; *Estatísticas Históricas do Brasil* 1987, 342).

This last observation leads us to the central point needed to understand the growth of coffee production in the Paraíba Valley—slave labor. In the 1820s and 1830s, it was commonly believed in Cuba that slaves cost double what they cost in Brazil (González Fernández 1989, 164). David Eltis's research confirms this perception. Until the 1850s the price curves for slaves acquired from the transatlantic trade for Cuba and Brazil are congruent with one another, but Cuban prices were always higher than Brazilian ones (Eltis 1987, 262–63). The explanation for the difference is simple. The traffic for the Center-South of Brazil was conducted by Luso-Brazilian merchants resident in Rio de Janeiro since the end of the seventeenth century. These slave traders primarily operated in the Congo-Angola zone. Their command of local operations, shorter voyages, and more solid contacts on the African continent made possible lower final prices for Africans who embarked as slaves. The efficiency of Rio's slave traders even allowed the importation of slaves from the east coast of Africa after 1811. In contrast, the Hispano-Cuban slave traders, despite being as efficient as their Brazilian and Portuguese counterparts, only began to participate in the traffic at the beginning of the nineteenth century, and they had to traverse much longer routes than those that went to the Center-South of Brazil.

However, the cost of slaves cannot be taken as simply an economic variable linked only to the law of supply and demand. Britain's systematic campaign against the transatlantic slave trade required a concerted political response from the expanding regions of slave production. In the case of Brazil, independence in 1822 exposed it to English pressure. Britain demanded that Dom Pedro I commit to ending the slave trade in exchange for formal recognition of the new sovereign state. This question was only resolved in 1826 with the signing of a convention that foresaw the abolition of the trade between Africa and Brazil three years after ratification of the agreement, which took place in 1837. These negotiations eroded a significant amount of the political capital of the first emperor and contributed to his downfall in 1831. While they were taking place slave traders and planters accelerated importations in the second half of the 1820s. Between 1821 and 1825 nearly 112,000 enslaved Africans disembarked in the part of Rio de Janeiro. In the following five years 186,000 captives arrived (Parron 2011, 18–53; Bethell 2002, 27–121; Florentino 1995, 59). This increase in the rate of importations clearly expressed the contemporary view that the slave trade would be effectively closed by 1830.

The years in which the greatest numbers of enslaved Africans entered the port of Rio de Janeiro (1828 and 1829 with forty-five thousand and forty-seven thousand Africans, respectively) correspond with the abundant harvests of 1834 and 1835 when production doubled the 1831 level. A considerable number of these slaves were destined for new plantations on the frontier of cultivation. Production revolved around this level until 1838 when it began to increase again until it reached a new plateau in the 1840s, beginning with 84,221 tons in 1842, 89,550 tons in 1843, 91,880 tons in 1844, and 97,440 tons in 1845. In 1846, production jumped to 123,300 ton and to 141,810 tons in 1847, the highest level before the end of the slave trade. It stabilized at that level until jumping to a new plateau of 181,290 tons in 1855.

The data for the harvests during the 1840s demonstrate the correlation between the growth of coffee cultivation and the increase in the slave labor force from the Atlantic slave trade. More specifically, the volume of the harvest from 1842 onward depended upon African slaves purchased after 1835. Nonetheless, the efforts of the planters of the Paraíba Valley combined with those political groups linked to the conservative reaction—the origin of the Conservative Party, or the Party of Order—was fundamental. In accordance with the terms of the Anglo-Brazilian Treaty of 1827, the slave trade came to an end in March 1830. With the objective of reaffirming Brazilian sovereignty in relation to the slave trade, Parliament, substantially strengthened with the fall of Emperor Dom Pedro I, approved the law of November 7, 1831, imposing draconian measures to combat the slave trade. From then on Africans who were introduced into the national territory would be automatically freed in anticipation of their immediate return to Africa. Those who violated the law, both buyers and sellers, were subject to criminal prosecution. Any person could denounce those illegally landing or possessing illegal slaves. Under the law, planters who acquired slaves from the transatlantic trade were subject to severe punishments. Usually regarded as a superficial measure to appease the British ("para inglés ver"), the decree of November 7 in fact was intended to put an end to the transatlantic slave trade and was understood as such by contemporaries. Consequently, between 1831 and 1835, importations of Africans fell abruptly, turning the traffic into a residual activity (Parron 2011, 53–115).

From 1835 onward, there was a profound reversal of this state of affairs. Pro-slavery views were again expressed in organs of public opinion. And a broad front of former moderate liberals and former *caramurus* (absolute supporters of the late emperor Dom Pedro I) together with the wealthier rural proprietors—the base of the future Conservative Party—advocated the annulment of the law of November 7 (Needell 2001, 259–308). The interplay of the demands of important social groups and the efforts of the coffee planters of the Paraíba Valley played a pivotal role in regimenting voters. By means of direct political pressure and by actions in the public arena, they demonstrated their desire to reopen the slave trade.

The representatives of the coffee planters threatened open resistance if the law, which would liberate slaves who had been imported after 1831 and prosecute their owners, was enforced. At stake were not only the slaves who had been acquired after the law went into effect but also those who would be purchased from then on. By making this a political issue from 1835 on, the agents of the Conservative Party signaled to the slave merchants and coffee planters that they would give the green light to the resumption of the slave trade. This strategy functioned well, as more than 150,000 illegally enslaved Africans disembarked in the ports of the Center-South of Brazil in the second half of the 1830s. In the following decade this number rose to 166,000. The conservative reaction succeeded in imposing its agenda on imperial policy (Parron 2011; Youssef 2016, 70; Mattos 1987).

Thus, it is clear that the advance of coffee cultivation in Brazil was highly dependent on internal political agreements that gave institutional protection to those who invested in this branch of activity. All of the slaves imported after 1831 were formally free, but at no moment did the Brazilian state challenge their effective possession by the planters. The mass of illegally enslaved Africans only became a political issue after 1865 when the social and political legitimacy of slavery had already been lost. Up to the mid-nineteenth century the coffee planters of the middle Paraíba Valley had an adequate supply of slaves. From then on, the replacement of this labor force as well as the acquisition of more slaves necessary for the expansion of coffee into new zones such as Cantagalo (Rio de Janeiro), the Zona da Mata Mineira, and the west of São Paulo occurred primarily by means of the internal slave trade, which was organized economically and politically at the beginning of the 1850s (Conrad 1972, 70–89; Slenes 2004, 325–70).

With abundant supplies of land and labor the coffee plantations of the Paraíba Valley distinguished themselves from those in other parts of the world by the extent of their landholdings and the number of slaves that they employed. Brazilian historiography has promoted the idea that coffee production in the nineteenth century was organized on great rural properties, usually employing one hundred of more slaves. Detailed demographic studies carried out in the 1980s sought to reverse this image. Based on sources that had not been used previously, such as lists of names of inhabitants and registration lists after 1871, these latter researchers called attention to the large number of small and medium slave owners engaged in coffee production. They emphasized that the average number of slaves per property was below the number that was traditionally accepted (Motta 1999, 67–108; Marcondes 2005, 259–81).

However, the question remains open. The great majority of these studies draw their material from the coffee municipalities in São Paulo during the first decades of the nineteenth century. With the exception of Bananal and Campinas no locality in São Paulo rivaled the volume of production and the relative and absolute size of the slave labor force of the great coffee municipalities of Rio de Janeiro, such as Vassouras, Valença, Piraí, Barra Mansa, Paraíbe do Sul, and Cantagalo, before the last quarter of the nineteenth century. Detailed demographic studies for these Rio de Janeiro coffee municipalities are lacking. Nonetheless, in a recent detailed study of Vassouras, Ricardo Salles indicates that, if property in slaves was diffused through the social fabric, with a great many freed men possessing slaves, ownership was nonetheless highly concentrated. The data gathered for the period from 1821 to 1880 indicates that the "mega-proprietors," owners of more than one hundred slaves, corresponded to 9 percent of the proprietors but owned 48 percent of the slave force. When one adds slave owners who had from fifty to ninety-nine slaves ("large proprietors"), 21 percent of the slave owners possessed 70 percent of the slaves. Salles further points out that the accumulation of slaves in the hands of these large and megaproprietors occurred in the phase of expansion of the coffee plantations from 1836 to 1850, while the illegal transatlantic slave trade was still in operation, not after it was closed (Salles 2008).

In view of this data, we can affirm that the great bulk of coffee production in the municipality of Vassouras was obtained from plantations with large slave labor forces, a conclusion that may be generalized to the other coffee municipalities of the mid-Paraíba Valley. However, a large slave force did not necessarily signify a large rural property. It was not unusual to find plantations with more than one hundred slaves with less than a hundred *alqueres* (480 hectares) of land. Moreover, studies of land tenure in the Valley indicate the substantial presence of units of less than fifty alqueres that account for the majority of the rural properties. This does not include the myriad of tenants (*agregados*) and smallholders who depended upon agreements with the big landholders in order to remain on the land. The usual size of plantations that employed more than one hundred slaves was from one hundred to three hundred alqueres, with a few proprietors having holdings above this figure. It was the owners of these properties who controlled almost the totality of the area of their municipalities (Motta 1999).

The distribution of rural properties in a patchwork pattern, with a chaotic mix of big and small plantations, small farms and tenant farmer holdings is linked not only to the particularities of the agrarian structure of the region, especially the role that this asymmetry played in the clientelist local politics of the region, but also the specificities of the labor process and organization of production (Graham 1997). On the one hand, coffee production was fully viable on a small scale on units that combined coffee cultivation with the production of provisions for the market. On the other hand, given the necessity of the spatial control of the slave population (Marquese 2005), the big plantations in full operation had a maximum size that was dictated by the time it took for the slave labor force to move from the slave quarters—always located by the big house and the work buildings—to the fields. This explains why many of the megaproprietors, owners of hundreds and at times thousands of slaves, established several contiguous plantations, each with its own slave quarters, drying grounds, factories, and warehouses, instead of integrating them in a single latifundia. Fazendas with more than four hundred alqueres required long roads from the slave quarters to the fields, with consequent unnecessary expenditure of time and energy of the workers.

The internal configuration of the plantations was discontinuous, to a large extent because of the hilly topography of the Valley. The strategies of land usage adopted by the planters further contributed to this pattern. The coffee trees were planted in vertically aligned rows on the distinctive hills of the Valley (*meia laranjas*), which had been clear-cut or burned. However, trees were not planted over the entire hillside. Depending on the altitude of the plantation, they were planted either on the side of the hill that received the morning sun (*noruegas*) or where they received the afternoon sun (*soalheiras*). While the trees were growing, beans and corn were grown between the rows of coffee trees. On the lowland meadows and swamps where coffee could not be grown, sugar and rice were cultivated. Trees that were planted in this manner remained productive for a maximum of twenty-five years, but their yield declined perceptibly after fifteen years. To maintain stable production levels, it was necessary to constantly plant new coffee bushes on cleared lands in order to replace old unproductive trees on lands ready to be converted into pasture, provision grounds, or waste (Stein 1985, 214–25; Laërne 1885, 253–382).

This scheme of landscape management, whose two essential principles were cultivation on cleared forest land and well-spaced, vertical alignment of coffee plants, was intended to maximize output. The practice of clearing the forest allowed the rapid preparation of the soil with the minimal expenditure of labor, while planting trees in vertical rows permitted close visual control of the working activity of the slaves. For preparation of the coffee fields, the slaves were organized in squads under the command of an overseer. Each group was assigned to a line of trees with the goal of having all the slaves work at the same pace. Because there was a considerable space between the rows (2.64 to 3.3 meters), the overseer positioned at the base of the hill could observe the slaves moving at the speed that was dictated by the slaves at the end of the line. At harvest time, the organization of work was different. It followed a system of individually assigned tasks and varied according the estimated volume of the harvest (Aguiar 1836; Werneck 1985; Marquese 1999).

The Brazilian slave owner thus combined two basic modes of organizing the labor process that were present in the other plantation regions of the New World, squads working under the unified command of the overseer or driver (the gang system) and the system of individual tasks (the task system) (Morgan 1988, 189–220). This arrangement allowed the planters to impose an astonishing rate of work on their slaves. In Saint-Domingue and Jamaica slaves were usually assigned between one thousand and fifteen hundred coffee trees each. In Cuba it was estimated that a slave cultivated an average of two thousand trees, a number similar to that in the Paraíba Valley at the beginning of coffee cultivation, where the slaves also grew their own provisions (Geggus 1993, 77; Higman 2001, 159–91). With the reorganization of fazendas in the Paraíba Valley greater workloads were demanded of the slaves. An account book of a coffee plantation in Cantagalo consulted by the diplomat Johann J. von Tschudi in 1860 registered thirty-eight hundred trees per field slave. The thesis presented a few years before at the Faculty of Medicine in Rio de Janeiro by Reinhold Tuescher, a doctor retained by Antonio Clemente Pinto (Baron of Nova Friburgo), also in Cantagalo, indicated an even higher number—five thousand to six thousand trees per slave (Tschudi 1980, 41; Mello 1982, 17). Such high levels of exploitation of the slave labor force resulted in erosion, soil exhaustion, and the precocious aging of the trees, which, in turn, required periodical replanting on virgin soil. Overexploitation of the workers and environmental destruction were the two sides of the coin of slave coffee production in the Paraíba Valley.

From 1840 onward the Dutch colony of Java in Indonesia was the only producing region in the world that was capable of competing with the Paraíba Valley. However, the trajectories of the two regions were quite distinct. While Brazilian coffee production registered a constant increase in production, that of Java remained steady at about seventy-five thousand metric tons annually. This discrepancy reveals much about the coffee complex in the Paraíba Valley. As we have seen, Java experienced a series of problems at the end of the eighteenth century. The efforts at reform after the fall of the VOC resulted in a new model of colonial exploitation after 1830, the "culture system" or *Kultuur Stelsel*. Its architect, Johannes Van den Bosch, judged that given the proximity to European markets and the low cost of slave labor in the Americas, it would be impossible for Java to compete in the world market using only free labor on large productive units belonging to private investors. Consequently, he proposed a scheme that was soon to be adopted by the Dutch government. Indonesian peasants were to be compelled to pay their tribute in kind, not in money. His policy reconfigured the old practices of the VOC on a new basis. Under the Kultuur Stelsel the peasants had to allocate one-fifth of their fields to the cultivation of products that were determined by the government without being supervised in the production process. They were obliged to sell the crops at fixed prices to government warehouses. Coffee became the backbone of this system and the principal source of income for the colonial state. The prices paid to the peasants were independent of the world market prices, which resulted in an immense transfer of surplus to the colonial authorities. The gains increased with the semimonopoly of the Nederlandsche Hendelmaatschappij, a company that sold the coffee on the Amsterdam market (Elson 1994; Clarence-Smith 1994, 241–64; Furnivall 1944, 80–147; Baardewijk 1993, 12–14).

The "cultivation system" permitted a remarkable increase in coffee production in Java compared to the eighteenth century, and supplied a significant amount of the coffee imported to Europe in the nineteenth century. However, the peasants were more concerned with the combination of activities that guaranteed them an income rather than with the maximization of coffee production, which was regarded as an imposition of the colonial state. Consequently, Javanese production could only increase in close relation to the increase of population.

The contrast with Brazil could not be more striking. In 1883, in the context of the crisis of slavery, C. F. van Delden Laërne, a Dutch agronomist with extensive experience in Java, visited the provinces of Rio de Janeiro, Minas Gerais, and São Paulo in order to examine the reasons for the great volume of Brazilian coffee production. After a stay of six months he produced a detailed report that even today is one of the best sources for the study of slavery in the Brazilian coffee economy. After evaluating the number of slaves directly employed in the coffee industry, Laërne stressed to his readers: "I invite particular attention to these calculations, the more that it seems to be generally supposed in this country [Holland], that coffee-planting in Brazil requires more hands is actually the case. In the chapter on coffee planting, we shall learn how it is possible, with so few people, to manage a crop of more than six million bales [360,000 tons]" (Laërne 1885, 124). The response to the enigma was simple. The open frontier and mobility provided by the enslaved labor force, together with the construction of the rail network and the adoption of advanced processing machines after the 1860s, permitted saving labor and releasing more slaves to the fields. Brazilian production was highly elastic, able not only to respond quickly to the impulses of the world market, but, above all, to dominate them.

It is interesting to note the contrast between coffee and sugar here. Sugar is a uniform substance. Sugars are indistinguishable from one another and differ only by the degree to which the sucrose is extracted from the plant. On the other hand, different coffees are distinguished from one another by different qualitative characteristics, which shape consumer preference. As a consequence of these characteristics, the difference between production in Brazil and Java created the differentiation of the world coffee market. Brazil pioneered the mass production of cheap low-quality coffee, while Java supplied the world market with expensive high-quality shade-grown coffee (Clarence-Smith and Topik 2003, 450–51). Thus, Java was able to maintain its strong position in the world coffee market during the nineteenth century where the sugar producers of Jamaica and Guiana were not.

Here we see the radically modern character of the Paraíba Valley. Brazilian coffee planters were able to mobilize nature and slave labor in order to produce massive quantities of cheap, low-quality coffee. On the basis of coffee production in the Valley, Brazil was able to determine the world price of a commodity that was inseparable from daily life in urban, industrial societies, whose work rhythms were marked by the consumption of the beverage. In factories, businesses, public offices, hospitals, schools, or in any other place where the cadence of work was dictated by clock time, this stimulant was omnipresent. In the United States, the appearance of large firms specializing in coffee roasting, modern roasting machines, packaging, advertising, and mechanisms for the mass distribution of coffee coincided with the expansion of the Brazilian coffee frontier. Mass production produced a mass market and mass consumption (Pendergrast 1999, 45–62). Not by chance, Brazil and the United States—the paradigm of the new industrial way of life and of mass consumption—were the two principal poles of the coffee commodity chain over the length of the nineteenth century, a link that became even closer during the following century. As at various other moments in the history of capitalism, the formation of a new commodity frontier for the supply of the core zones was directly articulated with the degradation of labor and nature in the peripheral zones. The novelty of the Paraíba Valley in relation to other commodity frontiers that preceded it was its scale, which was unprecedented. It planters not only promoted one of the most intense flows of enslaved Africans to the New World, part of which was done under the mark of illegality, but in the space of barely three generations also razed one of the richest forest covers in the world. Mass production, mass consumption, mass enslavement, mass destruction: these were the signs of modernity that shaped the historical landscape of the Paraíba Valley.

Notes

This chapter was originally published as "O Vale do Paraíba escravista e a formação do Mercado mundial do café no século XIX," in *O Vale do Paraíba e o Império do Brasil nos quadros da Segunda Escravidão*, edited by Mariana Mauze and Ricardo Salles (Rio de Janeiro: 7Letras, 2015), 21–56.

1. All data related to world coffee production cited in this chapter, except those for which we furnish another reference, are taken from the Mario Samper and Radin Fernando's carefully prepared appendix to Clarence-Smith and Topik 2003, 411–62. Data referring to the relative value of Brazilian coffee exports can be found in Pinto 1968, 152,

and Canabrava 2005, 166. Further, all references of the volume of coffee is in metric tons unless otherwise indicated.

Works Cited

Aguiar, Pe. João Joaquim Ferreira de. 1836. *Pequena memória sobre a plantação, cultura e colheita do café*. Rio de Janeiro: Imprensa Americana de I.P. da Costa.

Alden, Dauril. 1999. "O período final do Brasil Colônia, 1750–1808." In *História da América Latina*, vol. 2, *América Latina Colonial*, edited by L. Bethell. São Paulo: Edusp-Funag.

Arruda, José Jobson de Andrade. 1980. *O Brasil no Comércio Colonial (1796–1808)*. São Paulo: Ática.

Baardewijk, F. V. 1993. *The Cultivation System, Java 1834–1880*. Amsterdam: Royal Tropical Institute / Koninklijk Instituut voor de Tropen (KIT).

Bacha, Edmar, and Robert Greenhill. 1992. *150 anos de café*. Rio de Janeiro: Marcelino Martins and E. Johnston.

Bergad, Laird. 2004. *Escravidão e história econômica: Demografia de Minas Gerais, 1720–1888*. [Translation of English original.] Bauru, SP: EDUSC.

Bethell, Leslie. (1970) 2002. *A abolição do comércio brasileiro de escravos: A Grã-Bretanha, o Brasil e a questão do comércio de escravos, 1807–1869*. [Translation of English original.] Brasília: Senado Federal.

Canabrava, Alice P. (1971) 2005. "A grande lavoura." In *História Econômica: Estudos e perspectivas*. São Paulo: Associacão Brasileira de Pesquisadores em História Econômica-Hucitec-Ed. Unesp.

Clarence-Smith, William Gervase. 1994. "The Impact of Forced Coffee Cultivation on Java, 1805–1917." *Indonesia Circle* 64: 241–64.

Clarence-Smith, William Gervase, and Steven Topik. 2003. *The Global Coffee Economy in Africa, Asia, and Latin America, 1500–1989*. Cambridge: Cambridge University Press

Conrad, Robert. 1972. *Os últimos anos da escravatura no Brasil*. [Translation of English original.] Rio de Janeiro: Civilização Brasileira.

Costa, Emília Viotti da. (1966) 1982. *Da senzala à colônia*. São Paulo: Brasiliense.

Dean, Warren. 1996. *A ferro e fogo: A história e a devastação da Mata Atlântica brasileira*. [Translation of English original.] São Paulo: Companhia das Letras.

Dubois, Laurent. 2004. *Avengers of the New World: The Story of the Haitian Revolution*. Cambridge: Harvard University Press.

Elson, Robert. 1994. *Village Java under the Cultivation System, 1830–1870*. Sydney: Asian Studies Association of Australia / Allen and Unwin.

Eltis, David. 1987. *Economic Growth and the Ending of the Transatlantic Slave Trade*. New York: Oxford University Press.

Estatísticas Históricas do Brasil. 1987. Rio de Janeiro: Instituto Brasileiro de Geografia e Estatística.

Florentino, Manolo Garcia. 1995. *Em costas negras: Uma história do tráfico atlântico de escravos entre a África e o Rio de Janeiro (séculos XVIII e XIX).* Rio de Janeiro: Arquivo Nacional.

Fradera, Josep M. 2005. *Colonias para después de un imperio.* Barcelona: Edicions Bellaterra.

Fragoso, João Luís Ribeiro. 1992. *Homens de grossa aventura: Acumulação e hierarquia na praça mercantil do Rio de Janeiro (1790–1830).* Rio de Janeiro: Arquivo Nacional.

Fragoso, João, and Manolo Florentino. 2001. *O Arcaísmo como Projeto: Mercado atlântico, sociedade agrária e elite mercantil em uma economia colonial tardia. Rio de Janeiro, c.1790-c.1840.* Rev. and expanded ed. Rio de Janeiro: Civilização Brasileira.

Furnivall, J. S. 1944. *Netherlands India: A Study of Plural Economy.* Cambridge: Cambridge University Press.

Furtado, Celso. (1959) 1974. *Formação econômica do Brasil.* Rio de Janeiro: Companhia Editora Nacional.

Geggus, David P. 1993. "Sugar and Coffee Cultivation in Saint-Domingue and the Shaping of the Slave Labor Force." In *Cultivation and Culture: Labor and the Shaping of Slave Life in the Americas,* edited by Ira Berlin and Philip Morgan. Charlottesville: University Press of Virginia.

Girault, Christian A. 1981. *Le commerce du café en Haïti: Habitants, spéculateurs et exportateurs.* Paris: Centre national de la recherche scientifique.

González Fernández, Doria. 1989. "Acerca del mercado cafetelero cubano durante la primeira mitad del siglo XIX." *Revista de la Biblioteca Nacional José Martí,* no. 2: 151–76.

Gorender, Jacob. 1990. *A escravidão reabilitada.* São Paulo: Ática.

Graham, Richard. 1997. *Clientelismo e Política no Brasil do século XIX.* [Translation of English original.] Rio de Janeiro: Editorial Universidade Federal de Rio de Janeiro.

Higman, B. W. 2001. *Jamaica Surveyed: Plantation Maps and Plans of the Eighteenth and Nineteenth Centuries.* Kingston, Jamaica: University of the West Indies Press.

Johnson, Sherry. 1999. "The Rise and Fall of Creole Participation in the Cuban Slave Trade, 1789–1796." *Cuban Studies* 30: 52–75.

Klein, Herbert S. 1990. "The Supply of Mules to Central Brazil: The Sorocaba Market, 1825–1880." *Agricultural History* 64, no. 4: 1–25.

Laërne, C. F. van Delden. 1885. *Brazil and Java: Report on Coffee-Culture in America, Asia, and Africa.* London: Martinus Nijhoff.

Lenharo, Alcir. (1979) 1992. *As tropas da moderação: O abastecimento da Corte na formação política do Brasil, 1808–1842.* Rio de Janeiro: Prefeitura do Rio de Janeiro (Secretaria Municipal de Cultura).

Luna, Francisco Vidal, and Herbert S. Klein. 2005. *Evolução da sociedade e economia escravista de São Paulo, de 1750 a 1850.* São Paulo: Edusp.

Marcondes, Renato Leite. 2005. "Small and Medium Slaveholdings in the Coffee Economy of the Vale do Paraíba, Province of São Paulo." *Hispanic American Historical Review* 85, no. 2: 259–81.

Mariutti, Eduardo, Luiz Nogueról, and Mario Denieli Neto. 2001. "Mercado interno colonial e grau de autonomia: Crítica às propostas de João Luís Ribeiro Fragoso e Manolo Florentino." *Estudos Econômicos* 31, no. 2: 369–93.

Marquese, Rafael de Bivar. 1999. *Administração e escravidão: Idéias sobre a gestão da agricultura escravista brasileira.* São Paulo: Hucitec.

Marquese, Rafael de Bivar. 2005. "Moradia escrava na era do tráfico ilegal: Senzalas rurais no Brasil e em Cuba no século XIX." *Anais do Museu Paulista. História e Cultura Material*, n.s. 13, no. 2: 165–88.

Marrero, Levi. 1984. *Cuba: Economia y Sociedad.* Vol. 11. Madrid: Editorial Playor.

Mattos, Ilmar Rohloff de. 1987. *O tempo saquarema: A formação do Estado Imperial.* São Paulo: Instituto Nacional do Livro Hucitec.

May, Louis-Philippe. (1930) 1972. *Histoire économique de la Martinique (1635–1763).* Fort-de-France: Société de Distribution et de Culture.

Mello, Pedro Carvalho de. 1982. *A economia da escravidão nas fazendas de café: 1850–1888.* 2 vols. Rio de Janeiro: Programa Nacional de Pesquisas Econômicas.

Moreno Fraginals, Manuel. 1978. *El Ingenio: Complejo económico social cubano del azúcar.* 3 vols. La Habana: Editorial de ciencias sociales.

Morgan, Philip. 1988. "Task and Gang Systems: The Organization of Labor on New World Plantations." In *Work and Labor in Early America*, edited by Stephen Innes. Chapel Hill: University of North Carolina Press.

Motta, José Flávio. 1999. *Corpos escravos, vontades livres: Posse de cativos e família escrava em Bananal (1801–1829).* São Paulo: Annablume.

Murray, David R. 1980. *Odious Commerce: Britain, Spain, and the Abolition of the Cuban Slave Trade.* Cambridge: Cambridge University Press.

Needell, Jeffrey D. 2001. "Party Formation and State-Making: The Conservative Party and the Reconstruction of the Brazilian State, 1831–1840." *Hispanic American Historical Review* 81, no. 2: 259–308.

Parron, Tâmis Peixoto. 2011. *A política da escravidão no Império do Brasil, 1826 a 1865.* São Paulo: Civilização Brasileira.

Pendergrast, Mark. 1999. *Uncommon Grounds: The History of Coffee and How It Transformed Our World.* New York: Basic Books.

Pérez de la Riva, Francisco. 1944. *El Café: Historia de su cultivo y explotación en Cuba.* Havana: Jesus Montero.

Pinto, Virgílio Noya. 1968. "Balanço das transformações econômicas no século XIX." In *Brasil em Perspectiva*, edited by C. G. Mota. São Paulo: Difusão Européia do Livro.

Prado, Caio, Jr. (1945) 1985. *História econômica do Brasil*. São Paulo: Brasiliense.

Saint-Hilaire, Auguste de. 1974. *Segunda Viagem do Rio de Janeiro a Minas Gerais e a São Paulo (1822)*. [Translation of French original]. São Paulo: Edusp / Belo Horizonte: Itatiaia.

Salles, Ricardo. 2008. *Vassouras, século XIX: Senhores e escravos no coração do Império*. Rio de Janeiro: Civilização Brasileira.

Santamaría García, Antonio, and Alejandro García Alvarez. 2004. *Economia y colonia: La economia cubana y la relación con Espana, 1765–1902*. Madrid: Consejo Superior de Investigaciones Cientificas.

Schwartz, Stuart B. 1996. "Somebodies and Nobodies in the Body Politic: Mentalities and Social Structures in Colonial Brazil." *Latin American Research Review* 31, no. 1: 113–34.

Schwartz, Stuart B. 2003. *Da América portuguesa ao Brasil: Estudos históricos*. Lisbon: Difel.

Simonsen, Roberto. 1940. "Aspectos da história econômica do café." São Paulo: Reprint from *Revista do Arquivo* 65.

Slenes, Robert W. 2004. "The Brazilian Internal Slave Trade, 1850–1888: Regional Economies, Slave Experience, and the Politics of a Peculiar Market." In *The Chattel Principle: Internal Slave Trades in the Americas*, edited by Walter Johnson. New Haven: Yale University Press.

Smith, S. D. 1998. "Sugar's Poor Relation: Coffee Planting in the British West Indies, 1720–1833." *Slavery and Abolition* 19, no. 3: 68–89.

Stein, Stanley J. (1957) 1985. *Vassouras: Um município brasileiro do café, 1850–1900*. [Translation of English original.] Rio de Janeiro: Nova Fronteira.

Taunay, Carlos Augusto. (1839) 2001. *Manual do agricultor Brasileiro*. Edited by Rafael de Bivar Marquese. São Paulo: Companhia das Letras.

Tomich, Dale. 2004. *Through the Prism of Slavery: Labor, Capital, and World Economy*. Boulder, CO: Rowman and Littlefield.

Topik, Steven. 2003. "The Integration of the World Coffee Market." In *The Global Coffee Economy in Africa, Asia, and Latin América, 1500–1989*, edited by W. G. Clarence-Smith and Steven Topik, 21–49. Cambridge: Cambridge University Press.

Trouillot, Michel-Rolph. 1982. "Motion in the System: Coffee, Color, and Slavery in Eighteenth-Century Saint-Domingue." *Review* 5, no. 3: 331–88.

Tschudi, J. J. (1866) 1980.*Viagem às Províncias do Rio de Janeiro e São Paulo*. [Translation of German original.] São Paulo: Edusp / Belo Horizonte: Itatiaia.

Valverde, Orlando. (1965) 1985. "A fazenda de café escravocrata no Brasil." *Estudos de Geografia Agrária Brasileira*. Petrópolis: Vozes.

Youssef, Alain el. 2016. *Imprensa e escravidão: Política e tráfico negreiro no Império do Brasil (Rio de Janeiro, 1822–1850)*. São Paulo: Intermeios.

Ward, J. R. 1988. *British West Indian Slavery, 1750–1834: The Process of Amelioration*. New York: Oxford University Press.

Werneck, Francisco Peixoto de Lacerda (Barão do Paty do Alferes). (1847) 1985. *Memória sobre a Fundação de uma Fazenda na Província do Rio de Janeiro.* Edited by Eduardo Silva. Rio de Janeiro: Fundação Casa de Rui Barbosa/Senado Federal.

CONTRIBUTORS

Marcela Echeverri is associate professor of history at Yale University. She is the author of *Indian and Slave Royalists in the Age of Revolution: Reform, Revolution, and Royalism in the Northern Andes, 1780–1825* (Cambridge University Press, 2016) and coeditor of "Los écos atlánticos de las aboliciones hispanoamericanas" (The Atlantic Echoes of the Spanish American Abolitions), a special issue of *Historia Mexicana* 274 (2019). She is currently at work on a book-length research project about Gran Colombian slavery and antislavery between 1820 and 1860.

Anne Eller is an associate professor of history and an affiliate professor of Spanish and Portuguese and African American Studies at Yale University. She is the author of *We Dream Together: Dominican Independence, Haiti, and the Fight for Caribbean Freedom* (Duke University Press, 2016), which details the Dominican independence fight from renewed Spanish occupation (1861–65). She is currently writing a history of Caribbean politics in the 1890s.

Josep M. Fradera is professor of modern history at the Pompeu Fabra University in Barcelona. He had published extensively on the nineteenth-century economic, cultural, and political history of Catalonia and on Spain and its empire in continental America, the Caribbean, and the Philippines. His book on empires between 1780 and 1914, *The Imperial Nation: Citizens and Subjects in the Empires of Great Britain, France, Spain, and the United States*, was published in 2019 by Princeton University Press. He is currently working on the projects of social reform (labor, emigration, race, and political statuses) in the European empires from the 1780s to 1947.

Albert Garcia-Balañà is associate professor of modern history at Universitat Pompeu Fabra in Barcelona. His study of industrial work and popular politics in nineteenth-century Catalonia was published as *La fabricació de la fàbrica: Treball i política a la Catalunya cotonera, 1784–1874* (*The Fabrication of the Factory: Work and Politics in*

Cotton-Making Catalonia, 1784–1874). He has also studied the social and political links between metropole and colony in nineteenth-century Spain. Results from his work on metropolitan experiences of Spanish colonial wars before 1898 have been published in "Racializing the Nation in Nineteenth-Century Spain (1820–65): A Transatlantic Approach," *Journal of Iberian and Latin American Studies* (2018), and in " 'No hay ningún soldado que no tenga una negrita': Raza, género, sexualidad y nación en la experiencia metropolitana de la guerra colonial: Cuba, 1895–1898," in *Vivir la nación: Nuevos debates sobre el nacionalismo español* (2019), edited by Xavier Andreu Miralles.

Luis Miguel García Mora is a researcher and currently serves as head of publications at the Fundación MAPFRE. He has directed the journal *Debate y Perspectivas* (2000–2006) and the series *Prisma Histórico: Viejos documentos, nuevas lecturas* (2003–10), and was on the advisory board of *Revista de Indias* (2006–10) and the editorial committee of *Documentos Tavera* (1996–2006). He sits on the editorial board of *Cuban Studies* and the Antilia collection. A specialist in Cuban political history, especially the Autonomist Liberal Party, he is the author of various articles and monographs.

Javier Laviña is professor of American history at the University of Barcelona. He has been a visiting professor at UNAM Mexico, Central University of Venezuela, the Pablo Olavide University of Seville, and at the University of Puerto Rico's Río Piedras and Arecibo campuses. Among his publications are *Doctrina para negro* (Barcelona, 1989); *Resistencia y territorialidad*, along with Dr. Gemma Orobitg (Barcelona, 2008); *Les profundes arrels del conflicte Haitiã* (Barcelona, 2012); *African-American Spaces and Identities* (Barcelona, 2013); and *The Second Slavery: Mass Slaveries and Modernity in the Americas and in the Atlantic Basin* (Berlin, 2014).

Rafael Marquese is professor of history at the University of São Paulo and the author of *Administração and escravidão: Ideias sobre a gestão da agricultura escravista brasileira* (1999); *Feitores do Corpo, Missionários da Mente: Senhores, letrados e o controle dos escravos nas Américas* (2004); and coauthor with Tâmis Parron and Márcia Berbel of *Slavery and Politics: Brazil and Cuba, 1790–1850* (2016).

José Antonio Piqueras is professor of history at Universitat Jaume I in Castellón, Spain, and author of *La esclavitud en las Españas: Un lazo transatlántico* (2012).

He was the editor of the books *Trabajo libre y coactivo en sociedades de plantación* (2009) and *Orden político y gobierno de esclavos* (2016), and coeditor of the journal *Historia Social*.

Dale Tomich is emeritus professor of sociology and deputy director of the Fernand Braudel Center at Binghamton University. He is author of *Slavery in the Circuit of Sugar: Martinique in the World-Economy* (rev. ed., 2016) and *Through the Prism of Slavery: Labor, Capital, and World Economy* (2003), as well as various articles on Atlantic history and world-economy.

INDEX

Abolition
  Age of, 19, 28
  Atlantic, 19–22, 25, 27–29, 32, 35–36
  second (*see* second abolition)
  of slavery (*see* slavery: abolition of)
  of the slave trade (*see* slave trade: abolition)
abolitionism, 19–20, 28–32, 35–36, 142, 144, 148–49, 153, 155, 159
  Cuban, 142, 149
  Spanish, 28, 144
abolitionists, 79, 109, 144, 148, 152, 158–59, 160–61
  British, 29
  Cuban, 28, 33
Africa, 1, 3, 10–11, 13, 28, 48, 53, 89, 91, 108, 176, 188, 202, 211–12
  (destination), 88, 90, 92, 96–97
  Central, 202
  coast (*see* coast: Africa)
  fighting in, 54, 60, 62 (*see also* African War)
  Sub-Saharan, 177, 181
  trade with, 86, 211
  Volunteers in, 49, 51, 55, 58, 60–61 (*see also* volunteers)
  West, 128
  and Brazil (*see* Brazil, Africa and)
African War, 45–46, 48, 54, 56, 60–62, 71
  See also Guerra de África; Spanish-Moroccan War

agriculture, 68, 109, 116, 117, 130, 163, 179, 195, 203
Algeria, 3, 8
America
  Central (*see* Central America)
  Latin, 20, 23, 25–26, 28, 208
  North, 2, 5, 10, 200
  Portuguese, 1, 200, 202–203, 207
  South, 20–21, 24, 29, 30, 32, 36, 177
  Spanish, xiii, 3, 19–36, 80, 90, 101
  United States of, 1, 10 (*see also* Colonies: Thirteen; United States)
Americas, xi, 22, 24, 26, 32, 36, 175–77, 179, 181, 197, 216
Antilles, 2, 6, 10, 23, 143, 150, 155–56, 179
  Danish, 165
  French, 7
  Spanish, 84, 150
  See also Caribbean; Indies: West
Antioquia, 24, 29
antislavery. *See* slavery: anti-
  Cuban (*see* slavery: Cuban anti-)
apprentice, 119, 129, 144
  See also *patrocinados*; sharecroppers; slaves: former
Arango y Parreño, Francisco, 84–86, 101
Argentina, 20, 25, 32, 34
Army of Africa, 46–47
Arredondo, Martín de, 45–46
Asturias, 58, 96, 149, 168

229

Atlantic
  (ocean), 62, 177–80, 189
  (region), xi–xii, 22, 26, 36, 141–42, 150, 177–78, 198, 201
  British, 26–27, 47, 80
  circum-, 36, 176–77
  crossing, 71, 85, 158, 177
  history, xiii, 21, 27–28, 32, 176–78, 199
  North, 28–29
  sides of the, 142, 150
  Spanish, 21, 32
  world, xi–xii, 19–20, 22, 25–27, 30, 32, 35–36, 47, 51, 80, 143, 176–78
audiencias, 20, 63, 85
Australia, 10–11, 13
autonomism, 29, 144–46, 152–56, 158–59, 162–67, 197
Azua, 113, 115, 123–24

Barbados, 7, 108
Barcelona, 48–49, 52–54, 57, 60, 62, 69–70
Batallones de Pardos y Morenos, 46, 51, 71
blacks, free, 4, 25, 32, 45, 66, 119, 158, 197
  See also *libres de color*; *pardo/a*; *people of color: free*
Bolívar, Simón, 20, 30
Boston, 5, 95, 100
Bourbon, 32, 113, 200
  See also Crown: Spanish
Brazil, xi–xii, 19, 23–24, 34, 95, 194, 196, 203–204, 207, 212, 217–18
  Africa and, 211
  Center South of, 194, 202, 212
  history of, 193–94
  immigrants to, 167
  indenture in, 108, 130 (*see also* indenture; labor: indentured)
  monarchy of, 1, 203
  Peru and, 95, 108
  Portugal and (*see* Portugal and Brazil)
  United States and Cuba, (*see* United States: Cuba and Brazil)
  and Cuba, 23, 28, 200, 209–10
  and Java, 201, 209
  and Spain, 157
  and the United States, 218
  See also empire: Portuguese
Britain, 2, 5, 10, 12, 25–28, 31, 33–34, 80–82, 87–90, 95, 98, 108, 199, 201, 209, 211
  Cuba and (*see* Cuba and Britain)
  Spain and Great (*see* Spain and Great Britain)
  See also empire: British; England; United Kingdom
Buenos Aires, 20, 95

cabildos de nación, 54, 67
Cadiz. See Cádiz
Cádiz, 3, 31, 59, 62, 95–96, 117, 124
Caminho Novo, 202, 206
Caminho Novo de Piedade, 202, 204
Camino Real, 180, 184, 187–89
Canada, 5, 10–11
Canary Islands, 50, 58
Cantalago, 213, 216
capitalism, xi, 19–20, 23, 25–27, 35–36, 178, 218
  industrial, xi, 25
Caribbean, 1–2, 7, 23–24, 47–48, 50, 53, 56, 70, 94–95, 107–109, 142, 175, 196
  British, 2, 25, 107, 198–200
  French, 108, 196, 199–200
  Spanish, 25–27, 33, 35, 45, 55, 58–59, 71, 81, 106, 124
  See also Antilles; Indies: West

230

Cartagena, 24, 31, 181, 188
Castlereagh, Lord, 80–83, 85
Catalan Welfare Society, 51–52, 55
Catalonia, 48–49, 51, 54, 58, 61–62, 70, 96
Catholic
  (religion), 2, 5, 157 (*see also* religion)
  Church, 79, 113, 157, 169
  Majesty, 54, 83 (*see also* Crown: Spanish; Ferdinand VII (king); Isabel II (queen)
Central America, 21, 28, 175–76
Cepeda, Francisco, 144–46, 149–54, 159, 166–68
Chile, 28–29
China, 10, 108, 130
  See also Indochina
Chinese (people), 47–48, 119, 129–30, 163–64
  See also coolies; laborers, Chinese indentured
Cibao Valley, 111, 120
citizen, 6–11, 49, 65
citizenship, 7–9, 12, 24, 31–33, 128
Civil War (American), 13, 106, 165
Clavé, Josep Anslem, 49, 54, 61
coast
  Africa, 2, 88, 97, 177–78, 210
  Atlantic, 175–76
  Brazil, 206, 207
  Caribbean, 26, 175–76
  Cuba, 113, 120
  Dominican, 120, 126, 132
  Panama, 184
  Senegal, 47
  South America, 21
coffee, xi–xii, 143, 193–207, 210, 213, 216
  Cuban, 200–201, 206–207, 209–10
  bean, 205–206
  bush, 196, 199, 215 (*see also* coffee tree)
  cultivation, 194–98, 201–207, 210–12, 214–15
  export (*see* export: coffee)
  frontier, Brazil, 193, 195, 218
  municipalities, 203, 213–14
  plantation (*see under* plantation)
  planter (*see under* planter)
  price (*see under* price)
  trade (*see under* trade)
  tree, 204–207, 209, 215–16 (*see also* coffee bush)
Colombia, 20–25, 28–31, 33–34, 36
Colonies, Thirteen, 2–3, 5
  See also America: United States of; United States
colony, 113, 117, 119–20, 122–25, 150, 181, 186, 196–98, 200–201, 203, 207, 209, 216
  Dutch, 80, 98, 196, 198–99, 216
Concha, José G. de la, 50–51, 67
Congress of Vienna, 79, 81–83, 89–90
Consejo de Indias. *See* Indias: Consejo de
Continental Blockade, 98, 199
coolies, 47–48, 119–20, 130
  See also Chinese: people; labor: Chinese indentured
Cortes
  Spanish, 7, 83, 85–86, 150 (*see also under* Parliament)
  de Cádiz, 32, 149
  de Madrid, 85, 128
cotton, xi, 19, 25–26, 105, 107–109, 111, 118–20, 143, 193, 202–203, 205
  market (*see under* market)
  plantation (*see under* plantation)
  price (*see under* price)
Council of the Indies. *See* Indies: Council of the

creoles, 32, 47, 50–51, 62, 64, 67, 89, 99, 142, 145, 149, 163
See also *criollos*
criollos, 3, 5
See also creoles
Crown
  Portuguese, 203 (*see also under* empire)
  Spanish, 84, 112, 119, 121, 179, 183–84, 188 (*see also* Bourbon; Catholic Majesty; Ferdinand VII (king); Isabel II (queen)
Cuba, 22, 45, 51, 58, 60–71, 84, 87, 89–101, 105–108, 114, 120, 141, 144–54, 159, 200
  (colony), 45–47, 67
  (island), 19, 52, 61, 85, 116
  Brazil and (*see* Brazil and Cuba)
  and Britain, 25
  Catalans in, 52–54
  immigrants to, 47, 50, 60–71, 90, 97, 163–64
  and Puerto Rico, 21, 35, 48, 57, 71, 89, 105–106, 112–19, 124–25, 141, 143–45, 167
  and Spain (*see* Spain: Cuba and)
  urban, 54, 56–57, 142
  US South, Brazil and (*see* United States: Cuba and Brazil)
cultivation, 126–27
  coffee (*see* coffee cultivation)
  sugar (*see* sugar cultivation)
  tobacco, 118–19

Dominca, 108, 129
  See also Dominican Republic; Hispaniola; Santo Domingo
Dominican Republic, 59, 105, 107, 109
  See also Dominica; Hispaniola; Santo Domingo

Drake, Francis, 183–84

East India Company
  British, 1, 5, 8–9, 198
  Dutch, 196, 198 (*see also* Vereenigde Oostindische Compagnie)
economy, xi–xii, 19, 26, 84, 116, 143, 194, 197, 201
  capitalist, xi, 194
  coffee, 202, 217
  industrial, xi, 19, 147
  mining, 23, 26, 202, 206–207
  plantation, 19, 23–25, 31, 35, 179, 200
  slave, 200, 209
  world, 26, 35
Ecuador, 21–22, 25, 28
emancipados, 48, 111, 119
  See also men: freed; slaves: emancipated; slaves: freed
emancipation, 5–7, 30, 109–10, 129, 141, 143, 158, 160
  post-, 107–108
  self-, 6, 124
empire, xii, 1–11, 13–14, 49, 55, 108, 117, 141, 178, 203
  Atlantic, 3, 26, 32, 178
  British, 1, 3, 10, 25–27 (*see also* Britain; England; United Kingdom)
  French, 1, 6 (*see also* France)
  German, 1, 10, 13–14 (*see also* Kaiserreich)
  Habsburg, 10, 86
  Ottoman, 1, 3, 10
  Portuguese, 1, 203 (*see also* Brazil; Portugal)
  second (*see* second empire)
  Spanish, 1, 7, 19, 31, 33, 35, 46, 123, 156 (*see also* Spain)
  of Morocco, 55, 61

England, 79–81, 83, 85, 87
　See also Britain; empire: British; United Kingdom
Europe, 1, 3, 12–14, 20, 60, 66, 80–81, 87, 89, 116, 175–77, 196, 208, 217
export
　coffee, 193, 196, 204, 207
　sugar, 99–100, 147, 193, 196, 200, 203–205

fazenda, 195, 202, 214, 216
　See also plantation: coffee
Ferdinand VII (king), 83–84, 101
　See also Catholic Majesty; Crown: Spanish
First World War, 9
　See also Great War
Fort y Segura, Francisco, 50–54, 56–61, 70–71
France, 5–7, 10, 12, 28, 47, 69, 80, 86, 95, 197, 199
　See also empire: French
free people of color. See people of color, free
Free Womb Law, 29, 144
　See also Law of Free Birth; Moret's Law

García Léon y Pizarro, José, 84–85
Geffrard, Fabre, 57, 107, 109, 111, 129
gentes de color, 53, 65–66, 68 (see also *moreno/a*; *mulato/a*; people of African descent; people of color)
gold, 23, 26, 161, 175, 179, 202, 206
gradualism, 34, 144
Great War, 11
　See also First World War
Guadeloupe, 2, 196
Guerra de África, 45, 47, 53–54, 60, 70–71
　See also African War; Spanish-Moroccan War

Guiana, 108, 129, 217
Gulf of Guinea, 11, 47

hacendados, 84, 87
　See also owner: plantation; planter: sugar
Haiti, 2, 6, 28, 30, 54–57, 86, 105, 107–109, 120, 124, 181, 197, 204, 208
　See also Hispaniola; Saint-Domingue
Havana, 45–46, 48, 50–56, 63, 65–66, 69, 71, 85, 87, 90, 94–97, 100, 105, 113–14, 116–17, 123, 145, 149, 150, 152–55, 161, 163, 166, 200–201, 210
Hispaniola, 53, 60, 105, 127
　See also Dominica; Dominican Republic; Haiti; Saint-Domingue; Santo Domingo

indenture
　programs of, 108, 110–11, 121, 129–20
　in Brazil, (see under Brazil)
　See also coolies; labor: indentured; laborers: Chinese indentured
India, 8–9, 98, 109, 175
　See also Indochina; subcontinent: Indian
Indian Ocean, 5, 196, 196
Indias, Consejo de, 184, 187
　See also Indies: Council of the
Indies
　British West, 30, 98, 100, 198
　Council of the, 84–87, 101 (see also Indias: Consejo de)
　Danish West, 144
　See also Antilles; Caribbean
indigenous (people), 25, 32, 37, 182, 187
　See also labor: Indian; labor: indigenous
Indochina, 8, 48
　See also China; India; subcontinent: Indian

ingenio, 99
  See also sugar mill
Isabel II (queen), 64, 105
  See also Catholic Majesty; Crown, Spanish

Jamaica, 7, 13, 26, 30, 101, 144, 165, 198, 201, 204, 208–209, 215, 217
Java, 3, 196, 198, 201, 204, 207, 209, 216–17

Kaiserreich, 10, 13

La Gloriosa Revolución. *See* Revolution of 1868
labor
  forced, 4, 24, 32, 107, 111
  free, 4, 24, 29, 106, 108–109, 141, 163, 216
  indentured, 47–48, 105, 112, 119–20
  Indian, 32, 36 (*see also* indigenous; labor: indigenous)
  indigenous, 25, 32, 36, 179 (*see also* indigenous; labor: Indian)
  slave, 19, 24–25, 95, 107, 142, 148, 165, 179–80, 193–94, 198, 205, 210–11, 213–14, 216–18
  unfree, 31, 34, 36
laborers
  Chinese indentured, 47–48, 124, 129–30 (*see also* Chinese; coolies)
  wage, 108, 111, 147
Labra, Rafael María de, 142–46, 149–51, 153–54, 166–68
Labrador, Pedro Gómez, 82, 84, 86
law
  special (law of colonial exclusion), 6–7, 128 (*see also* specialness)
  of Free Birth, 20, 34 (*see also* Free Womb Law; Moret's Law)

legislation, gradualist, 21, 29, 37
liberalism, 12, 19, 27, 32, 35, 55, 81, 142
  economic, 35, 81
  political, 35, 81
libres de color, 46, 51, 67
  See also blacks: free; *pardo/a*; people of color: free
Lisbon, 3, 202
London, 68, 97–98, 107
Louisiana, 2, 120

Macau, 48, 123
Madeira, 108, 129
Madrid, 47–48, 53, 55, 59–65, 68, 70, 83–85, 123, 145–46, 149–51, 153–55, 160, 166
Malo de Molina, José, 113–14, 126
Manchester, 107–108, 128
Mandinga, Antón, 181, 187
Maranhão, 193, 202
market,
  cotton, 25, 107, 203
  coffee, xii, 193–95, 198–99, 207–209, 217
Maroons, 180–88
  See also slaves: fugitive; slaves: runaway
Martínez Villergas, Juan, 55–56
Martinique, 79, 125, 130, 196, 202
Mascarene Islands, 6, 8
Matanzas, 50, 58, 61–62, 64–69, 91, 95–97, 201
Matanzas Liceo, 60–61, 64–66, 68
Mediterranean, 101, 177
men
  freed, 197, 213 (see also *emancipados*; slaves: emancipated; slaves: freed)
  of color, 125, 197 (see also *moreno*; *mulato*)
Mexico, 20, 25–26, 28, 32–33, 48, 67, 106

234

Middle Ages, 49, 177–78
migrants, Asian, 13, 36, 120
Milicia
  Nacional, 49, 58 (*see also* Militia: National)
  Disciplinadas de Color, 46, 51
Militia, National, 57–58 (*see also* Milicia Nacional)
Minas Gerais, 193, 202–203, 207, 217
mining (activities), 179–80, 188, 194
  See also economy, mining
Monte y Portillo, Casimiro Del, 60, 64–65, 143
moreno/a, 45–46, 51, 62, 67, 71
  See also *gentes de color*; men of color; *mulato/a*; people of African descent; people of color; women of color
Moret's Law, 144, 158, 160, 168
  See also Free Womb Law; Law of Free Birth
Morocco, 45–58, 60–63, 70
movement, abolitionist, 28, 144
Mozambique, Luiz de, 181, 185–86
mulato/a, 66, 68, 70
  See also *gentes de color*; men of color; moreno/a; people of African descent; people of color; women of color
Muslims, 8, 48–49

Napoleon, 6, 81, 98
Napoleonic Wars, 1–2, 10, 87, 95, 98–99, 198–99
nation (state), xii, 4, 6, 9–11, 13–14, 22, 29–32, 45, 70–71, 80, 89, 143
New Granada, 20–24, 26, 29–30, 34, 85
New Orleans, 95, 100
New World, 176–78, 196, 215, 218
New York, 68, 95, 100, 205

Nombre de Dios, 175, 180, 182–86, 188–89
North America. *See* America, North

O'Donnell, Leopoldo, 46–47, 53, 59, 64
Ocean
  Atlantic (*see* Atlantic: ocean)
  Indian (*see* Indian Ocean)
  Pacific (*see* Pacific: ocean)
owner
  plantation 68, 96, 147–48, 152–53, 158, 161, 165–66 (see also *hacendados*)
  slave, 34, 68, 125, 156, 160–61, 179–81, 185, 189, 197, 201, 203, 205, 209, 212–13

Pacific (ocean), 11, 98, 175, 177, 179, 180, 189
palenques, xii, 178, 188
Panama, 22, 28, 33, 85, 175–77, 179–83, 185, 187–88
  Audiencia of, 20, 179, 182, 187
  Isthmus of, 175, 179–80, 188–89
Paraíba Valley, xii, 193–96, 202–207, 209–16, 218
pardo/a, 31, 45–46, 51, 62, 67, 71, 126
  See also blacks: free; *libres de color*; people of color, free
Paris, 5, 48, 68, 86–87, 152, 164, 197
Parliament
  British, 5, 7–8, 30, 80, 85, 90, 99, 144, 166
  Spanish, 149–50, 154–55, 157, 160, 167 (*see also* Cortes: Spanish)
party (political)
  Autonomist, 145, 151–53
  Conservative, 211–12
  Democratic, 48–49

235

party (political) *(continued)*
    Moderate, 49, 55, 57–58
    Progressive, 48, 55
patrocinados, 144, 151, 158–59, 162
    See also apprentice; sharecropper; slaves: former
patronato, 141, 144–46, 148–49, 151–55, 157, 162, 165–67
Peace of Zanjón, 151–52, 156, 165
peninsulares, 47, 50, 54–56, 58
people
    of African descent, 24, 29, 31–32 (*see also* blacks: free; *gente de color*; men of color; *moreno/a*; *mulato/a*; *pardo/a*; people of color; women of color)
    of color, 46, 51, 53, 65, 67, 71, 112, 124–27, 182 (*see also* Chinese (people); *gente de color*; indigenous; *moreno/a*; *mulato/a*; people of African descent)
    free, 46, 51, 67, 71, 112, 124–27, 182 (*see also* blacks: free; *libres de color*; *pardo/a*)
Persia, 10, 60
Peru, 22, 26, 28–29, 32, 34, 85, 95, 108
    and Brazil (*see* Brazil: Peru and)
Philadelphia, 5, 95, 100
Philippines, 1, 3, 7, 48, 88
plantation
    coffee, 194–95, 198, 200–203, 209–10, 213–14, 216 (see also *fazenda*)
    cotton, 105, 108–10
    Cuban, 35, 47, 113, 117, 209–10
    sugar (*see under* sugar)
    economies (*see under* economy)
    owner (*see under* owner)
planter
    Brazilian, 193, 205, 210–12
    Caribbean, 2, 5, 197

coffee, 112, 195, 197–98, 201, 204, 210–13, 215, 218
    creole, 51, 68
    Cuban, 51, 85, 119, 200–201, 210
    sugar, 197–98, 210 (see also *hacendados*)
Portugal, 2, 10, 79, 81–82, 87–88, 95
    Spain and (*see* Spain and Portugal)
    and Brazil, 88, 203
    See also empire: Portuguese
price
    coffee, 195, 199, 201, 204–205, 209, 216
    cotton, 107, 205
    sugar, 98–99, 146–47, 210
Prim, Juan, 48, 52, 54–55, 58
prison, 55, 123–24, 127, 149
Protestant (religion), 157
    See also religion
pueblo, 48, 115
Puerto Plata, 69, 113, 115–16, 118–19, 126
Puerto Rico, xii, 48, 53, 87, 105, 111, 113, 115, 117–19, 121, 125, 143–45, 167
    Cuba and (*see* Cuba and Puerto Rico)

Quito, 20, 24

railroad, 105, 113, 117, 120, 152, 164, 210
Raj, 9–10
Real Cédula, 88–89, 189
reformism, 32, 68, 142–43
religion, 89, 111, 115, 158
    See also Catholic (religion); Muslims; Protestant (religion)
republicanism, 20, 22, 30, 36
Restoration, the, 59, 80, 113, 144–45, 148, 150
Reunion, 3, 7, 196
Réunion, *See* Reunion

Revista de las Antillas, 145–46, 149, 153–55, 160–63, 165–69
Revolution
 French, 2–3
 Haitian, 20, 107, 197, 199, 201
 of 1868, 68, 143, 148, 150, 165
 (*see also* Ten Years War; war of independence: first Cuban)
Rio de Janeiro, 194–95, 202–207, 209–11, 213, 216–18
Rio de la Plata, 20, 23, 28
River, Paraíba do Sul, 193, 206
rochelas, 178, 188
Russia, 10, 13, 15

Saint-Domingue, 2, 5–6, 87, 101, 196–202, 204, 209, 215
 See also Haiti; Hispaniola
Saint Thomas, 116–17, 126
Saint-Hilaire, Auguste de, 204, 206
Samaná, 115–18, 121–24
Santana, Pedro, 53, 56–57, 59, 70, 105, 114, 117, 120, 122, 124–26
Santander, 95–96, 156
Santiago de Cuba, 48, 60–63, 67, 70, 95, 97, 117, 152, 165
Santiago de los Caballeros, 114–15
Santo Domingo, 50, 64, 70, 85, 120, 123, 125, 127, 178
 (island), 59–60
 (Spanish province), 112, 115, 124
 annexation, 53, 59, 70, 111–12, 115, 117, 124, 131–32, 137
 army of, 53–54, 59
 conflict in, 50, 54, 56, 58
 Real Audiencia de, 114, 130, 188
 recolonization, 33, 53
 See also Dominica; Dominican Republic; Hispaniola

São Paulo, 2, 193, 202–205, 207, 209, 213, 217
Schmidt-Nowara, Christopher, xii–xiii, 32, 34, 46, 68, 106, 141–43, 148
second abolition, 141–42, 144, 153, 159
second empire, 142–43
second slavery, xi–xii, 19, 22–23, 26, 28–29, 34–37, 86, 100, 107, 142–47, 193
Senegal, 3, 6–8, 47, 126
Serrano, Francisco, 45–47, 51, 59–60, 63–64, 105–106, 113–14, 116–17, 164
Serret y Capello, Antonio, 50, 60–64, 67–71
Seven Years' War, 2, 196
sharecroppers, 35, 109
 See also apprentice; *patrocinados*; slaves: former
ship(s), 9, 80, 83, 87–88, 91, 93, 95–97, 101
silver, 26, 175
slave trade, xii, 2, 4–5, 20, 25, 27, 29, 31, 34, 47, 111, 160, 177, 202, 209, 210–14
 abolition, 2, 5, 20, 27, 29, 31, 79, 80–82, 84–86, 88, 90, 100, 160, 198, 211
 African, 20, 79, 81, 86, 88, 93, 95–97, 100, 209
 Atlantic, 34, 211
 black, 82, 88, 91, 101
 illegal, 25, 34, 47, 88, 111, 196, 212, 214
 internal, 195, 213
 transatlantic, 79–80, 84–86, 89–90, 93, 95–96, 100, 183, 195–96, 198, 200, 210–12, 214
slave trader. *See* trader, slave

slavery, xi–xiii, 2, 5–8, 12, 19–36, 51, 53, 85, 88–89, 92–93, 106, 108–109, 112, 124–25, 127, 142–49, 151, 155–57, 159–60, 166–67, 175–80, 182, 195, 197, 199–200, 209, 213, 217
   abolition of, 20, 27, 31, 34–36, 85, 141–42, 145–46, 150, 154, 157
   abolition of (British), xi, 5, 20, 27–30, 79, 84–85, 90, 144, 165
   abolition of (French), 5, 28, 47
   abolition of (Spanish), 27, 31, 35, 85, 142, 167
   anti-, 10, 20–25, 27–33, 35–36, 68, 141–44, 209
   Atlantic, xi–xiii, 19–21, 25, 35, 51, 117
   Cuban, xii, 33, 51
   Cuban anti-, 33, 68, 142
   first, xii, 176, 178–80, 188
   pro-, 22, 29, 155
   second (*see* second slavery)
slaves, 4–7, 23, 30, 34, 48, 58, 68, 71, 82, 79–87, 97, 141–48, 156, 158–63, 165–66, 176, 179–88, 194, 201, 203, 209–17
   African, 88, 90–95, 99, 211
   emancipated, 160, 163 (see also *emancipados*; men: freed; slaves: freed)
   former, 6, 13, 144, 146, 159, 167 (*see also* apprentice; *patrocinados*; sharecropper)
   freed, 144, 162–63, 178, 184 (see also *emancipados*; men: freed; slaves: emancipated)
   fugitive, 124–25, 184 (*see also* Maroons; slaves: runaway)
   runaway, 178, 180, 185 (*see also* Maroons; slaves: fugitive)
   urban, 23, 67

Sociedad de Beneficencia de Naturales de Cataluña. *See* Catalan Welfare Society
South Africa, 10–11
Spain, xii–xiii, 20, 25, 31, 45, 50, 105, 143, 149, 201
   (metropolitan), 47, 49, 56, 58, 64
   (overseas), 63, 106, 112
   Brazil and (*see* Brazil and Spain)
   Cuba and, xii, 29, 148, 209
   French occupation of, 97
   and Great Britain, 79, 83, 87, 95
   and Portugal, 2, 82
   See also empire: Spanish
Spanish Abolitionist Society, 142, 144, 146, 149, 155–56, 160, 162
Spanish Main, 21–23, 25–29, 31, 34–35
Spanish-Moroccan War, xii, 45, 47–48, 52–53, 56–57, 71
   See also African War and Guerra de África
specialness, 6–11
   See also law: special
subcontinent, Indian, 2–3, 5, 9
   See also India; Indochina
sugar, xi, 3, 7, 26, 90, 97–101, 109, 120, 127, 148, 151, 177, 193, 195–206, 209–10, 215, 217
   Brazilian, 201–202, 204–205, 209–10, 217
   Cuban, 7, 100, 146, 200–201, 203, 209–10
   beet, 147–48
   cane, 24, 99, 112, 147, 204–205, 209
   cultivation, 197–98, 204, 210
   industry, 98, 147, 210
   machinery, 90, 99, 107, 112
   mill, 90, 147, 158, 200, 202 (see also *ingenio*)

plantation, 90, 97, 99–102, 109, 112, 147, 158, 198, 200, 209
planter (*see under* planter)
price (*see under* price: sugar)
trade, 100, 200
Sugrañes, Victoriano, 58, 61
Surinam, 130, 196, 202, 206

tariffs, 112, 142, 148–49, 160, 198, 201, 208
Ten Years' War, 50, 148, 150, 165
  See also Revolution of 1868; war of independence (first Cuban)
Tetuan, 48, 51–53, 58, 61
tobacco, 25, 106, 111, 118–20
Tobago, 108, 129
Tomich, Dale, xii–xiii, 19, 34–35, 143,
trade, 25–26, 81, 87, 101, 107, 111, 183–85, 188, 200
  coffee, 200
  free, 31, 81, 95, 98, 112, 142, 148, 200–201, 203
  global, 26
  interoceanic, 177–78, 182, 185
  sugar (*see under* sugar)
  world, 196
trader, 12, 90, 175, 188
  slave, 95–97, 101, 200, 210–11
Trans-atlantic Slave Trade Database, 92–93, 96
Treaty, Anglo-Spanish (1814), 83–84
  Anglo-Spanish (1817), 82, 88, 101
Tribuna, La, 146, 149, 153–58, 160–61, 163–69
Trinidad, 96, 108, 129
Turks and Caicos, 108, 129

United Kingdom, 80, 87, 98, 101
  See also Britain; empire: British; England

United States (US), 2, 7, 28–30, 33, 35, 50, 59, 67–68, 87, 90, 95–96, 105–107, 109, 116, 200–201, 208, 210, 218
  Brazil and the (*see* Brazil and the United States)
  Cuba and Brazil, xi–xii, 34, 36, 200
  South, xi–xii, 19, 30, 120, 125, 200
  See also America: United States of; Colonies: Thirteen

Valverde, Pedro, 112, 121, 124, 126, 131
Vassouras, 203, 213–14
Venezuela, 20–25, 28, 30–31, 34, 117
Vereenigde Oostindische Compagnie (VOC), 196, 198–99, 216
  See also East India Company: Dutch
Vienna, 79–84, 86
  Congress of (*see* Congress of Vienna)
Volunteer Corps, 150, 152
volunteers,
  Afro-Cuban, xii, 45–46, 51
  Catalan, xii, 46, 48–58, 60–62

Wad-Ras, 52–53, 60–61
war
  of independence (first Cuban), 50, 64 (*see also* Revolution of 1868; Ten Years' War)
  of succession, 2, 61
wars of independence, 2, 20, 23, 29–30, 32, 37
  See also Revolution: Haitian; Revolution: French; Revolution of 1868; Ten Years' War; war of independence: first Cuban
Washington, 68, 129
Wellesley, Henry, 83, 85

239

West Indies. *See* Indies, West
Westminster, 5, 80
women, 29, 93–94, 108, 120–22, 124–26, 142, 146, 183, 186
   of color, 125 (see also *morena*; *mulata*)
world
   -economy, xi–xii, 26, 35 194–95

Atlantic (*see* Atlantic world)
New (*see* New World)
trade (*see* trade, world)

Zeuske, Michael, 25, 34
Zona da Mata, 193, 202, 207, 213
zones, forbidden, 202, 206

www.ingramcontent.com/pod-product-compliance
Ingram Content Group UK Ltd.
Pitfield, Milton Keynes, MK11 3LW, UK
UKHW041917140426
5217IPUK00013B/197